Diary Of A
Rock 'n' Roll Star

Ian Hunter

Published in 1996 by
INDEPENDENT MUSIC PRESS
Reprinted 1996
Second Reprint 1997
This Edition is Copyright © Independent Music Press 1996
The Work is Copyright © Ian Hunter Patterson 1974
Originally Published in 1974 by Panther Books Ltd

The right of Ian Hunter Patterson to be identified as the author
of this work has been asserted by him in accordance with
the Copyright, Designs and Patents Act, 1988

British Library Cataloguing-in-Publication Data
A catalogue for this book is available from The British Library
ISBN 1-89-7783-09-4

Every effort has been made to trace the copyright holders of the
photographs in this book, but one or two were unreachable. The publisher
would be grateful if the photographers concerned would contact
Independent Music Press.

Independent Music Press
P.O.Box 14691,
London SE1 3ZJ
On the Internet: http://www.rise.co.uk/imp

Diary Of A
Rock 'n' Roll Star

Ian Hunter

Independent Music Press

London

INTRODUCTION

Thanks to a Melody Maker ad in 1969, Ian Hunter was singer with Mott The Hoople, a Midlands boogie quintet of sufficient stripe to incur a temporary ban on all rock gigs at the Royal Albert Hall and one saved from splitting-up when pal David Bowie lent them 'All The Young Dudes'.

On 21st November 1972, (it was a Tuesday) Hunter "mopped up the cat shit" from his kitchen floor and prepared for a five week tour of the States. His decision to document this latest trip, as "a letter to a fan in the front row of The Rainbow...as a buzz for the people who dig us" led to, quite simply, the finest and funniest insight into this life we call 'rock' ever committed to the back of a boarding pass.

It is not just the glorious naiveté of the age that endears (Day Two and Hunter is excitedly expounding the delights of air travel: "You get free meals, drinks, papers...the seats recline and they even have movies, a choice of two!"), nor the marriage of jet-set luxury and down-home Shropshire common sense (sunbathing on the roof of The Hyatt, LA, in "Woolworths trunks"). No, the magic of this little book, this dear diary, lies simply in the way the whole early seventies rock 'n' roll circus is distilled to its component parts by a bluff 28 year old Shrewsbury lad, high on Alka Seltzer, Medoc, Winston fags and life, caught up in the machinery of the Billboard 100, tour itineraries and "ladies of the lobby" hell.

With a star-studded supporting cast (Bowie, Moon, Zappa, Roxy, Sha Na Na), Hunter's observations - on travel, hotels, groupies, promoters, Hereford United and the perils of the tight trouser - resonate down the years, as relevant today as they were then to those of us hooked on the biz and the bollocks.

On picking up my own distressed copy of the book I was, as expected, thoroughly re-tickled, not just by the quaint spelling errors in the text ("Manhatten"), but by the original jacket's outraged enquiry: *"Who are they, these rock stars?"* No-one knew then, everybody knows nowadays, but it hasn't lessened the mystique of the dirty work that they do...

Andrew Collins, Summer 1996

PREFACE

This is a documentary about the band I'm in: Mott the Hoople. It covers the duration of a five-week American tour in November and December of 1972. It was written as it happened, on planes, buses, in cars, hotels, dressing rooms – anywhere I could put pen to paper. Sometimes I was tired, sometimes drunk, sometimes corny high and sometimes very down. For those of you who would like to hear lurid tales of orgies and the like, forget it. They did it all, rather sadly, in the film *Groupie*. I'm not about to reveal things that can happen to anyone, anywhere. Anyway – I'm a happily married man!

I'll begin at the beginning and I will write as simply as I can because I want the people to read it as it happens. It's not meant to have literary merit, nor to be a journalist's delight. No, it's more like a letter to a fan in the front row at the Rainbow, a diary to keep in touch. It's meant as a buzz for the people who dig us and will never be able to go to the places we travel. I hope the kids we play to will read it and that it will give them some pleasure.

I'm sitting on a T.W.A. Flight 761 on a $10\frac{1}{2}$-hour flight from Heathrow to Los Angeles – the only city in the world where they have ornamental oil rigs in town. The plane is a Jumbo 747. T.W.A. usually are better than most, and we're flying economy class because the price difference from that of first class is ridiculous.

I've been busy!

After leaving my mad black dog, Solveig, in the capable hands of Pete Frame (ZigZag), we gigged Saturday night in Northampton. As usual we had trouble. Two wagons and a car broke down, we had a lousy meal and Kim Fowley (Mr Nutrocker) got run over. Never mind, the gig was good and that's what matters (least that's what Kim said). The following morning I ship my American/Austrian wife, Trudy, to Long Island, New York (her home town).

Now we've got to look groovy so our manager, Tony Defries, gave us £100 each to buy clothes. That's O.K. but the clothes are all shit – Carnaby Street, Ken Market, Kings Road – ridiculous prices for rubbish that doesn't last five minutes – that's show biz; oh, and I saw Julie Christie on Kings Road, smaller than I expected but that jaw does something to me.

Trudy rings in the middle of the night – she arrived O.K. and there was also a call from Mainman (our agency) New York office. Apparently the work permits arrived late so we put back the flight a day till Wednesday.

Tuesday, 21 November 1972

Got rid of the cat to my friend and budding film producer, Richard Weaver. He and his wife, Edna, are a really nice couple. Crashed on the way – me and the guy shook hands and forgot it. It will cost a few bob though; I did the near-side headlamp and wing in. That's why I keep the Anglia, it takes all

7

sorts of knocks and miraculously still goes. Bought *Disc* and *Sounds*, average week, nothing really outstanding to read. It must be difficult for the trades while Bowie is out of the country. Still, they make up for it with Bolan. It's a wonder he hasn't committed suicide by now!

I cleaned the flat up a bit – mopped the cat shit up from the kitchen floor, had a bath and washed my hair. I don't look too bad. I've decided to travel in jeans and Mick Ralph's old shirt and my newly acquired afghan coat, and then change into black leather just before we reach L.A. C.B.S. will meet us and little ole poser me doesn't want to disappoint them.

Pull the T.V. plug out, pull the fridge plug out; stereo, Revox, hairdryer all pulled out. Send the landlord the advanced rent and settle the red electricity bill before it's cut off. Leave the keys in the car so Bill can pick it up and fix the damage – he's also going to spray it black and gold. (A black and gold Anglia – too fucking much.) Finally I had a bottle of Medoc and took a mandy (rock 'n roll sleeping pill) to ease the buzz building up inside. It's three o'clock in the morning by the bird on the wire – some day I'm going to strangle it. Doesn't time fly.

Wednesday, 22 November 1972

Well here we go on a good old-fashioned English morning – grey, damp and miserable. 9 a.m. the phone rings. I know it's Stan (our personal manager) 'cause the phone rings twice as loud as it normally does. I don't answer it as all he wants to do is wake me up. Somewhere in my dazed state a doorbuzzer ends an erotic dream, and I answer the door in my knickers. Stan gets annoyed, but no sweat as I've already packed. Clothes on and straight into a Mercedes limo driven by a nice girl – very courteous. Pete (Overend Watts, Mott's bass player) is already there. Half dead from an all-night chess game, and moaning about hair spray. It's later in the morning now, and the sun breaks through a little. It looks like it could be a nice day.

Off to guitarist Mick Ralphs. He lives in Shepherd's Bush, and it takes half an hour from our Wembley flat. Stan goes in and comes back. Poor old Mick's got it bad. Red in the face and crying – he's the world's worst flyer. He's on valium and mandrax to keep him sane, and the mood is quiet so as not to upset him. He really has a terrible fear of flying. I privately console him but I know it really doesn't do much good – still perhaps he realizes we care about him and that's O.K. if nothing else. Pete's all for putting him on a ship, but that means losing two gigs, and frankly we can't afford it. Bold Mick bears up even though he's petrified inside and we're already upset for him – it must be horrible.

Next stop Phally and Buffin's (Verden Allen, the organ player and Terry Griffin, the drummer), which is in bedsitter land, West Ken. Both are ready on time and Buff looks great in a red velvet and fur suit. He's really into clothes, studies Hollywood movies and Superman comics for ideas.

Whisper goes round about Mick and the conversation is general and lightweight all the way to the airport, deliberately avoiding the plane and flying, etc.

We make good time and me and Phally have a salad in the grill room and people start turning up. Dan Loggins (who signed us to C.B.S.), Nicky, an old friend from Polydor, and various other good friends who went out of their way to give us a send off. Through the immigration with no hassle and jolly remarks about the name of the group – 'Mott the what? – never heard of you – but I'm sure my nephew in Wigan has.' Yeah, yeah, and they all think it's the first time that funny was cracked.

For those of you who have never flown, I can tell you it's a buzz if you can dig it.

You get 'free' meals, drinks and papers, duty-free gifts and fags (200 Benson & Hedges for £1.50) and they get good wages to treat you like royalty. I've flown about 100 times so the novelty has worn off but I'll never forget that first flight. I was elated. Looking down at that land of clouds – you want to jump out and play in them and jump up and down. The seats recline and they even have movies (a choice of two). I'll be watching Steve McQueen in *Junior Bonner* any minute now.

For a pound you can get earphones which when plugged in

give a variety of music for every taste plus the sound track of the movie – which ain't bad. The plane's about half full and as I write, Mick's stretched out across three chairs. Pete and Buff are together in front and then Phally asleep beyond. The roadies, Phil, Ritchie and Dick sit conveniently near the escape hatch so as to be first out in case of an emergency. Ritchie's always been a macabre bastard. The others follow number one.

Over the windows there are pull-down shades which a chick just asked me to close because of the film. I feel good on a continuous supply of Schlitz, the traveller's companion, so I'll settle down and watch the action – see you later . . .

Well, the film was shit. The earphones didn't work for Steve McQueen so I saw Omar Sharif instead. Weak plot although bags of car-crash action.

My little window flap is up now and a moon-like surface greets my eyes. Mountains make groovy patterns some 39,000 feet up. Awe-inspiring sights become models when seen from so high. All I can see are snow-capped patterns, the odd road and a few glints which signify towns or cars or something. How people live there I'll never know.

It's not dark, and won't be. We're cheating the sun – flying from the dusk and just beating it. Our arrival time is roughly 5 p.m. in L.A. having left London at 1 p.m., so we lose nearly six hours in transit. Time changes can be difficult to adjust to. Everybody's groovy and all you want is some sleep. The plane is steady as a rock which is fortunate as yours truly has had one too many beers. A heave in the toilet brings me dangerously close, but not quite. The hostess delivers my third black coffee and I curse the day I smoked my first cigarette, whenever that was.

I'll tell you something; flying is an own up. What an infinitesimal flea you are compared with the sights you see. Somewhere below an Eskimo lines his igloo for warmth, catches fish, avoids polar bears in his back yard whilst I pass by pissed and unconcerned above his head. Yet another coffee arrives! Don't ever tell me groups see the sights – it's a fallacy.

And so white becomes a greyish brown, snow gives way to pastures and miniature settlements appear in tiny neat plots along the road. The sky from up here is cloudless so they must be having good weather and the mountains must be verdant. Huge mammary monuments discarding their overspill into the mouths of grateful lakes. I sometimes think if architects had seen London from the air it would have been a much easier place to drive a car. Please forgive my rambling thoughts but I can see it with my eyes, maybe not grammatically precise, but instinct should grab you. Still the scene is the same, so I'll meander a bit and give you a little information about the band I'm mixed up in.

Buffin is the baby of the band, unsure of himself, and paranoid about his nose. A guy lots of ladies like to mother, polite – sometimes too polite, and very into Mott. He goes out on all these formal outings with women. He met Lynsey de Paul – a singer/song-writer of some repute – a couple of times, but nothing serious. He's always broke, although he makes a bloody good screw. He's messy and lovable and breaks everything he touches. He gets uncontrollably drunk three times a year and we all have to get him, or what there is left of him, together. Usually he's too far gone though. The last time was Newcastle City Hall, where disaster upon disaster fell upon us. He was so pissed the roadies were feeding him black coffee during the numbers and stamping their feet in time with the beat so he could try to keep up. Needless to say he didn't. To cap it all the organ broke down and we beat a hasty retreat leaving a confused audience not knowing what was going on. If I die and go downstairs I would imagine hell to be like that particular gig. I felt suicidal. Now we've promised a cheap concert to make it up. Buffin's hard, gets easily bored and is quick tempered, but soon comes round if left to sort himself out. A brief excursion into new territory under the name of Johnny Smack fell far short of its intended expectations and Buff it is, was, and ever shall be. He's a drummer, man, a fucking great one at that so I'll leave him alone before he hits me with his camera. Scorpio.

Mick Ralphs is your original loner. He'll run for miles to escape friendship when it's the one thing he needs. He campaigned to get out of the group flat but having done so pan-

11

icked completely and met a rather skinny girl. Nina has since blossomed into a mature woman, beautiful sense of humour. She's just what Mick needs. She's delicate and sincere, her control of animals has to be seen to be believed. He relies on her a lot. He used to be the ace pusher, along with Guy Stevens, our manager at the time, and he pushed Mott down the throat of Chris Blackwell (of Island Records). Mick was the kind of guy who, if you slammed a door in his face, would open it again smiling; but all the shit we 'rock stars' go through has changed all that. He's now perplexed, uncertain and on the run all the time. His favourite answer is 'I don't know' – that's what the pressure does for you. He's totally committed to the group. Over the years Phally and I have come up for the boot, but both times he stuck out for us, and you don't forget things like that. Mick would dig it if it was all honest – this game we all play, but it isn't, so he lays back and plays the guitar, and I would say to other bands, 'You can't have him – he's one of us.' That's the way I feel about Mick.

Cloud is gathering and obscuring our view of Salt Lake City, Utah, so I'll move on to the character of the group, Phally. A product of Wales, he comes from the same tiny village as Marion Davis, just outside of Swansea.

It would take a book to describe Phal. He continually goes insane and comes back for holidays. Hypochondriac, fanatic, self-dramatist, Gemini. When he's down, he's down, when he's up he's within reason. Elaine puts up with him, helps him and loses weight because of him. Phally's head is continually troubled and he has great difficulty in living, the reason being he wants everything right – not a tall order you might say, but almost impossible to fulfil. Phally is unpredictable from day to day. He can storm out, grab you by the throat, be the most awkward bastard under the sun, but he's the most generous of us all. He's just started to write. The songs are in the main good and sometimes exceptional and each one takes countless hours of sleep away from him. A Van Gogh in a rock band's a difficult thing to be, but somehow Phal, with the help of God and Elaine, and a C3, manages to keep on an even keel. I should say at this early stage we're not into heavy drugs which

12

is just as well. The thought of Phal on acid scares me out of my wits.

And so on to Pete. Given a week's holiday he still gets to rehearsals two hours late, and we have them a quarter of a mile from his place in Hampstead. Two cats, Pam, and a one-roomed junk shop and he's as happy as a pig in shit. Selfish to the point of obscenity, we're all hip to the bugger's every little move and Pam's sussed him too, so now he relies on outside help. Pete would let you wash him, feed him, entertain him, clothe him and put him to bed and that would be the end of a perfect day. I must admit here in all honesty, I'm a bit like that myself too.

It's Pete though, who's perhaps kept us together more than anyone else. He's solid as a rock, always sunny, no matter what sort of mess he's currently in and he always tries to keep the egos up. He doesn't read the music press and spends bread like there was no tomorrow. Pam's just as mad – they're a crazy pair. When I think of Pete I think of kindness, gentleness, eccentricity – a complete upper in every way; and I appreciate him all the more because I know the kicks he's taken in the past.

Well, that's the band apart from myself, and I'm the writer so you'll have to make your own minds up, but I would like to mention the central core of the thing that is Mott the Hoople. His name is Stan Tippins and even the name, as most of his actions, are subject to strange excursions. Chiffon, Tilkins, Timkins, Rippof are but a few of the aliases credited to him by various inns and other forms of hostelry we have visited throughout the Western world. Funny, it never seems to happen to anyone else.

Our managerial fortunes tend to vary weekly – according to Hereford United Football Club's results. Many a cross-country dash has been made by Stan and Richard Weaver to give Hereford their support before racing to a provincial Mott gig. Stan knows directors, players, coaches, etc., and I believe his ambition is to have a bungalow situated behind the north end goal mouth and to be a groundsman for his heroes. Stan told me once he'd sung 'To be a penguin' at school for three years, before he found out from his sister it was 'pilgrim'. He'll also proudly talk of his Dad (a Basil Brush fan) who possesses a very loud voice, beating even Stan. Stan maintains that his father stood on a hill in the country just outside Hereford and shouted – he was heard four miles away. He's English through and through (keep the buggers out) and loves arguments, panic, rows, chaos and bull-shitting. He is also responsible for starting rumours. (According to him, Mary Hopkins hasn't got a rectum – she's too pure.) He also uses his powers of invention. Once, having been told an imminent gig was to be poorly attended, he promptly passed the rumour around that Mick Jagger was turning up. The gig was well attended. Need I say more.

Former singer with Mott, he shows no animosity towards me (I'd have gone mad) and has probably more loyalty to the band than the band has. He handles all the money carefully and we feel we can really depend on him. Long-suffering Sue, his wife, puts up with him, his madness, eccentricities, illnesses – from a runny nose he can force himself into a state of pneumonia. I could go on about Stan forever. Suffice to say he was with us at the beginning and he'll be there at the end. Stan you're beautiful – and you'll be so fucking embarrassed when you read this.

There we go, Las Vegas, Nevada – twenty-five minutes ahead of schedule and soon we'll start our descent. No fanatics on board, so it looks like we won't be stopping off at Cuba. If you've never flown it's difficult to describe. I wish I could take you all with us just to see the pleasure on your faces. Mountains, canyons, rivers, ridiculously long roads, and so straight, I wonder who uses them. See what I mean about fleas? You feel like a midge looking at time, and time's laughing at you.

During flights to the States you get all kinds of forms to fill in – customs, immigration, etc. I've now got to get into that, so excuse me for a while. Almost there – we're almost there! A bit of sun in November never did anyone any harm.

Well it's amazing. Seems like five minutes ago I was giving my flat keys to Miller Anderson's sister, Chris, and here we are slowly cruising down beyond the mountains to the flat land

and the sea of L.A. It lays before us, flat as a pancake. Orderly lines of houses, factories, etc. I can even see dinky toy cars moving up and down tiny criss-cross lines which meander on into the haze of the north and San Francisco. The wheels make the plane shudder slightly as they drop and there is an eerie silence as the giant tumbles downward.

The roads are larger now, it's a grey afternoon in the stars' back yard. Now I have to write quickly as the altimeter is beating me. The city looks dusty – L.A. is supposed to be 60 miles across. Sixty miles of freaks, stars, pretenders, and dollar worshippers – here we come! Toy palm trees, a baseball stadium, the dinkies become real cars. We're low and still no airport. You get that 'Will we hit the runway' feeling about now. Some American airports are frightening.

Down, down, down – we've landed – our American tour begins!

Oil containers, radar towers, Delta, Shell, Castrol, 'Fly TWA – L.A.'.

Captain welcomes us to the U.S.A. We're taxiing up now to the terminal, then immigration, then baggage. A feeling of relief and Mick's happy. It's all over – at least for a couple of days.

All goes reasonably well. A Cadillac limo meets us at the airport and a guy called John Porter is the driver. John has a fetish for drag acts and tells us all sorts of stories. Apparently Sly Stone always has to have a limo wherever he goes. When he hits a small town where there are no limos, the roadie (who catches an early flight) goes round undertakers hiring hearses. He's right in the middle of telling us about a row he had with Neil Young when a car draws alongside and a beautiful spade chick smiles – there's two of them. John's out of the limo quick as a flash and drags the one chick in. The other one, I think her name was Beverly, is driving so he tells her to follow. So there she sits in our car with this other car following. Nobody knows what to do as, sad to say, we've all got steady chicks, and we're all feeling guilty, not off the plane five minutes and we're already pulling. Forget it. Not worth it. Who needs it when it jumps in your car. We get to the hotel and ditch them in the lobby.

Now I wish a few of those conning bastards in England would come and pick up on American hotels. English hotels are really something. They can ruin your day.

For a start, we're pretty big in England. We use 4-star hotels which are the equivalent of glorified bogs. Oh, the foyer is groovy, but by the time you get to the sixth floor its beginning to look like Bradford railway station. The slobs that run these dumps really think we're long-haired hippies. You know, pockets full of shit and cases full of nicked ashtrays and towels. So they either patronize you or call you into the office and quietly tell you any trouble and we'll call for the fuzz. In the dining room they take the piss first and the order second. We don't tip on principle. Most places haven't got room phones, TVs or anything – you're supposed to get high on Radio 3 and the Bible. Misery and boredom. I sometimes wish we went to the old boarding houses, six to a room. I remember once putting a door under Ritchie's undersheet, and he didn't even know it – tramp.

Now, let me tell you about American hotels, specifically this hotel. We're on Sunset Boulevard, at the Continental Hyatt House. My room is as follows: two double beds, air-conditioning, a window overlooking the Hollywood Hills, table, two armchairs, full-length mirror, colour T.V. (with eight channels), a bathroom with toilet, bath and shower, a desk and stool, six different lamps and wall-to-wall plush carpet. This is my single room. There's also the phone on which you can get practically anything. Services listed include nightclub, coffee shop, barber shop, alarm calls, room service, garage, drinks, boutique, church, Hertz Rent-a-Car, laundry and valet, news-stand, taxis and travel tickets. You might think from this it is an expensive hotel, but it's your average 4-star equivalent – and Christ – what a difference!

Back to the group. It's the Hollywood Palladium on Friday and then the L.A. Coliseum on Sunday.

The Palladium's a downer because we're opening the show. A late gig, it was unavoidable as we only decided to do the

16

tour a couple of weeks ago. The Coliseum should be better. Sly's topping the bill with Chuck Berry, then come five name bands (we're one of them) and then about ten others. Still, we're fuck all here so I suppose we should be thankful. Incidentally, to set things straight our new single *All the Young Dudes* is a hit record here and the album is in the lower part of the charts. We feel we'll know that we're a large name band after maintaining this for at least 18 months. Anyway, Bolan and Slade didn't do too well so perhaps we'll fare better.

It's funny really – we're neither big nor small in America. There's thousands that haven't heard of us but then again there're thousands that have. If you want a rough comparison (and really I ain't too good a judge) I'd say we're about the same as the Velvet Underground were. Sort of a cult band. Now to be a cult band is great, our followers are fanatical in their support. I suppose that's why we're here. We've had enough messing around. It's about time Mott started thinking about money. We won't be kids for ever. Come on America, take us in out of the cold. We're trying hard to catch you but you're so fucking big.

Anyway, a couple of papers have been on the phone. We refer them to Stan as we don't really like doing interviews at the moment, ain't got much to say. There's a good write-up in *Circus*, I must get it tomorrow.

There's a famous club in L.A. which you may or may not have heard of called the Whiskey A-Go-Go. I rang them as we've got nothing to do and there's a couple of bands on every night, sort of like the Speakeasy in London. They know us, so we get in free and we have a table booked. The girl said the best time to go is around 11:30 p.m. – for the second show. The question is, will we stay awake. A bit of arithmetic tells you that 11:30 here is about 7:30 a.m. in England so we'll have been up quite a while. Perhaps that's why I'm in this business. I thrive on the odd hours, the unknown places and the things that can happen. Guess what! *What's My Line* was on Channel 9. Takes me back to Gilbert Harding and Katie Boyle. Well, into the bath and get rid of the travel sweat. Talk to you later.

17

Well, I don't know what the time is exactly, but it's somewhere around 11 in the morning English time. I've now been up for 25 hours and I can still manage a few lines.

Now this bloke Lee met us at the airport and he's looking after us until our manager, Tony, gets in from New Orleans tomorrow afternoon. Lee's great but his genders are a little mixed up. We talk about it as I don't want to embarrass him if it should come to it. So it was with Lee that we sallied forth to the Whiskey – at least the rest of the band did – I dozed off watching T.V. and finally made it to the club about 1 : 30 a.m. L.A. time.

In a yellow cab all along Sunset Boulevard I can see huge hoardings – unlike Britain, groups are billed here in a big way. Probably since Terry Knight took that huge space in Times Square for advertising Grand Funk Railroad. Huge ads for Roxy Music, West, Bruce and Laing, Sly Stone, and If (who have already disbanded) pass us by as we weave our way down about a mile to the Whiskey.

Now if you were born and bred in Shropshire like me, you've got to watch the Whiskey. People here are into so many games that when people are really nice to you, you blow them out just in case. Watch no one spikes your drink! Watch no one touches your arse! Watch the dose-ridden chicks – that's if you're interested.

Jill comes over – she might be genuine, but who knows. At least she works at the club so some degree of sanity is maintained. She's cute, buys me a drink, but she smells of onion and I upset her a little by giving her a breath freshener. I was only being nice. Some typical acid-high-type frizzied-hair looner asked me my name and says I have a funny accent. Pete's doing his strong silent bit, and Mick's past caring. Ritchie smiles contentedly on tequila and mandies, and Buff, Phal, Phil and Stan sleep soundly at the hotel. We'll take the piss unmercifully tomorrow.

There's two bands on. Mom's Apple Pie, whose main claim to fame is an album cover of a chick's cunt which has been banned. Terry Knight (former Grand Funk member and manager) making mountains out of molehills again. The other group are really beautiful. The Fabulous Rhinestones play laid-back funky music and I'm in the palm of their sticky hands. On top of this, one of my all-time-favourite bass players, Harvey Brooks is with them. Some of you will remember The Electric Flag.

I feel pleasant and Lee, who's proving to be really together, gathers Mick, me and a friend of his and gets us back to the hotel. Lee tells us gory tales of L.A. gay bars. The Blue Angel is a club where this two-ton drag artist stabs 14-year-old boys. It takes all kinds.

I'm trying to find out what time it is but the operator doesn't answer, so fuck it. There's a horror movie on Channel 10. English and mundane. I think I'll drop a mandy. Oh, just a mention about the food here. The names have different meanings. A sandwich is a full-scale preparation, not the type you eat out of a lunch-tin at dinner time. A salad is two bits of lettuce and half a tomato, but order a chef salad and you get the works. They have a way of making it look better to the eye than it tastes on the palate. Coloured paper and tiny tassled tooth picks adorn the plate leaving hardly any room for the food. Water is always iced here, and usually the orange juice is the real thing.

Somehow your body knows you've changed countries, you spend hours heaving on the bogs. There've been more than a few aching British arses since the bands started coming over. Still, you get used to it eventually. It's Harvest Festival Day tomorrow, they call it Thanksgiving, and I think I'll go and see the footprints of the stars Ray Davies talks about in *Celluloid Heroes*. I just heard he's putting it out as a single. I hope it's a hit, it deserves to be.

Thursday, 23 November 1972

Well folks, you won't believe this, but it's the 23rd November and I'm sunbathing on the roof of the hotel. My lily-white body naked, but for Woolworth trunks. On Thanksgiving the town is quiet and peaceful, and Spanish-style villas slope down

19

the one side of us. The flatness of this huge city lies on the other. It's been a long day. For some unknown reason we were all up at 8 a.m. and decided to check our bearings. We are, so the map says, situated in West Hollywood. So, taking the equipment lorry out of the car park at the rear we turned right and headed up past the dreaded Whiskey to the famous Beverly Hills area. Here we parked at the perimeter, commercial vehicles aren't allowed today. We started to walk along Sierra Drive. This is the part of Hollywood where the majority of stars live and it has to be seen to be believed. Ritchie, Phil and me sat on the corner of Lorna Vista and Usher Drive just taking it all in. We saw lime trees, olive trees, poplars, palms – you name it. Automatic sprayers click on with the air-conditioning and start to spray over beautifully tended lawns, and the morning papers lie strewn, waiting for Rita Hayworth to pick them up.

Way up on a hill above the entrance to Greystone Park we can see cacti. We try to reach it but stop exhausted half way. The houses could be Spanish, Italian, or Mexican in design. They are all low and the hallmark of poverty is a three-car garage. Cars are everywhere. The usual combination being a Cadillac, Rolls or Bentley and a cheaper Ford of some type (junior's runabout) and a Volkswagen for the missus to wreck. Talking of shops, there are none. One pictures huge fridges and bars piled high with champagne and Rothmans. The architectural designs on some of these places are really something. Some are shaped in semi-circles with gravel and rock roofs. Magic eyes stare at you from the trees and dogs growl and red pillar-box alarms duly alarm you. There are brilliantly coloured flowers; I don't know the names of them but I can dig 'em and all types of moss and fern. Huge gates compete for elaborateness. Was that Jane Russell I just saw in a Fleetwood? Rubber plants and other large-leaved climbing 'things' almost cover the windows giving those inside much-needed privacy from the daily bus-loads of sightseers – and us. An amazing house at the top of a hill to our left looks just like a modern Parthenon. Cord, Wallace, Doheny, Sierra and Chris are just a few of the drives and alleyways we tramped looking for stars to come out and play, but the lazy bastards must still be in bed. They even paint the fire hydrants a bright silver here. And so, somewhere inside, the occupants sit. Probably with the bedside T.V. on and wanking, the mirrors arranged neatly around them. It's Beverly Hills on a quiet Thanksgiving morning, 78 degrees; it must be one of the most beautiful suburbs in the world. It makes Wembley look silly.

The sun is high now, really hot. Having been weaned on English winters it feels like cheating sitting here cheerfully burning. We truck back to the Hyatt.

Just one more thing about the hotel I forgot to mention: it rates as another example which ought to be copied by those idiot English hoteliers. As I walked through the foyer there's a picture of a guy with long hair. Underneath a caption says – 'Treat this man with respect, he may have just sold a million records.' Right on!

Out onto the patio and in the distance I can see mountains with snow on 'em and I keep wondering why, if it's so hot, why the fuck is the snow not thawing? Must be part of life's rich pattern in Film City.

Up on the roof I sit with Phally and Stan. Phally keeps on about how his underpants embarrass him, but he's too tight to buy swimming trunks, and Stan rambles on about some American bloke who just came up to the pool, flung all his clothes off and leapt straight in. He swam frantically to the other side, then jumped out and fainted on the spot. I put my foot in gingerly – it's bloody cold! There's a Hertz clock on the wall that says three minutes to 1 p.m.

Everybody's happy, but adjusting – where to now? Someone suggests we go to Disneyland, but apparently long hair is banned. A lot of Americans live Peyton Place. Certain segments of the society, particularly middle-class families, annoy me. I find them nauseating and hypocritical. Over reaction and the tendency to almost act their way through life – a television nation. Too much self-indulgence – unreal is a word that's been used many times before, but that about sums it up.

Back in the truck with Ritchie and left down Sunset Boulevard. It's an experience I'd love those poor out-of-work North

East English kids to see. It's just like the movies, and I'm Neil Cassidy, hitching a ride on Ritchie's International Harvester. What a buzz it would be to drive this heap up the M1. We keep going down Sunset until it gets a bit boring. On the right the vastness of L.A. and on the left the word H O L L Y W O O D stands out of the hills behind and above.

Hundreds of hotels, motels, saloons, massage places, bars, clubs and dives. We stop at the corner of Hollywood and Vine – I once wrote a song about Hollywood an' Vine with Kim Fowley – who's still hustling for us to record it. Will his persistence pay off? Listen to our next album and find out folks!

So here I am on poetic Hollywood and Vine. How the hell can you write about the corner of Wardour and Old Compton? The people who named British cities, towns and streets want a kick up the arse . . . 'I left my heart . . . in Watford,' etc. . . . .

So we turn right and it's just your average houses. They're wooden with shutters and toy cars, basketball nets and well-dressed little chicks, tiny Mexican boys and early 60s cars. (There's much more character in them than the shit they make today.) Two dogs wait at the gate and a heavily lined spade parks the car after a hard day's work. It's good to see ordinary people in this extraordinary city. Back to Sunset Boulevard and more of those huge billboards. Mom's Apple Pie, The Bee Gees, Grand Funk and Chuck Berry – it's only a matter of time before Bolan's effigy adorns Piccadilly.

A shop called Sound City (no relation to the English one) sports a see-through drum kit and there's a club called Souled Out. Car lots sell their wares at what seem to be extremely low prices. I think of the ridiculously high prices asked in England for ancient Mustangs. '69 and '70 models go for a song here. Huge supermarkets with vast car parks making Safeways in Wembley look like a corner fag shop. Various sound studios and one film lot – all you can see is a hangar-like building – looks like a prison and probably is one.

We turn left on Sunset this time and intend heading for the hills but instead slow sharply as we find ourselves in a street full of adult movies and bookshops. I ain't got much of a memory for names but I do remember it was just off Hollywood Boulevard which runs parallel with Sunset. The pictures were closed so we went into the bookstore instead which was half porn and half straight. A door leads you to the porn section and a sign says 50 cents a look. Not feeling too randy I don't bother. Instead I get *Rolling Stone, Changes*, and *Rock*, the American equivalent of *Melody Maker, Sounds*, and *Disc*. There's a review of our album in *Rolling Stone* and it's great so decide to go back to the hotel and show the lads. On the way out I get *Close Up* and *International* . . . well, you never know – they're only cheap efforts. We pay the middle-aged spiv in charge, whose nose is a mess, his speech (if you could call it that) is slurred to the extreme, and I realize coke isn't just the property of kids here.

We get back to the hotel and saunter into Pete and Buff's room. Some chick called Rachel is ringing Pete once an hour and Phal's having trouble getting rid of a bird he said hello to three years ago. Excuses are made and the word's going round already that we're not going to bother this time around. It's all fucking boring anyway. They're lousy lays as a rule and you can never get rid of them once you let them in. They don't even listen to the music anymore and as I've said, you run a big risk in the dose stakes if you decide to dabble. The best thing to do, young and inexperienced musicians (if there is such a thing), is to whip their spotty little arses and lay back and enjoy a professional blow job; then tell them you got crabs and they'll be gone before you know it. Anyway, they don't make groupies like they used to.

Stan's red all over from spending too much time at the pool, and he's hobbling around in Mick's boots. They're new ones and Stan has smaller feet than Mick so he's wearing them in for him. Pete and I engage in a game of chess and we draw one apiece. Lucky old me, he usually does me every time; I can never concentrate. Buff's eating a very large hamburger and Phal's saying he's got to send some postcards. I go back to my room (603) and ring my Mum and Dad. They've never gotten a phone call from 6,000 miles away before so it will really knock them out. I also try Trudy but they're all out for Thanksgiving dinner.

And now I'm in the bath and Stan bangs on the door shouting Tony's in from New Orleans. He was with David Bowie last night at the Warehouse gig.

Tony Defries is our much maligned manager. David had seen us at Guildford earlier this year and dragged Tony along with him. Tony said, 'Do you want me to be your manager?' We all said, 'Yeah', but then explained we were up to our eyes in contracts and debts but it didn't seem to bother him, and now he's finally extricated us from our former bosses and placed us firmly under his wing. Since we've had considerable success in the short time we've been with him we are, needless to say, more than grateful. I simply think he's the best manager since Colonel Tom Parker. And I will continue to think that whether we continue our relationship or not. The fact that we're not even signed to him in any way should indicate the trust involved. Everybody slags him off just because he believes his artists should be treated properly – something that usually isn't done in the rock profession. He's young, Jewish and an ex-lawyer's lawyer. Still new enough in the business to take the simple sane decisions that seem to elude those more established managers, who all seem to disappear up their own arses at some stage in the game. He's quiet, calm, and careful. I've never seen him lose his temper.

We exchange notes; he wants to know how the London office is doing and we want to know about David's tour (which by all outside accounts has been a killer). He says Bowie's tired and the Warehouse gig didn't help. It was freezing cold there and the heating system didn't work. I remember doing that gig once in the summer; it was boiling hot then, so they want to get things together. It's the same old story – fuck the kids – fuck the bands – get them in and out – and MAKE MONEY!

He says Bowie got pissed and the guitars wouldn't stay in tune. It was all a bit of a drag. He doesn't want any of us to do that gig again. He also said that Mick Ronson (Bowie's guitarist) looks like a rainbow at the moment. Apparently Mick went bright red from swimming and sun bathing here in L.A. and the chlorine in the pool water caused his peroxide tresses to turn green. So now the Spiders have a red and green guitar player!

We then discuss plans for recording the next single. It seems likely we'll do it in New York in early December as David's tour will be over by then and we should be in the New York area. Buff wants to use Wally Heider's place here in L.A. but the timing makes this impossible. Tony makes a note of tentative places and dates as he has to liaise with Bowie, who, as I said before, is now very tired. He's going to need a couple of days' rest before recording. Tony also gives us the latest rundown on record sales. It looks pretty good. The single has touched the 30s in the American top 100 and has sold roughly 180,000 thus far, and the album is also doing well. David's got three albums in the charts, so Tony's well pleased for the moment and it's still early days.

Unfortunately, the royalties you make from selling records take a long time to come through and meanwhile Tony has to keep us all going. That's quite a sum of money going out every week. While we're on about money I'd better explain a bit more how money works for and against the band. The age-old question. Where does it come from and where does it go to? I'll try and keep it simple.

There're three guys you can get money from. The first bloke is commonly known as a financial backer. Briefly he's got a lot of bread and wants to get rid of some against his tax bill. He'll generally put in a few thousand in return of a percentage of the group's gross earnings. From the group's point of view this way ain't too good because you're already paying a manager 20 per cent of your earnings, plus an agency 10 per cent for getting you the gigs. Start giving a backer 10 or 15 per cent and by the time you've paid the hotels and transport you're left with nothing.

It's better to have the two other guys putting up the money. One's the manager; you need a bloke with plenty of bread. Now he still only takes 20 per cent of your earnings but he believes in you so he spends out a lot of money initially in order that his returns will be bigger. Really it's like backing a horse, but sometimes the favourites lose and the manager's broke and the favourite's back on a milk round again! Of course there're a lot of managers around looking for 'outsiders' but the outsider's chances get slimmer these days, as to present a group in any positive way at all is going to cost you seven or eight thousand pounds.

Of course, if you have potential then it becomes easier for the manager. He goes to the third bloke to help him out financially.

Now the third bloke is the record company man, a very shrewd operator. Stars rise and fall every day and like a greengrocer, the record man looks for commodities that aren't going to rot quickly after he's paid a good price for them. If the record man feels the band has a great deal of talent, he will prepare a contract, as does the manager, for the band to sign. This contract will hold the band to him exclusively and in return he'll dish out bread for equipment, lights, wages, transport, etc.

If the band is lucky enough to have three or four companies interested in them (as we were) their manager can then pit one record company against another emerging with an even bigger record royalty and money advance.

It is on these advances that groups exist until such times as they're earning enough on the road and on the sale of records to support themselves. I must point out that these advances are returnable so initially the band's got to sell a hell of a lot of albums and singles to make any kind of profit.

So the next time you see your rising idol roaring down the road in his Jensen think twice. He's probably got it on H.P., he's probably up to his ears in debt and he probably ain't got the price of a pint in his pocket. Mind you if you do hit the jackpot – gold albums, singles, huge money-spinning tours, etc., like the Moody Blues, Jethro Tull, The Rolling Stones, E.L.P., and Yes have done – there's no doubt about it. You'll live in luxury for the rest of your life. But everytime I see a hairy carefully unloading his Marshall Stack out of a battered Transit van I can't help thinking the chances are getting longer every year. After all, when I started all you needed was a Vox AC 30 and a Framus Star Bass an' you were nearly there. If you, dear reader, are thinking of starting on the road to fame and fortune, think again hard. But if you can feel the buzz, the ambition and the optimism, fuck the money – it'll come, eventually.

Red wine begins to tire me. Everyone else is tired too, even though it's only 9.30 so we split up and I wander back to my room, promising to meet the others later for the Whiskey.

I decide to sleep until midnight, but about 10:30 I'm woken by the phone.

'Hi! I'm Lynn. I'm ringing to ask you if you'd like to see L.A. Kim Fowley told me to look you up – oh, me and my friend Nancy too. No hassle really, I have a boyfriend already. We just want to talk.'

'Well I don't know, I'm a newly married man. I mean . . . *really* no hassle?'

'Really, no hassle man.'

'O.K.'

Five minutes later . . .

'Hello, we know Rodney at the E Club and Kim Fowley phoned Rodney and Rodney thought you might like to come round the club.'

'Well, that's real nice of Rodney.'

'Oh Rodney's a great guy – where's the rest of the band? Only we met Bowie, he's a beautiful cat . . . he taught us so much [I bet he fuckin' did]. And my boyfriend's group is going to back him in about a year from now, but I know how much we love each other [Christ] so I don't care.'

'Well thanks for dropping in. Give Rodders my humble thanks, but I heard all his ladies are ill this year.'

'Hey, I feel kind of weird. If you don't dig us just say so.'

'Hello, Nancy? How are you? No, I think you're both very nice, but I'm pretty tired at the moment.'

'See, some chicks are O.K., but there's a thing about – it's not Vietnam clap, but guys are carrying it around and there's a few down the hospital . . .' [Oh my God]

'Er, the roadies are in 606, why don't you nip round and see them. They're really nice people.'

'Do you really think they'd mind? I mean, we don't really want to hassle them in any way you know.'

'No. It's great – go and knock them up. They'll like you and they're nice guys. I'm sorry to be unsociable but I really am tired.'

'O.K. then. But remember to come and see us at the E . . . really, no hassle. You look tired, try and get some sleep.'

'Great . . . thanks for coming. We'll be around. Don't forget the roadies are in 606. Tara.'

10 minutes later . . . the phone rings. . .

'Cunt!'

Well now – that must have been 606.

Friday, 24 November 1972

Good morning, readers. The sun shines again – I didn't wake up for the Whiskey and it's 7:14 a.m. How long's it going to take to get rid of this time change.

Already Bugs Bunny leaps about the T.V. screen, closely followed by Batman and some film which I can't follow as I'm trying to write.

Phally says I'm getting fat so I'm trying to avoid room service. I've already smoked five fags. So many things I want to give up.

Anthony Scaduto's book on Dylan and Jim Morrison's *The Lords and the New Creatures* lie at my side. I never dug the Doors, but I dug the idea. The guy that Jim Morrison was got lost in an image cultivated by others as well as himself. Fine poetry got confused and lost in the rush to see the leather-clad arse, and he died, as Hendrix died, a mistaken identity. It seems to me you've really got to know what you are in the business of rock or you've had it. Those who falter or who challenge and fight what they are, usually wind up wrecks – or worse still – out of it.

Poor old George Best – he's having a heavy one at the moment. I got near to it once, but backed off after one drama-ridden, and very unsuccessful album. Rock is entertainment – a fun game; it shouldn't be taken too seriously. I find the press largely at fault for this dramatization of music. I just think we're all a bunch of kids playing a game with high stakes just doing what comes naturally. I'm grateful that I don't have to work in a factory like a lot of my less fortunate friends.

My only beef, one that really gets me going, is the press. These fuckers can ruin a beautiful day. I can never quite understand how a guy from a northern weekly local paper can be brought down to London and suddenly transformed into a knowledgeable critic – qualified to knock, laud or misinterpret the work of someone like Hendrix or Morrison. Sometimes you find these guys have been in bands themselves and think they're ten times better than the musicians they are criticizing. Basically, all but a very few journalists are fans. They set stars up then wait for the next issue to pull them down. They have their favourite artists who can do no wrong, and they have their little dislikes which they continually air. I remember once reading an article in *Melody Maker* saying, '. . . The 700-strong crowd at Liverpool Stadium went mad . . . ' The stadium holds about 4,000 people, but the reviewer disguises this because he digs the band. Had it been a band he didn't like, he would have put, '. . . A three-quarter empty hall turned up to see so-and-so – are they on the way out?' Oh yes. While we're at it, who chooses the letters for mail-bag, lads? And there's no way I'll ever forgive you for taking the piss at Screaming Lord Sutch (one of my heroes) and for continually going on about Craig Douglas – say no more. It's 10:30 Friday morning. Fuck it, I've got to eat!

The pressure has been building up all day. Phone calls – 'You don't know me but . . .' and various presents handed in at the front desk. One of the packages included Mott's Apple Juice and gay lib leaflets. These were sent by the Petit Bon-Bons – a group of lads who seem to have gotten us mixed up in the fag rock craze now sweeping America.

Now an American gig is really something. 5,000 kids are packed into the Palladium tonight, and the promoter, Gary, looks happy with the turn out. He seems a bit embarrassed about us opening the bill, bless him, so he sees to it that we get a decent sound check and ensures every kid is in the building before we open the show. Top of the bill is West, Bruce and Laing, second is Flash Cadillac and then us.

Flash Cadillac, contrary to their name, are a quiet bunch of lads; no inflated egos anywhere so the atmosphere is really good.

Anyway, the crowd is in and the Jupiter bit of *The Planets* we use goes on over the P.A. Straight into *Jerkin' Crocus* off the *Dudes* album, then *Sucker – Ready for Love* – and Lou Reed's *Sweet Jane*. All get a bit of applause before we do them so we know they know us and it makes us feel better. The sound's good too, but the lights are bloody awful. Union men doing artists' work and follow-spots lurch about the stage drunkenly. Still, it all goes very well and we come back on and do *Dudes* and *Honky Tonk Woman* for encores.

We've had to shorten the act for this gig and it's always a problem changing the sequences. This time it worked. I don't think we could have done better under the circumstances. A happy atmosphere pervades the dressing room. Happy, but cold as there's no heating on . . . and some fucker's pinched the beer! Ladies sit around and Tony comes in and looks well pleased. We've been paid by the promoter so we'll all eat this week and there's another gig tomorrow so we should be quids in. Columbia Records are helping out moneywise as it's our first tour with them so financially the tour should be O.K. The gig after tomorrow's is in a probably very cold Philadelphia. I'm not looking forward to leaving the Californian sunshine, but still, perhaps my wife will get there – and I'm beginning to get increasingly randy. She has no competition what-so-ever here. Fuck knows where all the starlets are supposed to be – they ain't here, and the coke that's flying around is unbelievable. I even saw a gas bottle and inhaler like an oxygen mask, but I can't tell who had it.

We change our clothes and we're happy. There's a good atmosphere; we're all relieved. James and Iggy from the Stooges both say they dug it more than three weeks ago in London. You can see I'm trying to convince myself that America is good for us – we're fighting again and the drama is high. Buff promptly proceeds to get pissed. Mick does his disappearing act – he always watches every band; Phally sits quietly relaxing and Pete dutifully talks to the slags (not too much, just enough for them to dig him and want to see the band again). Where chicks go guys are bound to follow – we've always understood this and gone out of our way to be nice.

I sit up the corner and enjoy a duty-free fag and an ice cold beer. The door opens and in walks Keith Moon, who sits down and tells us he is here for various business reasons including introducing the Coliseum show tomorrow. We get into talking money, and I literally marvel at facts and figures pouring out of this extremely sane guy who is said to be a nut. I always find that the more insane a guy's supposed to be the more sane he is in reality. I remember once talking to Alvin Lee (who was coming in for a lot of 'ego' criticism at the time) on our first American tour in 1969. I thought he was one of the nicest guys I'd ever met – and he didn't have to be - I wasn't a reporter he had to impress – just a small-time singer.

Poor old Alvin. B. B. King was doin' his cabaret act in the same gig, you know tuxedos, polite freakouts etc., and to be honest I never did dig him as much as Albert anyway. The Avalon Ballroom typifies Chicago. 4,000 kids trying to leave the first show battling with another 4,000 trying to see the second. Anyway, B.B. was top, Ten Years After second, us third and a couple of bands I've quite forgotten.

Backstage, the dressing rooms, alleyways – a huge shit house 'n Alvin sitting quietly reading an underground newspaper. Ten Years After were really hot at the time. Woodstock was out and our Alvin a superstar. Now this can cause trouble.

See, when you were a superstar in those days, the underground press often went against you. In other words, if the *Daily Mirror* was biased one way then *Oz* or *IT* was biased just as much the other so you got no fuckin' truth unless you read the *Guardian* and we all know they're a bit of a drag to get into anyway. Alvin slings down this underground paper, stalks on stage and proceeds to do himself in, the group in and the audience in finally smashing his beloved cherry-red Gibson onto his equally beloved amp. He'd definitely blown his top – pressure, at a certain level, always does that.

I picked up the rag Alvin had been reading. Three pages of pure personal invective against him. Real shitty Hollywood-type gossip done by some prat masquerading as a positive-type hippie. I can dig positive hippies but there're too many masquerading negatives. To cap it all this guy went on to say how Leo, Ten Years After bass player, was such such *such* a nice guy. The cunt was even trying to break the band up.

We once worked five gigs with one of *Melody Maker*'s pet bands and they were the biggest bunch of cunts ever. Never heard any bad reports about their egos though!

Noel Redding (Jimi Hendrix's ex-bassist) steams in and he sits and tells us he ain't played now for two years. He lives in L.A. and even though he seems really frustrated at not playing, he looks well. It looks like he's still living in Hendrix's shadow a bit, no matter how hard he tries to lose it. He's trying to start afresh and is on the lookout for a keyboard player and a bass player. Apparently Neil Landon reformed Noel's old group Fat Mattress and Noel saw them a few weeks ago but he didn't seem to like them very much.

Poker chips go round – plastic entrance tickets to a party afterwards in the arena's V.I.P. lounge. A C.B.S. rep puts in an appearance. He's young and hairy which, I suppose, is a good sign, and before we know it Flash Cadillac's set is nearly over. From the side of the stage I can see leather motor-cycle jackets, slicked back hair and shades, a white-suited pianist headstands on the piano and one guitar player hits Chuck Berry double notes as he sits astride the other guitarist's shoulders.

Jailhouse Rock, Roll Over Beethoven, etc. – you name a rock standard, they played it, and they did it well too. Arrangements – so much better and slicker than the original ones. The nearest I can get to describe them of course is Sha Na Na, only these punks are young punks – they're great and they go down a storm. Flash Cadillac – England, don't forget them!!

To be honest, West, Bruce and Laing were a bit of a let down to me. I feel involved, having known Corky Laing and Leslie West for so long but I still dug them more when Mountain were hungry and Felix's nose touched Leslie's, egging him on to new heights of guitar virtuosity. Now? Well, Les is playing great, but it does go on a bit and Corky started to muck about a bit too much. Jack Bruce, from where I stood, was almost inaudible and the place was so full (a tribute to their drawing power) that I couldn't move round to hear them from his side of the stage. A pity, as he's one of the finest electric bass players in the world.

Obviously, they went down incredibly well and encored, much to the delight of the audience. Moonie shakes his head, 'Fuckin' encores – leave them waiting for the next time! Encores are just not on – an apology for going on in the first place.' I agree, encores are a pain in the arse, but they are there and no one knows quite what to do about it. I mean seven times out of ten they're false, but it does give the kids another chance to shout their balls off, and who wants to go home anyway?

Out come the little poker discs and now we're eating bread and cheese and drinking filthy wine in the V.I.P. lounge. I talk briefly to a guy from *Crawdaddy* (another American music paper), about the gig and thank Christ, he dug it. It means a lot if you go down well on the first gig; it gives you extra confidence. Also, L.A. gigs usually get a lot of press, more than anywhere else in the States apart from New York.

We're all very tired and it's 2 a.m. John Porter, who's emerged as a great character, gives us a lift back to the Hyatt in the limo. Now I could say the limo was full of birds and we raved all night and lots of wicked things happened – and what of the Petit Bon-Bons? But I won't. Like an old film, I'll let today fade into romantic music, mist swirling across the screen, etc. See you tomorrow.

Saturday, 25 November 1972

Saturday morning and once again I'm awake at some ridiculously early hour of the morning. Never mind. Tom Mix woos perhaps his third generation of fans – I thought these films had long gone, but there he is. I forgot to tell you a couple of things we did yesterday morning. Buff and I went walking and I took his photograph bending over Marilyn Monroe's star on the pavement on Hollywood Boulevard. Then, just for a laugh, we went and checked on the prices of apartments here.

'Er, excuse us, but how much does it cost to live in this apartment block?'

A very tatty chick, well coked, 'Well gee man, you don't want to stay here – I mean they're up there on the hill with binoculars man. Like they're watching the place all the time.'

'Who?'

'The fuckin' fuzz man, I mean it's really bad. My old man got busted last week and there's no bread about.'

'How much does it cost you?'

'Well man, it's only about 140 a month, but them bastards are watching us all the time man . . . I mean fuck it man . . . they really interfere. Those fuckin' pigs are everywhere man.'

'And this is all your place?'

'Yeah man, it's really a groovy place if it wasn't for those bastards.'

'Well thank you madam, we'll return if we're interested. See you.'

'Well the guy that runs it is out now but if you get back around twenty after five he'll be home . . . see you.'

'Tara.'

But anyway it's Saturday, and nothing's happening except I've got to do an interview with a bloke from San Diego called Cameron who writes for *Creem* magazine and also helps with *Rock*. The sun beats down on the roof of the Hyatt as we sit and talk by the pool. It must be 75 in the shade. I look down over the back of the hotel railing and some freak opens his front door and starts hammering away at a huge drum that totally encompasses his front porch. Further away in the distance I can see a man hanging upside down from two rings while a chick seems to be pulling fleas out of his hair – don't ask me why. It was here at the Hyatt that a singer called Bobby Jameson stood on a ledge on the fourth floor contemplating the fact he wasn't quite making it at rock 'n roll. People hung out of windows below screaming, 'jump', and the poor guy had

34

to please the crowd – just one more time. He broke both arms and both legs.

The interview's over now and it's about 3 p.m. in the afternoon. I'm hungry so I go down the lift to the coffee shop with Cameron. I'd just sat down when in comes Keef Hartley who's been here since July with John Mayall and is quietly going mad (L.A. unreality), although he looks fit. We spend an hour or so reminiscing about Hamburg and sobering slightly as we discuss the recent death of Rory Storm and his mother – Keef was Rory's first employer.

To be honest, it's not for me to say much about Rory Storm. Suffice to say he had a band called Rory Storm and the Hurricanes right back at the beginning of Mersey Rock and Ringo was with him before the Beatles. I never knew him personally but he had his band, he was around but didn't quite make the big time and he just couldn't take being a failure. I'm sure he was a nice bloke, most musicians are. When you look at our various colours and creeds you've got to hand it to us. If we ran the world there would be no bother.

Although Rory wasn't a big name to be missed I get the same feeling of terrific sadness when I see musicians with 'broken noses'. Anyway, I bid goodbye to Keef – he has a gig a little while away and we're playing at the Coliseum tonight.

The best way to describe this place is to ask you to imagine Wembley Stadium. Security guards all over the place and we get that big-time buzz as people strain to see who we are through the darkened windows of John's limo. Down a huge ramp and the roar of the 35,000 strong crowd as Stevie Wonder finishes his set and is presented with a gold disc by a local D.J. who's acting M.C. until late in the evening when Keith Moon arrives to take over.

It's about 10 p.m. and the feeling is good. Passes tacked on our legs enable us to get to the backstage area and I get a good view of the Raspberries who aren't very good. I hang around for a while then wander back to the dressing rooms (vacated by American footballers for the evening).

Stevie Wonder is ecstatic at his reception and is surrounded by eager chicks. Chuck Berry slips by in an old overcoat (I saw him wearing that coat three years ago) almost unnoticed and almost uninterested too. He's due to go on soon. Meanwhile, Frankie Valli and the Four Seasons do a fine set. A huge screen to the left of the stage video reproduces the show as it happens, enabling the buggers at the back to get a good idea of what's going on. The sound's not too bad considering. Already the show's behind schedule and I say hello to Maurice Gibb in the corridor. They're due on after Chuck Berry – and we're due on about six acts later – far out mate.

Berry's bloody awful. His group (Yellowstone) don't know how to play; the sound is distorted, particularly the bass, and old Chuck doesn't really care. What does it matter? *Ding-a-Ling* brings his act to a storming finish and the best ovation of the day – or was it?

Merry Clayton's 20-minute spot turns into a 50-minute marathon and it becomes increasingly obvious that we're not going on stage until at least 2:30 a.m. We feel it's not on and as we're contracted to play before midnight, the guy says O.K. and pays us. The Eagles feel the same way too. There is a time at each gig when you should play. If you can't play at that time you should blow it out. We found out the hard way at Wembley and the Oval and I'm positive, in this case, we're making the right decision. We're just getting our bags together when the main man walks in. Sly Stone has actually shown up, contrary to everyone's forecasts, and he looks great.

Hair piled ridiculously high, he's like a black Mick Jagger, very friendly. We're probably seeing him in a good mood. He grabs John Porter and mucks about. He has a horde of spade hangers on plus the usual parasites and a few bodyguards for good measure.

Stashing away a few beers from a nearby bin we go out and wait for the limo and John takes us back to the hotel. In the foyer we meet two members of the James Gang, which is nice as we've always been fans of the sound they had with Joe Walsh. Apparently Joe's left now and is up in Colorado with a group called Barnstorm. I didn't meet his replacement, but Lee says we'll be playing with both bands during the course of the tour so we'll see.

Anyway, we nip down to the Whiskey for half an hour. The Rhinestones are going back to New York on Monday to record an album and I shall definitely buy it because they've grown on me. Back to the Hyatt and the lobby looks like Piccadilly Circus.

You know, I've got a bloody awful memory. I just met somebody in the foyer who knew me well and I knew his face but I just couldn't place him. You always try and explain about your lack of recollection but it never works. You always offend and the bloke always thinks you're a big-time twat. While not particularly caring what anyone thinks (life's too short) I've decided that I must improve and that's one of the reasons I'm writing this tour down; let's hope it works. And so . . . to bed.

Sunday, 26 November 1972

Bells tolling, then ringing shrilly, then screaming, then whining, then becoming clearer and clearer and eventually the drowsy awareness that the phone's ringing, wakes me up. Cameron, the reporter, says he's going back to San Diego as his business is finished here and wishes us good luck on the tour. Well, that's it – I'm awake now and it's Sunday and the weather's just the same as yesterday. A quick shower, a phone call, and I meet Stan for breakfast. Poached eggs, bacon and toast seem to be the safest things on the menu and the orange juice is a good average. Unfortunately, our eating is slightly spoiled by a freak hanger-on (there's a few bands at the hotel at the moment) and these prats continually shout and scream in an attempt to be noticed.

One chick annoyed with a lad in one of the bands . . .

'You God damned fuckin' bastard; you lousy cunt; you left me in Detroit with no fuckin' money – but I found you, you black bastard, and I'm gonna make your total existence a fuckin' MISERY!'

'Easy baby, the people are trying to eat. You'll get us thrown out. . . .'

'If I fuckin' get us fuckin' thrown out I'll take your whole stinking, rotten band with me, you rotten cunt – nobody, NOBODY, leaves me in a hotel room – and you didn't even pay the bill you bastard . . . ' etc., etc.

Meanwhile Stan and me are sitting like all well-brought-up English lads do, pretending nothing's happening. Now a huge Amazon chick with fleshy thighs comes up and I quietly pray she won't sit down.

'Where were you last night? You missed the party in Penthouse 37. There were 15 broads there and it was busted. You should have come, you would've got screwed.'

'Well, er . . . nobody told us, what a pity, eh . . . Stan, what a pity.' [Please . . . please go away . . . or I'll die, I know I will, I never feel good in the morning as it is.]

Then there's a silence and she finally takes the hint. Up to the pool with six cans of beer to combat the heat, and a meeting with two young ladies from a paper called *Zoo* which is pushed around for us to have a look at. Most American rock papers seem to be smaller versions of *Rolling Stone* – not contentwise but in the way they fold sideways. They're not as newsy as British papers and tend to concentrate more on letters. A few informatory items, a couple of real big features, and then the album, singles, film and book reviews complete the issue. They're definitely more political in nature, which I think is wrong, but they do really get into the bands much deeper than they do in England. I get the feeling they have more respect for musicians over here. Anyway, we do the interview which is fair and now Phally is trembling with anticipation as he's seen a Wurlitzer piano in a music shop he wants. It's older than the model he's got and it sounds heavier and more solid.

Ritchie, Mick and I go along for moral support (try and get the price down) and we also try out a Buick we've just rented on the way. Also, Mick wants his Echoplex checked over – it's been running a bit fast lately, and farting plaintively, as if in need of help.

We shoot down Sunset Boulevard. To our left we see a giant

Sheraton motor inn and dwarfed beneath it, the tiny shop where Phally's piano lies in wait.

While he's trying it out we have a wander round. There's a Danelectro amp (I've never seen one of them before), a local Mosrite Bass in great condition (remember the Ventures), and Fender necks hanging from shelves with no heads or bodies attached. Speakers are piled high and there's a huge assortment of sustains, wah wahs, echoes and other varieties of sound effect pedals, tuners and mini-mixers. Then there's a very small Fender with four picks-ups piled onto it plus a galaxy of apertaining controls. Over in the corner a couple of Telecasters are stripped down. The bloke's panicking because it's Sunday and he's the only one in the shop and he's certain we're going to nick something, and he could be right. For the third time I'm threatened out of the shop, and so I give up.

See, the only way to find bargains in shops like these is to poke about in dark corners, perhaps finding an old gem in the dusty back room. There's soon going to be a market for antique guitars – one usually finds their sound superior anyway. All you kids who eventually get enough bread together to buy a Gibson or a Fender, don't waltz in and buy a nice shiny new one. Find a ten-year-old battered one; the difference in sound between the old and new guitars will surprise you. And give Gretch and Mosrite a go too. These are great guitars, generally overlooked 'cos they're not groovy at the moment, but they'll come back into popularity one day. I have a Guild which I use on stage, and to my mind it's just as good as Gibson and the action seems to be slightly better. I say all this because although there's a bias towards Gibson and Fender, there are so many other good guitars around.

Phally gets his piano sorted out and orders a couple of sets of spare reeds in case some break on the road. Mick, still 'nosing' in spite of the bloke, finds an ancient Gibson amp (early 50s) which looks like one of those old leather-covered radios you used to buy – and it's only $80 (about £30). So there you are, we did find a bargain.

We come out of the music shop and the evening sun plays

tricks among the hills that front Laurel. Some turn red, others stay green; multicoloured neon dunes in the electric dusk.

Having attended to business, we decide to eat at a little place up by the Whiskey. We're on Hollywood Boulevard and we stop and look at this strange theatre that's been intriguing us every time we've passed it. It's called The Chinese something-or-other. In the forecourt there's a wax effigy of this guy who went to China in 1924 and, upon returning, decided to build a Chinese picture house. It's a real piece of Hollywood unreality and in the foreground there are famous prints of the stars that honour his theatre. Bing Crosby, Jean Harlow and Cecil DeMille are amongst them. Little kids stand in Judy Garland's foot prints and dream that someday over the rainbow they'll get everything they've always wanted. Of course they won't, and even if they do they'll pay for it through the nose just as she did.

Stars' lives don't seem to be their own at all. Daily guided tours take coachloads of sightseers round their houses and you can buy an assortment of books from kid street-sellers. I've bought one for you and one for Buff who has to know everything there is to know about Marilyn Monroe.

I told you before that Beverly Hills seems to be the main area and any Raquel Welch freak can find her, along with Danny Kaye and Fred Astaire on San Ysidro Drive. Lucille Ball lives on Roxbury Drive as does Jeanne Craine, Rosemary Clooney, James Stewart and as did Jack Benny. Beverly Drive sports a host of stars including Pat Boone, Stan Freburg, Betty Grable, Van Johnson (Christ, this brings back memories), Raymond Massey, Rosalind Russell, Jimmy Durante and Sylvia Sydney. Micky Rooney lives on North Rexford Drive as does Jane Wyman. Dean Martin lives on Mountain Drive, Charlie Chaplin has a house in Summit Drive and 'all American girl' Doris Day lives on North Crescent Drive. Phil Silvers has a house in North Alpine Drive and for the tit fans (it says here) Jayne Mansfield lived at 10100 Sunset Boulevard, which is where I am. Boot fetishists will find Nancy Sinatra at Carla Ridge. He-man Kirk Douglas at North Canon Drive, Burt Lancaster at Linda Flora Drive, Bel Air, and Bob

40

Mitchum at Mandeville Canyon Road, Brentwood. The king himself, Elvis, has a home in Beverly Hills.

The saddest one of all is the number of a house on Fifth Helena Drive which is listed briefly as 'last home' – Marilyn Monroe.

Ah well, over to the restaurant where we ate spare ribs and wined thoroughly. They have a silly system in some cafes here where they give you a huge flagon of wine which has horizontal lines going down the side of the glass. When you've had all the wine you want, they charge you according to the level the wine has dropped to in the flagon. The fiendish and subtle replacement of water can render you totally pissed and cost you next to nothing. Far out. I can't believe I'm the only one that's thought of it. It's about time they sussed it.

Mick decides he'd like to see Beverly Hills by night and when we get up there it is indeed a remarkable sight as we look down over L.A. It's like looking down on a massive field of electric potato plants, millions of them. A beautiful sight which proves L.A. can show off quietly and nicely despite what the people have done to its guts.

We returned to the hotel about eight o'clock and there's no gig until Wednesday so I thought I might go to see Loudon Wainwright III and Steeleye Span at the Ash Grove. It's their last night, and we met them briefly in the hotel. They all seem like nice people. My thoughts, however, are interrupted by the phone and the devilish tones of Keith Moon come storming through the receiver. He's been here a week, made his fortune (for this week) and goes back tomorrow. First he suggests we go to Dante's to see Murray Roman then, after a think, says he'll come round in 30 minutes and take me to see Frank Zappa in Laurel Canyon. I'd only met Keith Moon once, briefly, if you remember on that Friday at the Palladium, so this is a small example of what a nice lad he is. Now he's in the Who and I'm in Mott and they're bigger than us and so he breaks down that barrier which separates every on-the-way-upper from a made-it. Needless to say, I was knocked out and he'll probably be embarrassed to read this and mutter all kinds of words like 'cunt' but I am me and I thought it was a nice gesture; it made my day. I was also slightly apprehensive about meeting Zappa, whom I admit not having followed closely, preferring to accept his press image. Again the press is wrong – or maybe they just see what people like Frank Zappa want them to see. What I saw was a quiet family man with his lady, little girl, huge white cat and delightful Siamese kitten! I have a weakness for cats, we have one of our own called Saucer, and this little thing pulled the most amazing faces I've ever seen when Frank's wife scratched its nose.

But this is flying a bit. Keith picked me up in a Volkswagen which only went if he continually turned the lights on and off. It had to be parked on slopes and had what looked like a dog's kennel in the back – God knows where he'd found it. It steamed into the Hyatt forecourt scattering flowers of the female L.A. musicians' society. I was amazed and wondered if this was really Moon amongst the Cadillacs and limos. Joyfully he careered up the road in second muttering about his first solo singing role as Uncle Ernie in *Tommy*, which he did because Ringo was still filming and couldn't make it in time. Out to Laurel Canyon, finally farting to a halt at a three storey building set back amongst the trees. Up a flight of steps through strange-smelling brush and finally into Zappa's house. To describe his house, would be difficult and an invasion of privacy, so suffice to say the carpets were great for lying on and he has got his own studios in the basement. His quadrophonic was away ill but he still used four speakers for stereo. He played tapes done at Electric Ladyland with Jack Bruce which he hopes to release on a Frank Zappa album. He's also working on the new Mothers album.

Earl, one of the Mothers, was there with him. He seems to agree with everything Frank says. I don't – not with everything, so I stay non-committal, with my mouth shut. I have tremendous respect for him anyway. He's totally dedicated and can play you tapes for hours upon hours. He must edit for weeks to get the speed of change. Some of it was good, but some of it was boring too. I didn't feel overawed. I was annoyed at my memory for not identifying the musicians he worked with, and who was good and who wasn't. About 12 Keith wants to go and Frank still wants to play us more and show us a film he's got but Moonie wants to pay a visit to another of his friends, John Sebastian. I follow. It's a bit much to take in one day – these are people I've only heard about before. Still, if he's like Zappa, it will be O.K. I don't know what Zappa thought of me suddenly appearing. I'm sure Keith didn't forewarn him, but he was really quite nice and courteous to me. He said I could go back round there any time. I probably won't, 'cos that's the way things go.

Off again in the little V.W. and a hair-raising running jump at the steep hill that leads to John Sebastian's place. Don't quite make it but never mind; once round the block and the sweetest bit of cajoling I've ever heard got the little car up the second time. This bloke really likes his privacy. Several times I thought we were going to fall off the edge of the road – it seemed like the Alps. Well, John Sebastian wasn't home; the house was empty – just a ginger cat on the doorstep as eager to get in as we were. So, off to the Whiskey yet again. What scrubbers we all are. It was half empty but once again the Rhinestones slowly got us moving. The manager gave Keith a bottle of Champagne at two minutes to two (a.m.), and at two a huge black heavy wanted it back again. We gulped it down and Mick and Stan came over and helped. The 'own up' light went on and Keith and I exchanged phone numbers. The last time I saw Keith was in that slowly dying, but bravely hanging on Volkswagen. Never mind little car, he's going back tomorrow. Have a good flight Mooney, and a safe one – and thanks for the evening – I won't forget it for various reasons. I jumped into the Buick with Stan and Mick and went to sleep smiling. That was a buzz,

Monday, 27 November 1972

Tomorrow we fly east to Philadelphia. The *Los Angeles Times* gives us a flattering review for the Palladium concert so the atmosphere is good all round and we congregate at the pool for sundry photographs. The guys who are taking shots surround us. Supreme false security, 'cos they know, and we know, there's a long way to go yet. Still, they're nice, and it's all painless enough. No interview for Phally or me today, and, as I sit by the pool and write, Phal is sun bathing with Stan. Mick's doing his interview over in the far left corner. Beneath his feet fake grass abounds as do fake trees and shrubs. Still, I suppose it saves water!

Now I've just come back from the coffee shop, doing my observation bit. The guy at the till snorted coke while he was sorting out my change. Two groupies to my left looked quite reasonable while three hideous ones ogle from my right. One has on hot pants, velvet clogs and green tights; another wears a denim bib and brace with the arse sticking out of it and weighs about 13 stone and yet a third has on glitter lavender shoes, other assorted gaily coloured rags and this horrendous sight is completed by the application of bright red eye make-up, liberally daubed on with what must have been a trowel. Her only redeeming feature was the size of her tits, but even they hardly compensate for her overall appearance. Two Mexican birds walk by chatting excitedly, and a very tall bloke sits with an attractive bird at the top end. The place is a bar all down one side and seats and tables back onto the windows on the other. It's not unlike your Wimpy bar, except that the service is better and the carpet thicker.

'Welcome Mott the Hoople' still shines out over the foyer main doors – imagine the Railway Inn at Birmingham doing that!

The pool has emptied now as the sun cools downtown L.A.

and pollution covers the city. Even the hills the other side are slightly misty. Pete's now moaning about a chess opponent (American) who thought he was God and if I continue I'll get boring so I'll close for now.

Tuesday, 28 November 1972

It's about 1:30 p.m. and we're sitting in a 707 which is just about to take off. As I write we move slowly in line to the end of the runway, then turn and ascend.

As I told you, it's Philadelphia today. The California sun beams down on my writing pad through the window. Apparently it's snowing and freezing cold in Philadelphia and if I can find a doctor who uses a gun and not a needle I think I'll have $10 worth of flu shots. The flight today stretches from one side of the U.S.A. to the other. From California into Northern Arizona, then just tipping New Mexico, Colorado, Kansas on through Missouri, Illinois, Indiana, and Ohio, finally reaching Pennsylvania at about 5:30 p.m. Eastern time (8:30 Western time) – the time difference being three hours coast to coast. The sun's hot, really hot, as we go down a little bit of coast and take a last look at the Pacific before turning inland. Oil holders from the L.A. mining fields look like little orange buttons, and L.A. itself, with its vast suburbs (all apple, no core) lies neatly below.

In Arizona we'll pass over what's left of the once proud nations of the Hopi and the Navajo, squashed to the right of the Grand Canyon Park – it's desert as well. No kind of land for the American people to give the rightful landowners; this barren consolation. The sooner they get back on the fuckin' warpath the better. They are beaten right down into the ground and have lost more than the blacks. It is said that if you befriend an Indian for life he still hates you deep in his heart (a) because you are white and (b) because you are wrong.

Palm Springs lies below us and we are now flying at 27,000 feet, eventually reaching 39,000 feet and holding for the main part of the trip. I've just ordered steak from a choice of three courses. The film today, by the way, is *The Graduate* which I haven't seen and is highly recommended so I've invested a quid on earphones. They also give you a couple of channels of music. Richard Strauss plies for trade alongside Lindisfarne. Brahms competes with Carly Simon, and Beethoven's Gloria from *Missa Solemnis* is quite groovy if you alternate with *Piano Bird* by the Doors. Somewhere around is Petula Clark, Sonny Stitt, Junior Walker, and a Ruth Brown doing *Let It Be*. What a choice. Excuse me while I eat.

A nice meal, and now the little screen comes down and we put on our headphones for *The Graduate*. The first thing the man says in the film is, 'We are now landing in four or five minutes in Los Angeles.' Strange, we've just left. It occurs to me that you, reader, have probably seen *The Graduate*. So, if you have, the hotels in that film are exactly what most of the places we stay in are like. In some places the film drags a bit. It doesn't seem to be as good as its reputation would suggest, so I watch us slowly cruise into the night. The clouds below us, which obscured the terrain most of the way have changed from white to dark grey. The sky slowly sinks into deeper blues and yellows, and various golds line the horizon. *The Graduate* builds well at the end; the beginning only annoyed me as I have an intense dislike of the hypocrisy of American family life – difficult, as my wife, Trudy, comes from Long Island, and it looks like I can't avoid a confrontation with her parents much longer.

As Dustin Hoffman elopes with his bride on a Greyhound bus, the lights of Philly take shape below. As always the plane descends and lands deceptively quick.

Quickly through the terminal and into limos waiting at the front. Mick chirps up a bit. His fear of flying forces him to take sleepers but at least he's a lot better than if he flies straight. Brave lad, he knows we'd be in the shit if he let his instincts take over so he struggles on through. A passing black porter loves Buff's fur trousers. I really find much more comfort with the blacks in America; people take the piss at them all the time – just as they do to us. We share a mutual sadness in the medieval state of silly, stupid hypocritical bastards that dominate this world. Fuck 'em, I ain't got long enough to live to let them worry me, but they still bore and anger me. I just can't help that. I have noticed one thing personally, people who have taken the piss at me because of the way I looked have always been ugly themselves. Perhaps they delight in jeering at those they think subservient as an escape valve for the sadness their own images cause them.

The Warwick Hotel is in downtown Philadelphia and looks like a stately home inside. It's sedate and quiet; in fact, it's got no balls at all! I ring Trudy and she is coming down the 100 miles or so tomorrow on the Greyhound bus.

We cross the street to a small cafe as we only want a snack. The evening dinner at the Warwick is a mammoth affair, and two poached eggs, bacon and toast is adequate for my needs. None of us are too keen on the hotel, and we discuss moving to a nearby Holiday Inn tomorrow. We finally decide to give it 24 hours as Tony, David, the Spiders, Dai Davies, Mick Rock, Stuey, Pete, Robin and all the Bowie entourage are coming in. They're doing Pittsburgh tonight and are expected early tomorrow afternoon. I've got a feeling they'll want to move too as room service is only until 10:30 p.m. (which is unforgivable here), the phones are up the creek and the T.V.s are bad. Well, we'll see what happens tomorrow. Bowie is doing a 'walk on' with us tomorrow night and then he follows through with three nights at the same theatre. One good thing – it's supposed to be great acoustically. See ya. . . .

Wednesday, 29 November 1972

Here we are, Wednesday afternoon in Philadelphia on a grey and overcast English morning. Trudy wakes me up, looking beautiful, in a $100 green suit she has managed to con out of her Mum and Dad. Lee comes around and Stan is doing his usual panic bit. Nobody really is in the mood and his arm-waving and shouting are subdued somewhat by several slamming doors and early-morning cries of 'fuck off'. We sign a form for a radio station who want to record tonight's concert and put it out next Monday. Me and Tru cross Walcott Street and wind up walking down Chestnut Street – me on my never ending quest for pawn shops, and Trudy putting up with my mania sensibly. Nothing doing. Not a hock shop in sight and we get down to Market and 11th Street and read a sign that says, 'On this spot Thomas Jefferson drew up the draft for the American Declaration of Independence' – it's a parking lot now. Cute how they destroy what tradition they have.

Walking back up Chestnut Street we find a place called the Record Museum. My God I know a few people who would go mad in this place. You name it and they have it – all on original labels and all costing 65 cents. Not bad when you consider a new record costs 10 and something in England. They're still new records, some have been here for years; others I expect, although original recordings, have been repressed and the labels 'forged'.

I know the couple I was given, Jerry Lee Lewis's *Whole Lotta Shakin*, and Little Richard's *The Girl Can't Help It* were originals – on Sun and Specialty respectively; the guy also gave Tru Carly Simon's new record which is her current favourite. I say we were given them, because the bloke knew me from Mott and gave me a catalogue too.

The catalogue is unbelievable. All I can say is I bought 31 singles and God knows how many Mick and Pete will have. I know Mick wants the whole of Rick Nelson and the Buffalo Springfield output and that's about 25 before he starts looking through everything else. Pete will go mad – he always does.

I'm still frantically underlining masterpieces in the catalogue at the hotel, when Stan starts hassling for the sound check – a necessary evil when you are short of time.

We whisk through the evening rush to up around 65th Street and there we are. Top of the bill in America for the first time! There are just over 2,000 in a 2,500 seater and that's pretty good, considering the gig was just put in last Friday – only five days ago! Things start moving faster. Pete and Robin, Bowie's sound men turn up shattered from an all day's dash, but immediately throw in their lot for tonight's show. They don't get paid by us – they just do it because they want Mainman to be a family. They are inspiring, and what can you say about two blokes like that – they've got a night off and they sweat their balls off with us instead. Dick, our sound man, is getting into yet another P.A. while Phil's busily building a ramp as the theatre has a Rainbow-style orchestra pit which has to be crossed to keep contact with the audience; Ritchie slinks round – the ever present scowl. His last nickname's not going down too well – 'Snail Shit' – but he knows we love him. He's been there from the start and he'll be there at the end.

The sound check is great. The place is like your average ABC and everything's working but the organ which eventually farts into life and passes Phally's hypercritical try out.

Back to the hotel. We've only got an hour, and Trudy flies out for hamburgers and orange juice while I shave, shit and shampoo. She's great in a crisis.

Tony's in now with his lady, Melanie, and Sue (Bowie's hairdresser) shouts hello. She's with two other blokes in David's entourage.

David and Stuey (his bodyguard) and George (photos) are on their way from Pittsburgh in a yellow cab as something went wrong with his car. He's running late if he wants to introduce us. The adrenalin builds – I'm ready, and meet the lads in the huge sombre foyer. Into the limos and up to the gig. Security police pull back barriers (big time – great feeling) and straight in the back door. The dressing rooms are O.K. – the bare essentials – mirrors, chairs, a bog and a couple of aluminium dustbins full of ice,. beer, coke and wine; a system which English promoters never quite adopted. I wonder why.

Brownsville Station, the support band, are already playing and they're cashing in a bit on the current glam, fag rage. It's a bit upsetting to watch guys who you've played with before (we were in Chicago and New Orleans with them), who were hard driving and straight, turn poovy. Perhaps the manager's been working hard on them – it's time they were getting the gigs now. Good luck to them.

It seems all these acts have never seen David perform. David is David; when he goes on stage he is a complete natural, and his act is totally valid – he doesn't pretend, but dons a cloak. He's the only one who'll come through because he is himself and the talent is there. To see ordinary performers trying to imitate the extraordinary is the original sellout. Tasteless and temporary, I hate the lack of intelligence and cheap generalization in bands like these. They tend to clog the media, making it appreciably harder for the real artist to achieve recognition and validity.

Back in the dressing room. A low-level embrace between Trudy and Melanie (they are both the same size and get on well). Tony's happy. The ever present cigar in hand; two young guys are complaining about the lack of outlets for Philadelphia rock bands – I sympathize as I always have. Geography's got a lot to do with the make or break of a group. The crowd is restless now. Brownsville are off and chants are dimly heard from the dressing room. David, Stu and George appear just in time. Embraces all round – we haven't seen each other for three months and David looks tired but great. Looks like he's not been eating again; he's the only star I know who regularly suffers from malnutrition. The charming, disarming, urchin from Brixton who never misses a move or a point. Innocence, cruelty, the nearness yet the distance, all the qualities of the star he is – only *he* knows what he pays for this coveted title, but I've sometimes caught glimpses of the sadness.

Anyway, it's great to be together again and out he goes to a thunderous welcome. He comes off shaking like a leaf, and on we go to the final deafening crash of the tape. He's watching and sussing all the way through. It will be him tomorrow night. Half of him's with us and half with the audience. Come to think of it, that's the way I am. Mick does a blinding solo in *Ready for Love* and all doubt disappears after *Angeline* – it's the feeling, 'We've got 'em.' Off we come; beers go down in 30 seconds and then the wait for the right time to go back on. We hurriedly confer and decide to do *Dudes* and then *Honky Tonk Woman*. The chaos rises higher as Mott becomes six – David throwing out the harmonies with Mick and Pete. *Dudes* finishes, we acknowledge the guy who wrote our half-million seller, and then we finish on our own. A great gig – not a thing to moan about. That's two in a row – I can't believe it!

Back to the hotel now and David, although knackered from

51

his trip, troops down to the local all-night hamburger cafe with our lot. Tony puts Al Jolson on the jukebox. We talk of the tours – the eternal problem of Ziggy being Ziggy and Mott being Mott. There's always media confusion which has to be handled delicately. I tell him of the groups we've seen and he enthusiastically speaks of the New York Dolls – loves their attitude, and he's even more convinced about Iggy. Recording too, is discussed; the relative merits of various studios, etc. Anybody who thinks musicians work barely an hour a day is a mug. I've worked 16 hours a day for Mott since Mott's creation; so have Mick, Pete, Buff and Phally. Mott has been our lives; our love-life centres around it, inconveniences and long separations are demanded by it. A day can be ruined by a 10-minute interview or photo session, and 100 per cent cooperation is required at all times. Attitude is a big word if you *really* want to make it. In a group you're a diplomat, nurse, confidant, taxi driver, labourer, electrician, tailor, designer, and a few other things I can't mention, before you even get on stage.

It may look flashy, but it's over and you are finished before you know it – if you aren't already broken by one thing it will be another. They come and they go is the old saying, and you see it. Eyes. Record companies' eyes, promoters' eyes, agents' eyes, media eyes – they are all watching for that slightest slip – which will get around like wildfire. If this sounds like self pity, it's not meant to – you have to be realistic, and the rock business is a dirty business full stop.

Thursday, 30 November 1972

Well, my first American train ride the 10:15 express from Philadelphia to New York. We missed the 9:45 Metroliner so we have stops on the way. It's a grim, grey day and the slag heaps of New Jersey rush by for 90 minutes – wrecked cars piled 30 high, swamp, waste, construction sites, a timber yard, sidings with Rock Island Line, Canadian International, Canada Pacific, and North Western wagons standing by. Into the tunnel of New York's Pennsylvania Station and a cab takes us to the City

Squire – a nice place, but busy, situated on 51st Street and Broadway. Trudy is off to Kennedy Airport to meet Elaine.

We check in, walk out and it's Christmas on Broadway. Snow falls lightly and Phally and me dodge in and out of cinema foyers avoiding the wet. Police sirens bring back memories of earlier visits – they're so loud you hear them clearly in my 17th storey room. Phally is on the 7th. Broadway in the dusk – I think it's great but a lot of people would tell you different. Gaudy and flash, the Orange Julius, drink kiosk on the corner, reminds me of Larry Friedman's second-hand guitar store. I mentally check the prices at Larry's so I can ring Mick in Philadelphia, and recite them dutifully.

By the way, you're probably wondering why the hell Mick's still in Philadelphia and it's all my fault. Excess wine, women and song are taking their toll so I'll put you in the picture. See, after the gig at the Tower Theatre, Phally and me came to New York the following day. Phally's bird, Elaine, flew in from England and we had to meet her in New York and take her to Trudy's place where she's staying for a holiday. Mick, Pete and Buff, being country lads at heart, have decided to stay in Philly. The next gig's on Saturday at the Palace, Providence, Rhode Island so John (Trudy's brother) will take me, Trudy, Phally and Elaine and we'll meet up with the rest of the band at the hotel prior to the gig. Got it? Far out!

Old movies flicker through your mind. Hollywood stars shopping in the snow on Broadway in Christmas films and strange enough in this frightening city we feel safe.

Into a hamburger joint and friendly Italians, larger than life, pursue a non-stop comical conversation with a very old regular. They are trying to get him a job at Macy's as a Santa Claus. The old fella laughs away enjoying the only company he's probably got. And the guys behind the bar know it, bless 'em.

Phal has a mania again – when will it end. This time he's gone berserk over a cassette recorder and insists on stopping at every cut-price hi-fi store that speckles Broadway. Finally, we go in and he gets the one he wants for $69 which magically reaches $89 with accessories. A non-stop hysterical barrage of salesmanship, and a T.V. goes from $125 to $75 dollars in two minutes. We manage to get out alive but then Phal's forgot to get a receipt so we enter the madhouse again for a further 20 minutes of hair-raising talk which leaves me exhausted and Phal elated. Like Stan, he loves panic – I wish Stan could have been there, he'll be sorry he missed it.

So here I am and I haven't seen my lady properly for nearly two weeks so who knows when I'll write again. Think about me about eight tonight. Phal, Elaine, Trudy and I will be eating shepherd's pie and drinking good wine at the Haymarket on 8th Avenue, and I'm really looking forward to it. See you. P.S. Batman's on the telly.

Friday, 1 December 1972

We decide to go out walking. Meeting New York is rather like meeting Cassius Clay head on and then slowly finding out he is really a nice bloke.

We cut through to 8th Avenue, the porny one to upper classes of N.Y.C., but sometimes convenient for end-of-day businessmen. It also has numerous pawn shops which have guitars or at least used to have guitars. Now the Japanese imitations abound and are of fancy prices. Friends tell me some of the Jap copies are good, but to us in the band the old originals are the best and finding an old Les Paul Junior in a junk shop is the equivalent of a stamp collector finding a Penny Black. Trouble is now the pawn shops are hip. One asks $200 for a Melody Maker and we walk all the way out of the shop laughing.

We turn left into 42nd Street which is even dirtier. Handcuffs, masks, whips and all are on sale here as are the inevitable books and vibrators. Tru's gazed at lasciviously and you get the feeling she'd be raped on the spot if I weren't here. Up the top end we are nearing Times Square – the huge convergence of buildings which isn't really a square at all, and it's getting so cold now we seek the warmth of a yellow cab. The driver is about 60 and came from Poland 52 years ago. He thinks I'm Australian. On down town to 8th Street and 6th Avenue. 8th

Street takes us through the West Village and I conjure up the inevitable dream of seeing Dylan riding by on a bike or something but no such luck. The icy wind again, and we cut across to Bleecker Street. The legendary Bitter End and groupies' paradise Nobodies. We wind up in a bar called the Dugout and have a drink and something to eat. This was where Trudy and I had our first date a couple of years ago. We thaw out over beer, shrimp and broiled chicken. After being warm again we find it's twice as cold outside, when we eventually brave it, and so we get a cab back to the hotel for a rest. Dick rings; the roadies are in town en route to Rhode Island where we play tomorrow. Nothing new to relate except Buff's had a tooth out in Philadelphia. I don't envy him. My fear of dentists is almost pathological. I get up the courage to get there about once every two years, and then it's a full-scale operation.

We get restless watching *Batman* and *Batgirl* and all the other late afternoon shows so we go out again, and, not trusting the wind, we get a taxi straight away to Lexington and 62nd Street where Iggy buys his quite amazing stage gear. The place is called Skin Clothing – only a little shop and for some reason the young guy in charge locks the door, opening only when somebody tries to get in. We chat on a while about music and he says he's got a tape with Freddie King on one side and Jeff Beck on the other and that's all he plays. I order a black leather one-piece which he'll have to make so he takes all my measurements. The idea is that I do the design then ring him from wherever I am and describe it in detail. A dodgy procedure but there is no other way when you are continually on the road. It'll be a miracle if it works out, and I've also got to find $175-200 which is going to take some doing. We take our leave and at a little chemist on Lexington Avenue I get some new shades for $8. The last pair have finally bit the dust but they were loyal and I appreciate that.

We walked back across the avenues then turned left down 6th – the buildings, 30-40 storeys line up on either side. It looks like a bus queue of giants. The weather is more peaceful now. Elaine's dragged Phally off to see the Empire State Building and I wonder how they are getting on. It was nice to see the excitement in Elaine – it's her first time here. Have you ever ridden on a bus from London Airport and tried to explain something of the sights to excited tourists? I always get a kick out of it. It's like watching somebody's face when they get a present.

Well tonight I meet Trudy's parents. Johnny, her brother, is coming in to meet us. I'm really very bad company at this sort of thing, but I'm hoping my manners stay intact as her Mum and Dad have been good to us in the past. My emotions are usually quite uncontrollable and I have to rationalize with myself continually. Wish me luck because I'm going to need it. It's six o'clock now and John's picking us up at seven (he must be O.K. – he's got a Martin) so I think I'll have a shave.

Well it's all over and Trudy's Mum was a delight and her Dad was easy to talk to. Younger brother Kevin regarded me as the enemy and I came away drunk. Trudy's Dad kept saying, 'Get him another beer', and he could have adopted me willingly by 11 o'clock that night. I had pre-arranged with Phal to ring me at 11 just in case I needed to get out of trouble but in the end I became so engrossed in conversation with her Dad that her Mum had to practically kick me out. Anyway, nuf said, the evening was painless and, like a visit to the dentist relief flooded me as John sped us home in the Merc.

A bacon sandwich for me, chicken salad for Tru and a pint bottle of 7-Up from the 24-hour deli across the street led us into deep sleep – oblivious to the never ending sirens which speed all too often to their usually tragic destinations.

Saturday, 2 December 1972

Saturday found us awake at 11 and as John was coming at 12 to take us to the gig we had to hurry. Me like a lady in front of the mirror trying to make myself look like a pop star, and Tru making up an inch from the mirror her head encaged in those vulgar curlers peculiar to the American female species. Dozens of arguments have proved fruitless and so this Martian-

56

like creature delays my morning ablutions in her position on the toilet seat in the bathroom in front of the mirror.

To get to Rhode Island is pretty simple. Johnny U-turns (to his disgust) back to the Long Island Expressway and over the Throgsneck Bridge into the Bronx. Huge blocks of flats make you wonder about the gangs there. Out onto Route 95 and straight to Providence about three and a half hours away. You never know mileage here, it's always given to you in hours. Into Connecticut and the New England area; names like Colchester and Shrewsbury crop up, English names everywhere. The scenery is dull and ordinary, more or less like the Black Country to look at.

We discussed the relative expense involved in a trip like this in America and in Britain. Here they have no road tax as such but instead you pay yearly for the number plates – £27.75 in John's case (it goes according to the weight of the car). On top of this you continually pay freeway tolls – 25 to 30 cents a time, so if you travel a lot and have no expense account it can hit you hard. The one saving grace is that petrol here is cheaper. The Mercury was fully tanked (14 gallons) for about $8 (approximately £3.20). In all I think your average American who works and takes the birds out at the week-end is better off.

The weather (by the way) is really mild – contrary to what I had been told it was like this time of year. We had a quiet meal in a restaurant and then down to the Porchester Palace where we were supporting John McLaughlin.

Now the Palace plays a small but memorable part in Mott's history. It was here on a previous tour we did a walk-off after 10 minutes. We'd not had that all-important sound check that day and hadn't even been billed outside the theatre. When we got on the sound was awful and instead of getting better, it got worse as the guy in the sound box got more and more stoned. In short, I'd thrown my guitar across the stage (an upside down Firebird at that!) and stormed out. This had produced chaos; we refused to go back on and no kidding, our treatment had been so bad that the promoter had paid up in full. So here we are again, and it promises to be another bummer. Putting us on the same bill with McLaughlin isn't a great idea. On the one side rock 'n roll and on the other rangeless sounds and never-ending two-chord jams from brilliant but misguided musicians.

There were about 2,700 people in the 3,200 seater and we went on first about 8:30 to good applause. Now the sound wasn't good, but it wasn't bad either, slightly blurred at the front but clearing as it got to the back of the hall and was pretty good on the balconies. All went well until just after *Ready for Love* when I started to hear spasmodic cries of 'play music' and 'fuck off'. It came from only a few people to the right of us and I could dimly see them waving their arms about. This lot were definitely not here to see us.

I made a brief statement to the effect that they were stupid, narrow-minded bastards and we launched into *Sweet Jane*. This went down well too, but I had to silence the hecklers again while Dick tried in vain to get a good grand-piano sound. He didn't, and the audience had to put up with a very loud vocal and a very quiet piano throughout *Seadiver*. Applause again and on to *Angeline*. We must have been two-thirds of the way through when the music suddenly stopped. I was at the front without guitar, singing with a hand mike. What the fuck was happening? Buff was off his drums, white faced, and Pete was swearing through his mike. Phal looked bewildered and Mick shouted something about a bottle hitting his guitar. I jumped off the stage. Buff was right behind me, and Ritchie leapt from the side. Instinct led me to pointing fingers and a guy ran from his seat hurriedly collecting his coat. I screamed at him, 'Who was it?' and he pointed the guy out before running for cover. The bloke sat back in his seat. Search spots swooped over the now standing crowd and he looked squarely at me as I swore at him. I knew it was him so I let him have it – right between the eyes. The crowd erupted and Mick started the beat again. I ran back over the rail into the orchestra pit, flash bulbs popping all the way, and climbed back onto the stage . . . rip – my trousers split – oh no, not now! – Quick, I squatted on my haunches and sang the last verse in that position pointing to the area of the incident. We finished and the whole crowd were up – what an ovation! Fuck 'em. Nobody gets an encore after a bottle's been thrown. The promoter's going mad (he'd given us a guitar-shaped cake in good faith). The police want Mick to press charges but he won't so they take the guy outside for a once over. And fucking right too. Had the bottle been a couple of feet higher and it would have been Mick's face.

And so on to McLaughlin – peace reigns. The man has found the ultimate in happiness. The songs start in the middle and end in the middle, and the audience loves it. Too frameless, tuneless, formless, but as I said the kids loved it. Perhaps love and happiness add up to utopia, but to be without hate, jealousy, envy and greed you're just not alive. You're a fucking Zombie – and that to me is what John is, although I admire his principles. Phally disagrees; I take a mandy to avoid an argument and I don't even see the journey back to New York, waking only briefly for a deli bacon sandwich thrust down my throat by Tru back at the Squire.

Sunday, 3 December 1972

Valley Forge is just outside Philadelphia. It's not very far from New York. At 42nd Street we go through the Lincoln Tunnel past the rocks where I'll swear Dave Mason posed for *Alone Together* and out onto the road. I read *Rolling Stone* and it tells me how Carlo Santana went religious from John McLaughlin, and the ins and out of a band I never really dug anyway. Each to his own.

The radio's going strong for underprivileged children, perhaps the products of the Vietnam War. It's funny how Nixon was considered such a weak president when he entered office and is now considered so very strong. Apparently he's shitting on everyone at the moment. The election's just been won – his great campaign over the heads of everyone. He has problems.

Dutch barns fly by and one is reminded of the people who were more brutal than even the British – or was that just an illusion. Again, that Black Country scenery – nothing – and into Valley Forge. The Howard Johnson's motor inn is just off the turnpike and we check into room number 114.

John, Neil, Trudy and I have a look at the room. Howard

Johnson's like Billy Butlin gone mad. Every turn off sports a Blue-Boar-like Howard Johnson cafe, and motels are everywhere as well – although this is the first I've been in. We are on the upper deck of an L-shaped two-storey building. A half-empty, filthy swimming pool is in the centre of a lot which is full of girders and planks waiting to form a foyer and restaurant – which will file us in, feed us, fuck us, and file us out – but that's the future. Meanwhile mine and Tru's room is quite nice. Asbestos for a roof and ye old wooden beams. Colour T.V., chequered carpets, walnut walls, leather chairs, bath and shower fill our needs. I mean, everybody knocks Holiday Inns, Howard Johnsons, Sheratons etc. but they are O.K. by me. The basic amenities are there for speed and quick adjustment. You need this on the road. My bowels are in a ridiculous state and Trudy braves the smell like a trooper.

The gig which goes under the name of the Valley Forge Music Fair is . . . weird. Not unlike Belle Vue on wrestling night. The seats surround a central stage, so someone is going to lose out no matter what. We sound check with a crew who belong to Savoy Brown. Savoy are paying them, but they are trying their best for us as our lights just finished off Bowie's tour the night before. Strange stories of naked Spiders knocking on every door in the Warwick – it's great when the heat's off. They are in New York to record new records whether they be singles or albums.

Meanwhile, a voice on the outside speaker placates the irritable cold, waiting crowd and we learn that the third band has given up having been delayed in Ottawa, so its just us and Savoy. A bloke says, 'Right you guys, sound in 10 minutes.'

'FUCK OFF!'

Forty-five minutes later, we take the stage to a partly fanatical partly indifferent audience. An hour later we leave to almost total satisfaction, having done an atrocious version of *Dudes* and a great version of *Honky Tonk* as encores.

A load of groupies looking like Tussaud's Waxworks wait for us and I tease them. Not too successfully though because they suss me and say they've had nothing to laugh at all night. This calls for a throating and the chick amends her statement to 'someone to talk to'; then I release my grip. Tru watches in amusement. Well, I was pissed and they were stupid; it was six of one and half a dozen of the other. John tries my old Echo and doesn't say much. I try to con Tony into buying Trudy a fur coat, but Mick puts the block on it thinking the band would have to pay but I wasn't trying for that. I was trying for a Mainman coat.

Tony's happy with the gig and he and Melanie will be with us non-stop from now on as David's tour is over. It's nice to have your manager around, something we badly missed with Island.

Tru, Elaine, Phal and I go back to the hotel and after a meal discuss the eternal argument. Elaine is very pro family and that's everything I am against. See I'm anti parents. Ireland is a typical case in hand. I really believe the only solution to Ireland's problems is to take a generation of kids away from their parents at birth. I know this sounds inhuman, but is it any more cruel than the bombs, left snidily in cars that blow up innocent people? Parents are steeped in religion and Victorianism, relics of a bygone age. I'm not knocking religion – it's the way it's used by people. An excuse for power, terror and oppression. By all means believe in the 'Good Force' but when it comes to an old white man with a beard, a virgin mother and totem poles – count me out. I'm a confirmed agnostic. Kids lie to keep their idiot 'betters' happy and who wants lies? Kids – my God, kids are beautiful. Kids and the old folks are the most beautiful people on earth – it's those bastards in between that worry me. How old am I? I'll answer by saying I'm twelve years of age, and I'll stay that way until I'm suddenly sixty-five. Still Elaine's Elaine and I'm me – who's to say who's right? All I can say is reader, think for yourself, if you don't you'll miss life altogether. Anyway, Phally can put up with all her parental dramas, but I can't help putting myself in his place and I think I would have gone mad by now if I were he. Fortunately for Phal, he's had a very close family upbringing and he can appreciate Elaine's philosophy. The discussion is broken by Mick returning from the end of Savoy's set, extolling Jackie Lynton. Jackie is a pro and an amazing singer – nuf said. I always thought Savoy Brown were a dirge blues band, but they are good, not new, but they are really good. I think Kim Simmonds has a point about England but he should tour again with Jackie. He was a legend in Hamburg and Hamburg knew who was who, whether they were big or small. Jackie and King Size Taylor along with Tony Sheridan were three of the English all-time greats who somehow by a trick of fate just missed. Some people are just meant to miss, I hope I'm not one of them.

Mick says a trip to the Martin factory is in order tomorrow. Neil and John bid us goodbye. Tru and Elaine will go back to Trudy's place on Tuesday as the band moves out to St Louis that day for the next gig. So far four out of four, and for the States we are still remarkably fit and optimistic. As I write, the hour is 2 a.m. and Trudy is asleep to my left. An English horror film is on T.V. and a Budweiser rears its untapped head invitingly. Two standard abstracts decorate the wall and my clothes are strewn about the floor. You are just about to get up for work in Sheffield; I'm 3,000 miles away and I'm thinking about you and the City Hall. Cheers – all the best – up the lads! My God! Hereford United have done well on the quiet. Norwich comes to mind – I've always loved pirates, but my teams Northampton and Shrewsbury and Hamilton remain infuriatingly middling in the lower leagues. I can't believe Shrewsbury's consistency – they've been in the same place for God knows how many years. Of course the rest of the group support Hereford fanatically – and secretly so do I! Dave Bowen – do it again for fuck's sake! If I were a millionaire – but that's another tale altogether. Goodnight. I just remembered, I told one of the promoters to fuck off when he tried to get us on stage at 8. I hope he didn't take offence. I offered him some wine afterwards and he accepted. People are like models in a fleeting painting. Worries come and go and paranoia swings from side to side like a Satyricon see-saw. The 'art', the real art is to avoid and calculate, but I fall sometimes. That's my nature; I'm a mug. In fact, I might even call this thing *I'm a Mug*. That's what it amounts to – or does it? Ah, bollocks. I'm just a rock 'n' roll bum. . . .

Monday, 4 December 1972

Valley Forge was held onto bravely by George Washington for a whole winter against the evil British. That's what someone told me, and frankly I didn't see what the fuss was about. Perhaps I'm on the wrong side of town. Anyway, there is a historical park here which, if I were John Betjeman I would describe in detail, but I'm a musician so today you are going to get C. F. Martin instead. In case some of you don't know, Martin is a famous make of acoustic guitar; so famous that I've never quite been able to afford one, but I admire them anyway so there's no harm in going. Mick rings them up and they say they'll take us for a tour round if we get up there at a reasonable time.

C. F. Martin, Sr, was born where all good inventors are born, in Germany. Markneukirchen, Saxony to be exact, and as all good beginners did at the time, he emigrated to New York arriving in 1833. The first Martin guitars were made there but as his wife did not like New York, he moved to Nazareth, Pennsylvania, where a lot of Germans had settled; just to keep her happy.

Nazareth is not far from here so Buff, Mick, Trudy and I get into the car and away. First the wrong way and we muck about in Philadelphia before more or less returning to square one. At last onto Route 76, east and then a left onto the P.A. Turnpike, north. Turn off right at Allentown and a tyre bursts just down Route 78, west. This still doesn't deter us and our resourcefulness pays off. We get to Nazareth at about three in the afternoon. The snow has been falling here and chunks of hail lie all around. A typical American quirk brings Northampton, Barry, Bethlehem and Nazareth within a few miles' radius, but if you are pushing romantic illusions, don't. If Jesus decided to do an encore here, he would have to find a parking meter first.

63

A small sleepy midland town, Nazareth sits comfortably about four miles north of Route 78. Sure enough, there is a definite European flavour in the architecture. No hedges separate, that's the thing that's always peculiar to England. In England we've always had hedges. A signpost says the winner of some big race, I think his name was Andretti lives here. We pass a road diner that looks like a couple of buses knocked together, a couple of baseball grounds, and ask the way from a sleepy man at Trumbowers back yard.

Life-size Santas stand in the porches of houses as the district gets better along South Broad Street. The C. F. Martin sign watches us as we steer into the visitors' parking lot. Frozen rain on other cars tells us it's pretty cold in Nazareth, much colder than in Valley Forge.

Martins is a one-storey, wide, rectangular building, about the size I had imagined, employing perhaps 200-300 people. The firm is still as family as it was back in the 1800s. Frank Martin is the latest head of the family and he's only 39 years old so there's no sign of them 'going public'. Consequently, the product is reputable, and indeed handmade. Obviously machines are in use, but the necks of Martins, the graceful curves at the back are all hand carved. The various woods (mahogany, rosewood, cedar and ebony) are stored high in one corner. They're imported mostly from Africa and South America. I'd always wondered how they bent the sides of guitars and here was a guy soaking wood in boiling hot water and bending it by hand around a wooden mould. Seams which the eye can't detect hold the bottom of a Martin together and the top of the guitar (the bit with the hole) has small slate criss-crossings on the inside; the more delicate in size, the softer the tone. Frets are inserted by water. The wood loosens slightly enabling the fret to be hammered in, then the water expands the wood, holding the fret in firmly. No glue is needed. Beading is glued on the lips of the side of the guitar for a bigger glueing surface to connect the top and bottom. You can see hundreds of clothes pegs around every frame holding the beading until it dries. Fine wood is checked by passing it across a special light which exposes any flaws there might be in the wood. If there are any flaws the piece of wood is thrown away. The neck has to be chipped and filed in order to fit the body perfectly and then, when it's together for the first time, it is cleaned thoroughly in a machine. Now they fit a small plastic cup inside the hole in the body to prevent lacquer from messing up the sound. The guitar is then lacquered and sanded up to seven times! Fret boards have previously been put on over the neck which houses a wire rod to strengthen it. Mother of pearl inlays, not done with strips as I had thought, but with tiny lengths of sea shell. Very patient ladies take up to two months on one guitar getting them perfect.

The chick who is showing us around, a little officious blonde with baggy pants, says it takes six months to finish one of the better guitars, their current pride and joy being the D-45 Dreadnought (rosewood) which would cost $1,650. The average Martins, the D-35 and D-28 come cheaper at $610 and $570 respectively. My mate Miller Anderson has a D-35 and it's great. The girl says, 'A lot of people are saying Martins aren't as good nowadays, but like good wine, they mature with age. The older your Martin gets, the better it sounds.'

Any chances of a cheap 'second' are dashed when she tells us any Martins with final flaws are destroyed immediately. Underground stories, however, mainly from roadies, suggest there are indeed a few Martins around which should have been destroyed. Unfortunately, you aren't allowed to talk to the men who work there, thus rendering a quiet word almost impossible unless, of course, you want to risk a right hander at the gate.

We are hungry, so back to the hired station wagon and Mick speeds us back to Valley Forge and the dubious Howard Johnson's menu.

Taking no chances this evening I have an orange juice and chef salad, which is a glorified ordinary English salad with turkey, cheese, eggs, tomatoes and a whole load of unwanted lettuce. This, combined with Trudy's hamburger platter and Coke costs $4.75 (just under £2) which is reasonable by American standards. We try to get Buff to order a huge sundae, but he passes, brave lad.

Today is one of those days when nothing is happening

although I did see a couple of painted ladies about and Pete's been getting obscene phone calls again.

Phally comes in with Elaine, tired. They are the usual demonic pair. Ideas come and go, arguments won, lost and forgotten, all in a matter of seconds, and they are gone. Trudy sits bored while I write so I suppose I'd better pack it up for today. She has to go back to New York tomorrow as we're flying out to St Louis so I think we'll relax a bit now. Everybody needs a little relaxation now and again. P.S. for Bowie – seen *Salome* (Oscar Wilde). It's just been on the telly – great!

Tuesday, 5 December 1972

Today is muggy in Valley Forge. Stan wakes us too late, only giving us 40 minutes to get ready and we are all a little disgruntled. Down into Philadelphia, missing the best route, as usual, and running the gauntlet of Broad Street traffic lights, before passing the heap of wrecked cars again. Over the bridge and out to the airport. Trudy and Elaine are dispatched to the railway station terminus, New York bound. We wind up in the airport snack bar chatting to a couple of barbers who saw the show and were suitably impressed. My gut's starting to protrude, and, as pop stars are not supposed to have a gut, I've decided to slim again. No beer and no breakfast. I sit sullenly and watch Buff attack his tuna fish sandwich – an orange juice my only consolation. Pete's half dead with exhaustion and Mick is worried about this tape we've just acquired of our show at the Tower Theatre. Owing to the hijacking precautions, they put you through the metal door-frame detector for guns etc. Mick reckons it might fuck up the tapes. Pete's also worried so Stan says he'll handle the situation. As usual, with all Stan's well laid out plans, the operation ends in disaster. The guy lets him through the door, but instead of passing the tapes around the outside as requested, the guy says, 'Oh, you forgot your tapes,' and puts them right through the door into Stan's hands. Stan just looks amazed. The usual fight with inefficient airline officials at the boarding-pass desk, and once more we enter the

carpeted short mobile hallway that leads us on to (this time) a
T.W.A. (Ambassador Service) 727. Down to my seat (14-D)
and Phal sits to my right and Buff and Stan over the passage
way to my left. Pete's asleep behind and Mick's way back somewhere trying to forget himself. All airlines have their own magazines and usually they're pretty lousy, but there's an article on
Charles Munroe Schulz, the creator of *Peanuts*, perhaps the
world's most famous cartoon strip. Anyway, that grabs my
attention for a little while.

I think this plane's got something to do with India as there's
a sign with 'Bombay' on it just inside the pilot's door, and
there's also faint orange paintings of Indian-type buildings on
the fuselage walls. I hope we haven't gotten on the wrong one
by mistake.

I heard Ritchie, Phil and Dick were put on the wrong plane
last night. They usually fly on earlier to sort out the sound
equipment, and some idiot put them on a plane to Chicago.
They found out while they were still on the ground, but the
stewardess wouldn't let them off as the engines had started so
they flew north instead of southwest. Now O'Hare Airport in
Chicago is probably the worst place to land in the country and
when they finally did get there, they had to circle one and a half
hours before landing. Sometime later, three spitting-tempered
roadies got a morning flight to St Louis. . . . Remind me not
to speak to them today.

We've got a choice for lunch today. A pizza snack or a
chicken dinner. Looks like the chicken dinner, but that means
a long hungry day until tomorrow. Perhaps I'll just eat the
side salad. By the way, I'm smoking a pipe instead of fags now
and everyone is taking the piss. They say it makes me look
older – they should see my birth certificate. (Phally's just taken
a photograph of me writing so if you see it you'll know when
it was taken.) These airline dinners are good you know, but I
always seem to leave an inordinate amount of mess all over
the place. Everything down to tiny salt and pepper pots are
stuck neatly in the holes provided, but somehow mine end up
wandering down the aisle to be crushed by some stewardess's
foot. I must compliment T.W.A. on this lot of stewardesses,

they look really nice, no instant wigs and false gushing smiles – more natural.

Now and again someone comes on and apologizes for something, and it's all bullshit. I mean, at the beginning of this flight somebody came and said they were sorry for any inconvenience incurred in the searching of our baggage before we boarded. They're not sorry at all! If I'd said, 'No, you can't search my fuckin' bags,' they'd have thrown me out. I know there are hijackers about, so why apologize? Turn me over man; be careful with the heroin though, it costs a lot. It's getting to the stage where it's a case of, "Oh shit, man, you've only got coke, where's the lugers man, where's the guns?" Soon the kids of ten in the school bags won't be choking themselves to death with an American equivalent of a Woodbine – they won't even be having a sly snort – it'll be target practice; you know, photos of teachers on the wall – a few rounds between the eyes before geography. Where is it all going to end? Random thoughts flash through all the time – too quick to write; some of them right and some wrong – everybody's human. I tried using a cassette player to get them down, but I feel (a) like a twat and (b) like Kent Walton . . . so I stick to the pen.

The group's talking about vitamin pills now – I mean are they any good? Pete takes them and Phally is a yeast fanatic. I take them too, but I feel just the same. Still, if I wasn't taking them perhaps I'd be feeling worse than I do. The people who make these pills are crafty fuckers.

We've just gone over Indianapolis and the captain's told us that we're slowing down because the St Louis airport, only 33 minutes way, is 'inoperable'. In other words, it's fuckin' shut, and if it doesn't open again soon, we'll have to take our custom elsewhere. We've just found out that the weather in St Louis is too foggy to land so it looks like Kansas City may be our destination. The captain still hasn't made it official. This just isn't our day. People immediately go to the toilet – isn't that amazing! I hope Peter's not scared. He does horrible things when he's scared and he's sitting just behind me. It's really hard to think of a foggy St Louis far beneath us as the sun beams through the portholes onto my pad. If we all live up here after

68

we die it's a good scene but you'd have to duck now and again. We've been up to 31,000 feet but I can feel us descending now and nearing the clouds. Christ, the bloody things are solid. Why couldn't they gang up somewhere else? It looks like we're circling now. Blue from the left and white approaching from the right. Phally's looking at watches in the little booklet that sells airline goods and decides that the one with an alarm in it must release a needle into your arm when it reaches the given time. Believe him if you like. There we go, it's official, St Louis is still fogbound; no planes landing there so Kansas City here we come, 45 minutes and 300 miles further on. I hope we don't run out of whatever they use for fuel. Apparently there's snow as well in St Louis. It looks like we're in for a couple of hotel-bound days in the city. The captain says a guy will meet us to sort out alternative travel back from Kansas City and business-men slap their knees in frustration and nervously scratch the remaining hairs on their heads. Meetings delayed, perhaps business lost, and loved ones waiting for nothing below. What with Ritchie, Phil and Dick and the rest of us all having trouble we hope it's not a bad omen for the gig at the Keil Auditorium in Market Street, downtown St Louis tomorrow. Fleetwood Mac are topping and I haven't seen them for ages so that will be interesting. We're on second with Bloodrock and Danny O'Keefe bringing up the rear.

The arguments start. Pete won't go to St Louis unless there's a train. Buff won't go in a car. The stewardess says there should be a bus waiting to take us, so maybe it will be O.K. after all. Stan's a bit worried, but then he's always worried. Still, we've never been on a Greyhound but, it's another experience. I've noticed buses here, especially long distance ones, have aircraft seats in them and travel at an incredible speed. Take note England's Midland blushing Red.

Perhaps that's libel so I'm only kidding – really! I vaguely remember hearing the news on T.V. last night. Nixon's stepping up the bombing again whilst Kissinger hints at dramatic happenings at the meeting in Paris. The defence bill expected to be dramatically cut is, instead, to be increased. The amazing thing is that Americans and English alike have grown to accept lies from politicians and take it as a matter of course. I wonder if it's true that Coca-Cola sales help the bombs drop. It's like something out of Walt Disney. They wouldn't let us into Disneyland because our hair was too long; you can buy a colour T.V. and watch the shows though. I wonder what Lennon's doing now; he's probably just having breakfast. Bacon and eggs Japanese style. Good luck mate. But how can you tell everything to the people, and how can you escape piss-taking and the biggest media weapon? Do the thick masses you try to reach really want it? Sometimes the happiest people are the thickest. You know, they touch, miss and back away. It's happy to be dumb to a degree; and how frustrating for you, John. Obsessives can't stop and usually die as miserable as they lived. It's not fair! It's like God saying, 'Don't poke your nose in or I'll squeeze it', but I'm sure that's not so.

The plane wobbles as the clouds bite us and the undercarriage goes down. The table I've been writing on has to be stuck back onto the seat in front, and my pipe smoulders out in accordance with the no smoking sign.

Well me and Phally are sitting here opposite Terminal 29 in Kansas City Airport. Confusion and Stan reign supreme. We stood in the plane for about 20 minutes before the captain said St Louis was open again and would we go to Gate 29. When we all rushed up there (about 100 of us) the T.W.A. official took one look and disappeared, only the tannoy system brought him back with an assortment of pilots. He was applauded by us all. An announcement says, 'Well, ladies and gentlemen we are going back, but if the weather doesn't clear in that area we will have to come back again.' Pete's pissed off, Phally smiles, Mick's white and no one really wants to take another go at it by air. Stan's gone off somewhere to find a bus or a car or something.

Later . . .

Well it's now 5 p.m. Central time and we're still sitting here. The lot that went out on the 2:35 plane have come back and the airport's in chaos. On top of this the place is new and there's no telephones.

Later still . . .

St Louis opened for 30 minutes and then shut again, so it looks like it's going to continue that way. T.W.A. have just given Stan $162 for fuckin' us about, and we can't get a car without that magical credit card that gets you anything you want. So it's the bus; a four-hour Greyhound journey which leaves from somewhere in Kansas and Kansas City is 20 miles away I just found out.

Later, later still . . .

We sit upstairs in the restaurant and Mick's still eating, we'll go when he finishes. It's getting dark now and the supermarket music plays out carols, a smooth cover to hide the panic going on underneath the airport's veneer. Still, it's a day in the life. We saw Crazy Horse briefly and heard that Danny Whetton (the guy who wrote one of our singles, *Downtown*) died. The media seemed to have ignored his demise – perhaps he wasn't big enough.

Pete excitedly tries a huge six-string with really thick strings owned by a passing Mexican group who don't speak English. Buff keeps writing his cards; he must have written as much as I have since we've been here. Phally tries to stave off his hunger and makes do with an apple. The eternal slimming battle – we're like a load of old women! The things you do for a fuckin' rock 'n' roll band. The porters, they're all black for some reason, come up. I'm writing and walking at the same time so I'll stop.

Well, I'm on a Greyhound bus now and we're mobile. The cab drive was great, the driver talkative and I sponge what little knowledge I can get out of him for future references. Apparently there are two Kansas Cities; the one we're in is the big one – Kansas City, Missouri. The Kansas City in Kansas has a population of only 65,000 and is just the other side of the Missouri River.

It's strange going into Kansas; you have the total traveller's dream. On our left freight cars crawl slowly along the railroad. We crawl slowly along the road. The old airport, still in use for small craft, and then the river swimming down to its date with the Mississippi in St Louis. The cabby says soul is big

71

here. Rock music is confined to occasional concerts due to roughhouse tactics by various segments of the local community.

Bond houses line up over on our left close to the police station and the prison. A fortune is made by these guys who bail out suspected villains on H.P.

The Greyhound bus station is just here and the cabby helps us with the luggage up the stairs into the station. Stan runs up and panics again. There is a bus in now at Platform 4. We run like hell, bags all over the place, and here we are. Me and Pete and a game of chess.

And the time goes by. I'm beaten twice and we play boxes which I win. Then we play noughts 'n crosses which is a farce. We plug in earphones to the radios above (England, again take note) and when Pete loudly says how good the chicken sandwiches and cokes are a miniature lumberjack leaps up and says 'Where?' Lights, darks, flash by and although inside the bus it's warm, the rain freezes as it hits the bus outside and we stop a couple of times en route for the driver to clear the front window.

Finally, about 10 p.m. this bloke Sam who sat across the aisle from me and talked so much I can't even tell you what he said, walked off to see his mother who is ill. She was 98 last Sunday, so the grand old lady is entitled to sag now and again if she wants to. Sam is full of sorrow. Phoney tears seem not far away and whisky shines on his young female companion's face. Sam, in a tarzan suit, for when the night comes has to reveal his 245 pounds for the chick to see. He knows every trick does Sam, and he knows what he is too, but he's decided to go along with it. It's easier this way. He's like a pleading little fat dog but he'd slit your throat for five shillings if he decided it would benefit him in some small way. They're a breed – small, fat, lots of greying hair, moustaches and beards; sort of flash Boston gear and hip flashy things – watch those fuckers. Don't be taken in by the chat. Goodnight, Sam; hello, St Louis.

The cylindrical Stouffer's Riverfront Inn is situated in downtown St Louis, 200 South Forth Street to be precise. We stayed somewhere else last time when the Gateway Arch, St Louis's proudest possession, stood miles away; now we are right up close to it. It's a huge thing about 650 feet high and you can go over it in a lift. I don't quite see why it's there, probably to hide certain other things here which the St Louis council aren't so proud of. St Louis is one of hundreds of American cities that have areas where a cab driver won't go, whether he be black or white. He won't be seen with you. St Louis ghettoes are a famous part of the blues tradition; if you go to the edge of them it's easy to see why. Once they built a huge new ghetto like a modern council estate to house the blacks that team into St Louis; they wrecked the place completely and the last time we passed it looked like a monument to architectural inhumanity to man. I wonder how many people cooped in like battery hens around estates elsewhere wish they'd have had the guts to do the same thing.

People died before they finally got the message, and that's how blues are written. They do live life you know, they don't let it pass without commenting. And what a fuckin' commentary it's turned out to be.

I don't know what got me on to all that so I'll get off it. I had a beer tonight in the Rag Bar two storeys under the lobby, with Phil and Dick. Huge bowls of peanuts and the nearest thing to wine I could get was Dubonnet. Fleetwood Mac walked by, having a good look, sussing the opposition. Nothing said despite my hand waves, so fuck 'em if that's the way they want to be. Each to his own. That Fleetwood guy's as elegant as ever and I tell a lie, the bass player did smile, but his missus didn't. Perhaps they've heard advance tales of our flash egos etc. It's amazing how reputations can belie.

Back to the room and I'm just in bed when Ritchie rings. They've got the tape of the Tower Theatre Show in 510 so down we all go to drink Ritchie's white wine and listen to what is supposed to have been good. Dick operates the tape he's just hired and as it's 10 in. we have to wind slowly and edit onto a couple of 7 in. He gets it going and it's bloody awful. Stan says it was nothing like this. *Dudes* is terrible, makes you want to stop doing it. We've never done that number well live. Oh my God, I can't believe it – take it off. Some of that stuff doesn't sound too bad, but the balance is awful. The bass and organ disappearing and the voices and lead guitar always too loud. It sounds like it's 70 per cent his fault, 20 per cent our fault and 10 per cent the tape's fault, which is playing slightly fast. Bloody hell, I can't stand it. Me and Pete go back up to the room.

Wednesday, 6 December 1972

And so today in St Louis the snow lays crisp and even. The sun shines. Pete's gone down to breakfast with Mick so I think I'll nip down as well. We're going out pawn shopping. Stan just rang. He says we have to fly tomorrow even though it's only about 90 miles or so and this is upsetting to Mick. He also says Tony's flying in from New York.

Later . . .
The pawn shops were shut. It's strange to find everything closed in a predominantly black area because of a Jewish holiday, but that's the way it is around here. We went down to Franklin Avenue and Easton, then approached Dr Martin Luther King Drive. This drive may one day reflect the size of the man's heart it is named after. At the moment it could be a tribute to the changin' times or, at face value, could be taken as the street Dylan referred to as Desolation Row.

Barbers, pool halls, underground clubs, cheap auto dealers mad missionaries all have the same fronts. Cheap, hand painted with the nature of their business scrawled do-it-yourself style, the letters dribbling down below their intended endings. An old cleaners, a wall, a tower and a cinema are left looted wrecks. Tiny pieces of grass brave their way through this 16 degree December day surrounded by frost-covered chairs, prams, and other junk, once warm in people's homes.

They are slowly knocking the place apart and a lump comes to my throat as a shivering dog tries to sleep at the side of the road. Another stands in the porch of a vacated house, orphaned by rules laid down by new landlords, and almost too skinny to be alive, waiting for the old days to come back. Old buildings stand here and there, the standard black houses of a

74

bygone day. Brick blocks, maybe three stories high with wooden porches, rails, staircases, chairs and other bits of wood stuck on the front giving the overall impression of a cuckoo clock.

Some are still lived in. Articles of clothing hang here and there but not a soul in sight. It's much too cold, what a bloody sight. At least, as I said, they are pulling it down and sightseers in years to come will probably marvel at the flash hotels and beautiful restaurants and parking lots. But I'll always remember the cold, misery and squalor that is the street called Dr Martin Luther King Drive.

Perhaps the next street over might have been nicer, perhaps upper-class blacks have good lives here and perhaps the Indians are worse off. All I can say is nobody should have to live here. It is 12 noon and a really drunk black man sullenly avoids his chick's outstretched arms. When you hate help, hope's been knocked out of you. It's the end.

Mick makes a few phone calls about 2:30 and we finally find a place open on Olive Street, not too far away, called Sam Lights. An overweight (but dieting) guy shakes us by the hand and announces himself as Larry Bird. Potential star, dreamer of Las Vegas, he says he destroys the world every night before supper. Pawn shops here are both creative and destructive. Guns hang next to guitars, flick knives next to jewellery, suitcases, drums, T.V.s, clothing – they really get into it. A man told me of a guy in Albuquerque who walked into a shop with a sub-machine gun squashed inside a Martin case. Most owners will tell you stories of young rich college kids or bewildered older people selling ancient Les Pauls for $10. Alas, we never have that kind of luck! I make do with about the only decent guitar, and E.B.O. bass which I buy for $75 complete with battered case.

Larry's a great conversationalist. He rings round friends to see if they have anything. There's a woman who can't get over the accents, especially Phally's, and we stay there for about 90 minutes. Phally takes photos before we leave. Hundreds of hats are in a huge bin. They give us one each and we feel like 'dudes'. I give a Negro a cigarette in the doorway. He's frozen stiff and trying to keep warm, but they won't let him in. Even when I offer the cigarette though, he smiles gently and asks me if I need matches. I'm not rich, but I feel fuckin' rotten – really rotten.

My hat says 'Barrister of Philadelphia' inside it. I wonder whose it was. Once again a talkative cabby – who tells us about the huge Bush Stadium which houses baseball, American football and soccer, apparently soccer's on the way up here. A sign outside the Bel Air Hotel just down the street from here says 'Welcome Los Angeles Rams' they'll probably be gigging at the Bush.

The promoter rings up and says half the audience is coming just to see us, and they have the best groupies in the U.S.A. We're beginning to realize this is standard business procedure to put you in a happy frame of mind, but we feel good anyway. I try to ring Trudy, but she's out picking her Mum up; I'll try again later.

Pete sleeps on the bed as I write. He can sleep 14 hours a day if he's not working. I haven't seen Buff, and Stan doesn't answer so he must be at the gig. Phally's gone back to his room with Mick. As I haven't got a watch I can only guess it's about five o'clock. There's a Chinese documentary on Channel 2. The sound is off the telly and Cat Stevens sings about the wind in his hair on the radio. I think I'll visit the bogs for a marathon. American food does my staid English gut in, even if it's only salad. I just glanced out the window; it's dusk now. The swimming pool's iced over and there's a light in the church across the street. The other way a bridge spans something I can't see and a huge office block slowly goes to sleep, it's windows like hundreds of eyelids shutting as the working day comes to an end. Stan rings; sound check in 20 minutes. There's another band added, Dick Heckstall Smith's new band, but we're still second from the top, so that means we can come back to the hotel to get ready. Pete's £70 thigh-length boots have been mended and Trudy rang to say she's in now so I'll ring her. I still haven't had that shit yet.

It's 7:30 now and the sound check leaves us in the hands of the Almighty. We'd just gotten switched on for it when 4,000 people invaded the front stalls leaving Mick amazed, stranded half way through *Ready for Love*. Needless to say, Stan panicked and a poor second-in-command whose name is Rob takes everything he says with shrugged shoulders.

There's a dispute between Bloodrock and ourselves over second billing. Now this may seem petty, perhaps flash, to the reader, but illusion plays a large part in the game of rock 'n roll and any guy in a band will tell you this is an important facet. The rows I've been through over billing in my life must be in treble numbers, and the result about 50/50 depending on where we were and how big we were. If you are expendable, if you've got enough bread to carry out your threats and fuck off, that counts too.

I chatted to Mick Fleetwood who was very shy but extremely nice, and a couple of musicians from Heckstall Smith's group including the man himself. They're opening every gig because Dick doesn't want to use Mayall and Hiseman as stepping stones. We wish him luck.

As I said, the promoter's not here yet. Still selling hi-fi's in his stereo shop somewhere, so we don't even know now if we'll go on. The *brrrrr* of the hairdryer signifies Pete's drying his hair before applying that silver stuff which will stink the room out and I'm waiting my turn. Just had a grilled cheese sandwich and orange juice with Stan, Phal and Mick. Buff's had a letter from home saying *Disc*'s called us a one-hit wonder. Silly bastards. Buff's camera lens is missing so he's a bit sad, but he'll come out of it himself. You can't sympathize with him or he gets more angry. Tony's flying in with Melanie from New York, but I haven't seen them yet.

Hangers-on bang on the doors and we have to be rude. If you just say hello you are subjected to endless conversation which leaves you behind your schedule. When you do finally get them away they turn nasty anyway so you might as well do it straight away. Chicks knew our names, but then again they make that their business. I should imagine it happens with every group.

One reporter in L.A. told me he'd seen girls asking me exactly the same questions as they'd asked Bolan a couple of weeks before. Well, at least I'm in good company. The adrenalin starts to build; that excitement we get at every gig no matter how big or small, top of the bill or bottom. It will be a sad day when it's not there anymore.

Thursday, 7 December 1972

Well it's now 5:15 p.m. and I'm sitting yet again on T.W.A. going to New York City in seat 14B. Things have slightly altered so now I'm going to tell you (as much as I can) what really happened yesterday.

We got to the gig last night and it was absolute bedlam. As was expected, Dick Heckstall Smith opened, and then absolutely nothing happened for over an hour. The crowd was really hostile and backstage it was a deadlock. Bloodrock were refusing to go on before or after us. Fleetwood Mac didn't want to end the show but Bloodrock wouldn't either. The arsehole promoters hadn't got a bloody clue, they just stood there hopelessly. Why do these silly sods promote? They'd given Bloodrock a second-on-the-bill contract and we had an identical one. Bloodrock would not budge an inch and neither would we; finally we gave in at the time we'd originally planned to do and went on. The poor kids had waited so long because the promoter was totally ignorant, or extremely snidy and just let the incident occur.

What with no sound check and all the hassles back stage, we went on pretty miserable. If ever a gig should have been pulled out, it was this one. Tony just wasn't sure of the procedure on down-the-bill acts and let it happen. We went on even though we shouldn't have. The sound, although good out front (as we found out afterwards) was terrible on stage. We slowly dissolved in front of a curious but non-committal crowd. Two spots comprised the entire lighting system, Bloodrock not even allowing one of their lights to be used. And the spots careered crazily around the stage missing most of the points in the music. We bravely carried on, me waggling my arse in a none-too-hopeful attempt to attract a few females. What an act. I felt like a prostitute – it was nothing to do with music. It was a professional con, forced on us by circumstances, and we hated

78

every second of it. *Angeline* fared well and we finished with *One of the Boys*. A good ovation but stamping died too quickly for a reappearance, and we trooped angrily back to the dressing room. The atmosphere was electric. We can't stand bummers, especially those not our fault. We'd sold out on the gig and it left a horrible taste in our mouths. We all knew now it should have been a walk-out. We would have had every right to, but it's too late now. We played.

Tony says it's totally his fault – his first experience of a terribly disorganized gig in the States and he finally decides that things will have to change.

We try to discuss it seriously and Bob C., a light man who's watching us and getting ready to light the five or six other headliners we have to do, gives us the benefit of his considerable experience. Big Bob reckons on him going out early with Ritchie the next day to Springfield to check out the lay of the land. If it's at all dodgey Tony will cancel it altogether. By now Bloodrock have actually gone on and we have a quick look at them before leaving. They are going down about the same as us. I like the singer's red velvet trousers with the squiggly yellow line down them, but that's about all.

I turned, and at the side of the stage the little assistant guy was talking to a couple of at least 50 chicks who were hanging around. As a parting gesture, as I passed him I whispered, 'That's what happens when you treat your groups like shit.' I walked onto the ramp, happened to turn and saw him waving his fists egged on by the girls, who'll agree with anything and anybody. I walked back and calmly shouted, 'The people you work for are a bunch of utter cunts,' into his face.

'What?' came a yell. And five guys, one I knew as a promoter, ran over. 'What the fuck are you talking about?'

'You're fuckin' useless; you shouldn't be allowed to run gigs.'

'You fuckin' jackass, get out of here. Go on, get out you fuckin' jackass, you jumped-up cunt. Your group sucks. Get out before I put a hole in yuh.'

'Bollocks, you load of fuckin' idiots – you fuckin' idiots.'

The little one came first, first pulled back, and I squared onto

79

him. He held back and the promoter came up near – really near. He threatened and I just stood there facing them. The blood had gone from my face and my lips were quivering. Tony pulled them away as calm as ever and they waved their fists and yelled. All I could shout was 'fuck off'.

We walked down to the lower level. There were no bottles anywhere. My lips were twitching and I was in that cold rage you get when nothing could hurt you. Tony just took me out and we got in the car without exchanging a word. I don't know what he must have thought; I knew what I thought though. I knew I had been what the guy said I'd been. A jackass. I knew the group had been bad, but I also ·knew that the pathetic apology for a promotion by complete idiots was the reason. The band had missed the whole episode, Tony and I being the last out of the Convention Hall and now they all ached to go back. The police were there now. The streets were silent as we travelled back to the hotel. How was I going to get rid of the rage? As Pete and I lay on our beds, we talked of the suspicious disappearance of Wishbone Ash's equipment from this same town, which put them into debt again and caused them to break off their tour half way through. The mirror in the room broke at the top from my badly aimed ashtray. Pete expertly finished the job off with a tumbler.

Stan rang for another meeting with Tony. This time in his suite on the 21st floor. And so up we troupe for a rambling discussion – getting slowly to know Tony better, and he us.

He's decided not to mess about on this kind of gig anymore. Out go three or four suspect gigs straight away, and instead he wants us to speed up the act for the all-important headliners.

Good news from Cleveland where we're doing a three-thousand seater. 1,000 seats have already gone by mail order without the gig even having been advertised. It stands a great chance of selling out. Detroit is also selling well. It's on these gigs we must concentrate. We'll take second or third bill only on proven, up-front, well-organized gigs. Last night had been a lesson in a way, and could prove to be a valuable one.

Mugs. Never again. Go and hit a wall, but don't play at any cost. It'll do more damage in the long run.

80

The meeting over we go down to Mick's room. It's about 3 a.m. in the morning and the room is packed. Fleetwood Mac turn up to see this guy Ed's guitars. Mick rang him earlier and asked him to come. Various ladies hang around but get pretty much ignored in the quest for Ed's guitar bargains. He's well known in group circles and well respected as a purveyor of musical instruments for English bands. We've met him before in various towns. He buys continually around the pawn shops and then goes to where the bands are and sells them. Mick Fleetwood grizzles a bit about going on late and I don't blame him. I just hope he didn't think it was us who fucked him about. They soon leave and various other people slowly follow. I've had a mandy and try, somewhat the worse for wear, to get Ed's double pick-up, upside-down Firebird down from $300 to $250, but he just won't have it. Mick eventually gets a small Gibson amp for $60 and Peter gets a bargain, a 1941D-18 Martin Concert in beautiful condition for only $130. I have no luck at all convincing Ed that $250 is a good price and off he goes into the lift with his friends, covered in amps and guitars.

Pete and I return to our room and survey the damage. It looks like the Armada's been through it. Fuck it. My eyes sag heavily; it's 5 a.m. and we may be going to Springfield later today.

But that was yesterday; now I'll get onto today when we almost missed our flight to New York.

The radio wakes me at ten. There's a cold chill in the room. The temperature is zero degrees. I pull my coat onto the bed and huddle back into that nowhere snoozing land. Twelve o'clock comes and Stan rings to say the Springfield gig is off. Bob C. and Ritchie think it's as bad, even worse, than last night's mess. Tony suggests we go to New York instead and do a few interviews which are outstanding so we set 3:45 in the lobby as the leaving time for the airport. Room-service coffee takes ages to come and then, about one o'clock, Pete realizes he has no case for the Martin. We ring Mick; the pawn shops are open, why don't we go for a quick shuffle. Trouble is Mick's just ordered breakfast so it's about 2:30 before we eventually get a cab. Franklin has nothing, but a lightning dash back to

Larry Birds gets Pete a $5 case. It's great for the price—a black one which looks new. The time is tight though, and the cabby joins in the spirit of the thing speeding from one pawn shop to another in case of *that* bargain. Bingo! A shop called Ace discloses from somewhere in the backroom of junk, a clean long case. He opens it revealing a shining Fender Jazz bass in immaculate condition. The guy says he won't mess around, he'll quote his lowest price and that's that – $125. Pete's in like a shot. Borrows $70 from Mick and another 25 from me as he is, as usual, broke. With the guitar safely in his sweating paw we joyfully enter the taxi. A great buy – the feeling an antique dealer or a stamp collector gets when finding something valuable at a very low price.

A clock on a building lights up 4:06 in bulb letters and we are almost back at the hotel when Pete discovers he's left behind his T.W.A. bag containing his various walking-about accoutrements. Sullen moans of 'You fuckin' idiot' have no effect on him and he cheerfully redirects the cab back about 40 blocks to Ace. Mick and I sit in the back glumly. Stan's going to bollock us for this. We may miss the plane, and Buff hates it if he's kept waiting. We get back to Ace. The bag is where he left it and Peter tries to ring Stan to no avail while I rush to make a last-minute appeal for a Gibson Melody Maker. The guy's sticking at $100 and I think that's $10 to $20 too much by Detroit prices so I decide to leave it. Mick says I did the right thing, and we speed downtown. A couple of cardboard cartons hit the car from a small gang of jeering Negroes. We got away just in time by the look of it. Back once again to the hotel, the limos are waiting, one for us and one for Tony, Mellie, Lee and Stan.

We speed to the airport and I'm still marvelling at how we managed to catch the 5:15 to New York. If it hadn't been for the new search regulations, I think we'd have missed it, and that would have meant another day in St Louis as the other planes are flying out full. I wouldn't have liked that. I'm a bit petulant with Tony about the promoter. I can't forget it – I don't suppose I ever will. But he assures me that neither David or we will do a gig for him again. Nuf said.

And now my ears are beginning to pop signifying our slow descent to La Guardia, New York's domestic airport, and I've forgone chicken and roast spuds to write this lot down.

Ah, the lights of New York City. It seems like returning home after doing a gig in Manchester. How many lights down there? It would take a lifetime to count them. The plane's a metal ball, cruising up the groove at the side of the largest pinball machine in the world! Above the dark blue of the darkest drinking bar.

Elizabeth, Newark and over the river to Manhattan. The Statue of Liberty and we might turn in over the Yankee Stadium. Everybody in the world should see the world. It should be made compulsory. The kids from Bradford, Newcastle, Liverpool, Sunderland and all those northern towns whose only buzz is signing on Wednesdays and Fridays may never get to see the sight I see now and I'm woefully inadequate at translating it to paper. Whoops, a bumpy landing, but a safe one and I've got to go. See you.

Now American hotels are expensive, a single in this place (which is really a double, but only one person is booked) is going to cost you $30, so what we try to do is smuggle Trudy in to save a bit of bread. It's all paid for by the travel agency as are the air flights, but Stan's got to settle up at the end, and obviously the band shouldn't pay for somebody's lady.

Trudy and I have wine and shepherd's pie at the Haymarket with Phally and Elaine, and we return to the hotel via Times Square. I must compliment Winston fags on their huge sign in the Square. This bloke's smoking away and real smoke comes out of his mouth and forms rings in the crisp night air. The temperature here is about 30 degrees. It's a funny thing about the cold here; it's a dry, clean sort of cold, and providing you're not out for too long, it's not unbearable at all.

Anyway, we go back to the hotel and it's one of 'those'. Now most hotels are groovy. You're paying a lot of bread for a room so they turn a blind eye if any 'guests' happen to drop in, but not this bloody place. You get the feeling a $10 bill will solve the problem but fuck them, they overcharge anyway. The thing is they're being funny about letting the ladies in and this can ruin a good Haymarket meal. Indigestion creeps up on me! Only one way. All great statesmen have used it to great effect throughout evolution. In a word bullshit's required – and plenty of it. We storm the desk.

'What is this, a bleeding kindergarten or something? How old do you think we are, 15?'

'I'm sorry sir, but we have a new general manager here; he won't let guests up after midnight unless they register.'

'Fuck your general manager. Ring my manager, Stan Tippins, we're leaving, the lot of us, first thing in the morning. This is disgusting. The lady is my wife and lives on the island with her parents while I'm working here, so what are you implying?'

'Look sir . . .'

'We're not looking anywhere, I'm ringing Stan . . .'

'Nuts.' [This time we're at the internal phone.]

'SIR! JUST A MOMENT.'

We return to the desk.

'Look sir [he calls me sir, he thinks I'm a twat], just sign your (ahem) wife in and then it's O.K. No extra charge at all.'

'Oh, well all right – that's different. [Cough, feeling like a twat now.]

'But don't forget, sir, no ladies can stay the night, all night.'

All fuckin' night – forget it. He's just got to say that so he can say he said it – but I think it's O.K.

Up to our room, watch a Bob Hope film then try to watch a Bing Crosby film. Finally move Tru's sleepy head over gently and nip up to switch the T.V. off. It's just about 3 a.m. and I wish that episode hadn't happened – it means we've got to watch out. If it happens again, I think we'll either register properly or move to another hotel. It makes Tru look like a scrubber, and I'm *not* having that – NO WAY . . .

Friday, 8 December 1972

And now it's raining, 'like hell on a fire engine' as Stan would say. The open curtains reveal a huge block centre, at least 50 storeys high with a red neon 'Grants' stuck on top. A master-piece of understatement. 'Hotel Edison', 'Hotel Madison', '–otel –aft', (that's all I can see) and more immediately oppo-site, an 18-storey office block with girls busily working type-writers and a man looking straight at me watching if I'm looking at him. Neither of us can tell, as we can't see each other's eyes.

Down below *Crescendo* is playing on the right of 7th Avenue. 'Off Track Betting', 'Jack Dempsey's Bar', 'Chock-full-O-Nuts', buses, taxis, hundreds of those huge American cars (which look as normal here as they do abnormal in England). I can see one of those Volkswagens with Cadillac radiators that they are selling at the moment. Immediately below, two fountains, one of which is drained in front of a huge 80-storey building with no name. Rain everywhere and people scurrying. Christmas is in the air. A block across and a few streets down is where I wrote *Angel of 8th Avenue* – looking at Manhattan three years ago, after a very drunken night at 'Nobodies' in the Village.

It's one of those days in which nothing happens at all so let me skip to about 6 o'clock in the evening when we find that Stan's got us tickets to the Jethro Tull, Roxy Music concert at Madison Square Garden.

You've probably heard of this place; if you can imagine Wembley Pool only twice as big, you've got the picture. We all meet in the lobby at 7:15 and Pete says he's tired because he's walked round looking for guitars all day, and Buff's not bother-ing either, so it's me, Tru, Phally, Elaine, Stan and Mick for the evening out.

Phally, me and the girls pile into a yellow cab hailed for us by an oilskin-covered doorman. He stands out in the middle of the rainswept street madly gesticulating and blowing his whistle. Other whistles can be heard from rival doormen and the avenue is alive with the chords of sirens, cars and whistles.

Straight on down Broadway, past Allied Chemical (where you can get a very thin *Daily Mirror* if you get up early) and about half a mile on down to the Garden. I give the cabby $2 and we run under the cover of the foyer. Dozens of escalators, lifts everywhere, makes you feel very small. You clutch your ticket in amongst thousands of kids all jostling to get in. We sway through with the crowd to the ticket gate. On the way, people shout the sale of T-shirts, photos, and tickets; others shout they want tickets. Tower D – Gate 14 – Seat 35A; there are so many numbers on this fuckin' ticket you've got to be an accountant to work it out. Up three escalators and finally we find the gate. A health-food bar is opposite the entrance and I notice coconuts with straws in them. Avoiding this stall we pass onto the next, and I felt distinctly unhealthy buying 'a pack' of Marlboro cigarettes for 70 cents. Incidentally, you must buy cigarettes by the 'pack' here; if you ask for 20 Marlboro, you'll get an incredulous look and a carton shoved in front of you. Upon explaining that you really only wanted 20 actual cigarettes, abuse will be hurled at you, and you won't forget the next time. I haven't anyway.

All the lights are on and the Garden is about half full of people who all seem to be walking about. It's a raunchy atmosphere; everybody shouting including doormen and security guards, but it feels good and I don't get that uptightness you sometimes get at venues. The theatre is like a huge rectangle, people high in the gods and below on the floor. On stage the usual pandemonium is in full flight. The P.A. is stacked high above on scaffolding; only two columns on the stage making it better to see. A roadie talks through one of the mikes to the guy on the panel somewhere at the rear of the front audience area. A huge fat man directs which coloured panels should go into the lights above. A guy hangs precariously following his instructions. This is where it all happens and I look at the middle of the floor expecting Mohammed Ali to be jogging around somewhere at his old gig.

The first frisbee is thrown and a cheer goes up in the audience. These little saucer-like plastic throwing toys are always thrown at American concerts along with wafer thin plastic rings and balloons. This doesn't happen much in England. I remember we once threw 200 out at our gig at the Albert Hall in London. Not knowing exactly what to do with them the crowd promptly hid them under their pullies as souvenirs of the event. Four or five college kids sit excitedly next to us shouting madly if somebody throws a frisbee a long way. The applause varies according to the length of the throw and often winds up in cackles of laughter if some poor unfortunate gets it on the head whilst looking another way.

Stage lights flash on and off. A moog farts obligingly denoting it is working and an electric piano blares out a pot pourri of notes from the horny hands of a roadie. Finally, right in the middle of the chaos, the promoter, the young and well-respected Howard Stein (we worked for him in Porchester a couple of years back) calmly announced, 'From England, Roxy Music'.

A reasonable cheer went up, signifying the crowd didn't really know who the hell Roxy Music were. Eno looked like a Spider and Bryan Ferry like a Dracula-type Presley. The first number was a complete mess and *Virginia Plain* was ruined by the bass refusing to work until about half-way through the number. Right away you knew that Roxy never had a sound check. By the time the sound was right they were wilting under pressure although I thought they held on extremely well. To my mind doing Madison Square Garden without a sound check is like Marc Bolan fighting Joe Bugner for the English heavyweight title. Roxy tried, did their best, and failed – through no fault of their own.

You can't tell an audience why they failed, it's one of those things. They paid their money, they want a show. But what can you do when they are still putting lights up for the headliner when you are on? What can you do when the sound guy you totally rely on hasn't a clue what you are about? People are jumping about distracting you from your job and the headliner's fanatical fans howl abuse, not because they dislike you, but because they are impatient to see their heroes. Roxy passed like a vague irritation before the mainliner, and I for one know that in two years' time those same people will be lauding them. Tonight, though, it will be of no consolation to the band and many a gig like this will give them sleepless nights before they eventually break through.

The lights go up and it's the interval. Stan flies off with Howard Stein backstage and comes back with backstage passes.

I really want to console Roxy but I don't know them, so adopting correct procedure Stan goes up and inquires first. This saves any embarrassment. Maybe they never heard of us; maybe they don't like us. Maybe they want to be on their own, or maybe they don't want to know – it takes all kinds. Stan comes back and says for us to go up and we pass through the security guards to the backstage area. Well-dressed gents, huge greasers (I don't know why) and assorted groupies, all in their garnished uniforms of the night.

Out through the back curtain into a land of folded up boxing and wrestling rings, huge canvas rolls, fire apparatus, wagons and pipes and air-vent tunnels. The crowd noise grows faint as Stan leads us through a door and along a tunnel lined with photographers, managers, agents, record people, their women and the like. We pass the door marked 'Jethro Tull' and opposite a little way down we come to Roxy's dressing room.

It's full of people. Photographers, writers, hangers-on, managers (the same ones who used to manage ELP and Tyrannosaurus Rex a few years ago). The bass player comes over straight away, seems nervous and talks about a variety of things. He says he saw us at The Temple and he met me at a party at the Kensington Hotel but I swear I've never been there but he swears I have, so I might have been. Mick talks to the guitar player (as usual) and the sax player comes over. They are really polite, shy and extremely nice people. Eno smiles everywhere, his gaily painted locks, make-up and stage dress still intact. Poor bugger doesn't get a chance to change, with us lot around. We get offered champagne but I have a coke instead and I feel sorry for Bryan Ferry. About three people are talking to him all at once. He tries to answer politely while probably feeling quite sick inside about the gig. I'd love to sit and have a chat with him as his voice is really good and I just like the ideas he has, but it's bloody hopeless. Apart from a brief five minutes exchanging pleasantries it's all over. Photographers trying to get them here, there and everywhere – together and individually.

I have a quick chat to their manager, he's a pal of Chris Blackwell's and I know him slightly. Then I whisper to Trudy we ought to get out. Our presence only adds to the hordes of people and they need a bit of space to breathe.

Back through the curtain to the side of the stage. We can faintly see faces in what were our seats so we decide to stay put. Jethro Tull are half way through their particular brand of magic to a now-capacity Madison Square Garden crowd.

The balance is beautiful, the dynamics perhaps the best ever by a rock band when utilized in Tull's intricate arrangements of which Ian Anderson is mainly responsible. Anderson is a master of the art, the complete musician. Showman goblin music played by goblins, evil, delightful, cheeky and tongue in cheek, yet spot on musically. I'm not keen on the weather forecast bit of the act. The rabbit and gorilla don't particularly impress me either, but the rest is faultless. Tull are beautifully set on a little branch of the tree of rock 'n roll. No comparisons can be made and their music is entirely their own. Their influences are either cleverly disguised or they are a proto-type of their style. You can't say too much more about Tull. They fully deserve the acclaim they get and that's unanimous – they're just one of the greats, full stop.

Like all posers I decide we must leave before the end of Tull's performance to avoid the rush. We signal to Phally and Elaine still somewhere in the audience and they slip out with us. Stan and Mick are lost somewhere in the crowd. Just before moving through the barricade of the backstage area, a hand touches my arm. Martin Barre says hello whilst the drummer pounds his solo. Martin is one of rock 'n roll's nice quiet lads. He's always so modest it's painful and if you say Tull is great he gets very embarrassed. He's always overawed by everything and only wants to sit and talk guitars with anybody interested. Tea is his only weakness, he always wants a cup of tea. He asks about Mick and asks me to tell him he'll ring him later.

Out we go, down the escalator, and finally, after a couple of wrong turns, out into the rainy street. Straight into a cab and up to the Haymarket again. Old habits die hard and here we are again, shepherd's pie and wine. Well we know this place and feel safe here; nobody bothers you and the service is good.

The wine is a bit expensive this time around though: $1.25 for a small glass – should have brought my own.

Back to the hotel, no guards to stop us and relief as we get into bed with a bottle of Budweiser and a packet of nuts. C.B.S. have an 'In Concert' on and by sheer luck we see Chuck Berry, the Allman Brothers, Poco, and Blood, Sweat and Tears. The new singer sounds good with B.S.&T. Poco are 10 times better than I expected them to be and the whole show is dedicated to the Allman's bass player, Berry Oakley (included on the film) who died recently in a motor-bike accident.

Tab Hunter follows, fighting the Indians in a typical western movie which nearly sends us to sleep. Then on to the one o'clock movie – Marilyn Monroe and Richard Widmark in *Don't Bother to Knock* which woke us up again. It was good. And that was Friday.

Saturday, 9 December 1972

Good morning Saturday, or should I say good afternoon as it's 2 p.m. and New York is dry contrary to the forecasts of a wet weekend by the various weather reports. Nobody rings so Tru and I wander through the streets around Broadway. All the cinemas, niteries, restaurants, liquor stores, drugstores – you name it, it's all here. A huge Soho. Porn everywhere; they have papers called *Screw* and *Swinger* which don't even give you a hard-on, they're so graphic. Who wants to see an 18-inch square fanny. Like a cock they are pretty unsavoury when viewed in the cold light of day. Most hi-fi and stereo shops here sport Sony and Panasonic, very popular radios and cassettes. Gone it seems are the days when Japanese goods were considered a joke. Now they make shit-hot stuff – and at competitive prices.

Plastic nude models front a nudie bar and eager New York Puerto Ricans laugh as they peek through a hole in the curtains. We get back to the City Squire and I find Stan lunching with Pete in the restaurant. Buff and Mick are up in 508 doing a *Circus* interview and I complain to Stan I'm being ignored. Nobody rang me, and all that shit.

He tells me he has been given various free records from C.B.S. and again we're going to do the classic Mott record-picking routine. This consists of the records available being stuffed under the bed sheets and then one or the other of us picking blindly at whichever album you feel first. Unknown records are treated cautiously by the recipient. Known lousy albums cause the rest of the group to laugh at the unfortunate new owner and a good album brings cries of delight from the chooser and groans from those who'd hoped to find it. When the albums are all gone from under the sheets a brisk bargaining session takes place and like a zombie I wind up with two Poco (both the same) and Edgar Winter's new album. Never mind, I can always flog them to Brian in the North End Road if I don't like them.

Angela Bowie rings up arranging a tentative party with Bowie, the Spiders and ourselves after David finishes recording but it's not certain, just a maybe. David rings Mick too, to find out how Roxy went. He never misses keeping up the tabs on the competition. Tony's out Christmas shopping with Melanie and it's been decided that Stuart and Zee, David's heavy men, will now accompany us on the remainder of the tour, owing to the St Louis incident.

Penny Valentine in *Sounds* showed her ignorance when confusing the reasons for David having Zee and Stu on his tour. They are not supposed to protect him from over zealous fans, they're just there to keep him from maniacs who haunt him every time he visits the States. Today I took a walk to the Sam Ash Music Store and on the way a guy asked me if I'd like to jam in the Village. I politely (and I mean politely) declined. He then changed from a groovy guy to a complete bastard. 'You ginger headed cunt, who do you think you are? A big-headed English bastard musician. You're all cunts!' Well it's cunts like me that make these pricks stand to attention (a seasoned cunt's answer). Acid freaks stare at me and I don't know what is going through their minds. All sorts of scenes I can't handle. I'm not a heavy, I just sing – all hail Stewey – the sooner the better. I just want to stay nice and sane. I don't need all this. God knows what old Rod, Elton or Jeff go through,

Perhaps we're all right where we are; forever on the way up.

I should mention the American press here by the way. It's full of appreciation. It's been 100 per cent. If there's been a bad one then I didn't see it. A *Fusion* I bought today had a great write up as did *Rolling Stone*, the *L.A. Times* and others. Makes a pleasant change from the English press.

Have you ever heard of a telethon? These are marathon television programmes which run all evening and all night designed to raise funds for one deserving charity or another. Tonight it's the Sickle Cell Telethon. Sickle Cell is a disease which affects mainly little black kids who get it when very young. It's something which prevents the cells forming in the proper way; it causes grave illness and even death. A slim-line Aretha Franklin co-hosts the show and will be here on Channel 9 for nearly 14 hours. What happens is stars come on this show free of charge; a phone number is continually shown on the screen (212-985-9940) and all the stars that perform on the programme, when not performing, sit and answer the phones whilst pledges pour in from all over New York City. They also continually announce the money coming in, citing the pledger's name and address. Money comes in from all over. Quantities vary from $1 to $5,000. At this time, 12:05 a.m. they've managed to cajole $56,000 out of the NYC audience. I can't for the life of me think of a better way of raising money. People, even if they don't want to give, can't resist hearing their name mentioned. It's 'in' to contribute, and for whatever reason they give, they *do* give, and unfortunate children benefit.

Acts come and go. Some you've heard of and some you haven't. It's nearly an all-black cast. Most notable of all was a double act by the name of Nick Ashford and Valerie Simpson; watch out for them. I get a feeling of envy watching this show as it's an almost all-black community show and I'm white and I feel left out. They say some blacks have tried to dye themselves white; well I knew a few white musicians who'd dye themselves black, if they only told the truth. Now it's $62,400 and Ferranti and Teicher take the stage and the piano sound is really good, considering it's a live show. Half a minute. I'll just count the channels; 9, 11, 2, 4 (Johnny Carson), 5, 6, 7 and back to 9 again. An extremely good selection, all in colour but all plagued by commercials which are really annoying at times. They come without warning at all. Just flash on, unlike I.T.V. in England where they do at least show you the title, and then fade to a commercial.

Ferranti now bows his head over the keys and plays *West Side Story*'s *Somewhere*. Ah, wonderful memories of Jim Proby immortalizing this song. The ace punk of all times. His own worst enemy, so what. P. J. Proby's the greatest – he's a fuckin' pirate in this world of drudge. Wherever you are P.J., the world needs you now. My God, England was the worst place to pull your stunts. I don't think you ever really knew that. In England all the extroverts are cunts and all the introverts (no matter how stupid, false, and generally fucked up they are) are the nice guys. See Jim, we are the products of one of the most civilized societies in the world. In other words, if someone cuts your tool off, stop up the blood before you go to the hospital – it might offend someone.

The telethon has now linked up with Chicago. Chicago grossed $1,500 in the first ten minutes, and the total is now $70,000. No phone call from Angie or David so Phally and Elaine are going out to eat you know where, you know what – so see you tomorrow. Love – me.

P.S. United Artists just contributed $2,000 – where are you Columbia?

Sunday, 10 December 1972

Well Sunday's 'family' day. We stop in bed only getting up about 4 p.m. to get ready to go over to Trudy's place on the Island. I only thought it was going to be dinner so I just shoved a country-style shirt on and wore my jeans. They used to have studs in them but I got fed up with them and ripped them out. Now there are little ⅛-inch holes all the way up both outside legs of the jeans. Slinging on my afghan, Tru and I wait for Phally and Elaine (they are coming too) and then we all go down to the lobby to wait for John who is picking us up in the Merc.

93

Hillside Boulevard is, I suppose at a guess, American hard working but reasonably well-off upper middle class. A very wide road, the houses set a little way back off the road and mostly wood fronted. Greens, lavenders and whites are predominant house colours, plus the usual brick-built residences. Christmas is near now and they have competitions every year for the best lit house. Kevin, Trudy's youngest brother, has been working for two weeks solid on the lights for the house and you could see it half a mile away. Looks like a Swiss cuckoo clock. The Americans have an uncanny knack of making all adult things extensions of children's toys. Everything is attractive on the eye as everyone was once a child.

Well, it turns out the whole family has come round to inspect their new member and if they were appalled by my appearance they didn't let on. We had dinner downstairs in the basement which is made much more use of here than in England. Trudy's dad had had a couple of walls knocked down and the basement is a huge area housing snooker and table tennis tables, a rifle range, and a frame with a net attached to it. You throw the ball and catch it at whatever angle it happens to rebound at.

Kevin's bedroom is rigged out like a capsule. He can lay on the bed and press a button which will make anything in the room go up, down, open, close, turn on or off. He was on about an electrical course he's taking and by the look of his room he won't have much trouble. He's also got rifles on the wall on a rack.

A couple of hours later John's sort of hanging around while I'm still playing with Kevin's rifles and I think it's time to go before Trudy's mum kicks me out again. We say our goodbyes as I probably won't see them again for quite some time, and John rips us back to the City Squire.

The rain has stopped and we stop in to say goodnight to Stan on the way to our room. Stuey rings up while we're there and he says he'll come round and pick us up and take us to David's hotel to hear some of the tapes he's just been doing. Thirty minutes later Stu stands in the doorway looking like one of the Mafia; dude suit, fedora, wide tie, and large collar brimming with typical Stuey-style enthusiasm. Some guy Charles is in tow who's an out-of-work sound man and sings with a group in Ohio and has a Bowie hairdo so he's got to be a hanger-on, or somebody's boyfriend. You never know nowadays, do you?

We left Phally and Elaine having a row and just walked back to the Warwick. It was cold but not unbearable and a guy in a dressing gown and pyjamas was buying groceries in a deli. Up to the 18th floor and my first meeting with David in a little while. The room's long and adjoins a bedroom and the window overlooks 5th Avenue. He's got a tape machine, a stereo, and a moog sprawled around the floor and large room-service tables are everywhere. It's about 2 a.m. Angie's still up and is wearing a silver Japanese dress. Spider Trevor Burton looks tired, his elongated side boards hang unsprayed. Stu arranges himself neatly in a cottage chair and Tony and Melanie wander in on their way back to their own place. David looks surprisingly well. He's got a Japanese bell tent top on with huge bell trousers and clogs. He's really into Japanese clothes at the moment.

He plays *Drive-in Saturday*, a beautiful song which grows on you. It's Dylanish and it's got a hell of a chord run down. He says he's putting it out as the next single. A new version of *Dudes* on the next album is a possibility if David's satisfied with the final mix. To be honest, I much prefer our version. This seems too slow and he's done it in a lower key. The sax sounds good in the hookline though – flows right through it. He talks about his plans for the new album. He's calling it *Aladdin Sane*. It's also the title of the fourth track he played which hadn't yet got a vocal, but sounds great anyway. He's really got the saxes back together again now and talks of using four saxes when he gets back. Three altos and one bari, and they've all got to wear white wide-lapel suits and have Mafia frizzled hairdos with glitter stuck on. He stands there describing it and his eyes are six months into the future already. He's holding up well under pressure. No sign of a crack-up anyway and he talks enthusiastically. This supreme self-confidence shouldn't be confused with ego. It's great to see someone so positive. Guy Stevens told me that to think positive was the all-important clue to success and Bowie's a walking example of this. People tire about 4 a.m. and there's only Tru, Angie, David and me left. Lenny Bruce *Live at Carnegie Hall* plays on the stereo and Angie shoves it off, as she's determined to eat. We get into a cab and go back to 7th Avenue to eat at the Stage deli. It's an average looking place, but the food and 24-hour service is excellent. David and I then get down to talking about Mott. Both of us fighting to get a word in as we both talk a lot.

We finally split about 5:30 a.m. Bed calms our tired limbs about 6 and it seems like five minutes later that the phone rings and Stan is banging on the door.

If success is measured in terms of audience hysteria ... !

n and
ife, Trudy.

That inimitable superstar, David Bowie.
RCA

The author with Gibson in hotel room.

Their show's still one
of the most exciting
around.
*Courtesy of London
Features.*

The inscrutable Frank Zappa.
Courtesy of London Features.

The Author.

Elvis Presley's hous

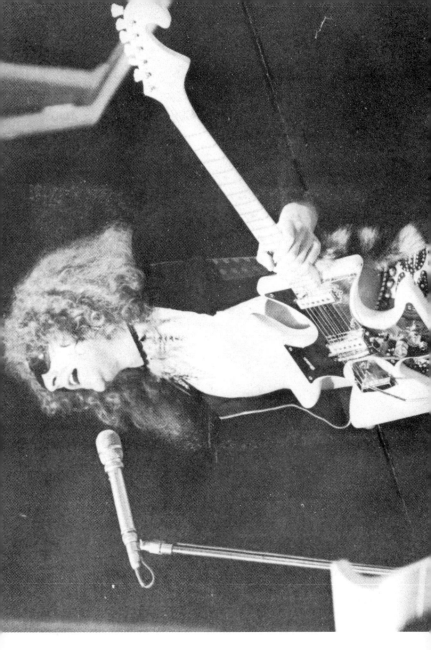

The author with his famous Maltese Cross.
Courtesy of SKR Photos International Ltd.

MOTT line-up.
CBS

Monday, 11 December 1972

It's 10 a.m. and Trudy wearily packs my bags as I stagger round trying to dress myself. I try to take in images of Queens on our way to La Guardia but it's no use reader. I'm too tired and all I can see are huge blocks of flats and shops and people starting another week. A Boeing 707 stands waiting to take us to Fort Wayne. Fort Wayne is in Indiana. A small place for a gig but not too far from Detroit where we fly tomorrow. We have to stop on the way at Cleveland though, and all eyes watch Mick anxiously. He's liable to make the first half of the journey and not the other. Poor bugger, it's really doing him in and nothing is worth that. He sticks it out though, and we reach Fort Wayne about three in the afternoon. It's a midwestern. town which has grown out of an area once alive with Indians. There are three rivers here and the Indians used to live near the water so as to fish for the tribe's food. Somebody told me Fort Wayne was the first French fort in America in the old settlement days, but I couldn't swear by it as I didn't get any local history pamphlets.

Fort Wayne doesn't have limos at all and the one that does turn up has come all the way from Indianapolis to take us around. A bit bloody daft really, but I suppose it looks good. We check in at the good old Holiday Inn. I'm in 201 and I don't even have time to powder under my arms before the sound check.

The place is called the Embassy. It's your average 2½-thousand seater cinema-type place and the billing is strange. There are four bands on – Storm (from Mississippi), Bull Angus (from New York), Flash (from London) and us from Hereford. Arguments over billing have led to Flash being top on the posters with us underneath, but outside the theatre we are on top. Probably the promoter being nice and keeping everyone happy. Flash are big here; much bigger than they are

97

in England. They've already had a hit single and album, and apparently were great at a festival in Indiana earlier on in the year – hence their rebooking at the Embassy. Of course we kick up because they would never headline in England and that goes to show what pushy fuckers we are. I make no attempts to deny it. Anyway, may the best man win – that's what I say.

Very funny sound here, small and dead on stage. Pete's grizzling because the only way he can get a decent bass sound is to have the amp on full treble and only half up, and he can't hear himself. A string on the H guitar goes. Everybody's playing their own little things and altogether it's a bit of a nonner sound check.

The promoter cheers us up, telling us a club is staying open especially for the bands after the show. Storm's going to play there and we can all have a blow if we want to.

Back to the Holiday Inn and we've got two hours to get ready. A meal is followed by hair washing and shaving etc. and I try my suit trousers on. Trudy's Mum fixed them for me and they fit really tight now. I'll have to play knock-kneed to keep them from splitting again. I wish we could just wear jeans. I'd feel much more comfortable.

Back into the limo, down to the gig and Bull Angus leap around like we used to in the good old days of '68 in Aylesbury. Trouble is, they give too much away – just as we had a habit of doing. Wine, beer and groupies are in abundance. Me and Mick lock ourselves away with the guitars in a little room. The heat and the cold are both here depending where you happen to be and the tuning fluctuates accordingly. My new string needs pulling and hitting so I can ged rid of the slack before we go on.

Finally *Jupiter* comes on the tape and on we go to 1,700 people. Some have heard of us and we get quite a shout when we go on. Our act is laid back a bit and after the initial impact they settle down. The sound is considerably better than the afternoon check. Apart from Mick's Echoplex which plays him up a bit when we go on, the gear runs smooth. Bob, the light guy, does wonders with the inadequate lighting system. The people are really good, the atmosphere relaxed, with none of the tension found on the American coasts. We're a bit tired and perhaps it shows a little, but we go at the end and *One of the Boys* and *Angeline* does the trick. We walk off to moderate applause and Phil unlocks the dressing room door for us. I'm half undressed when we realize the moderate applause has grown and grown and it keeps going for four or five minutes. GREAT! Get back on to a great reception and we do *Dudes* well (sometimes the harmonies are dodgy) and straight into *Honky Tonk* which finishes the set off nicely. A great gig. I can't tell you about Flash. We were discussing changes in the act right through their set so I just can't say. It was a good discussion. So many end up in arguments, but this one was fruitful. For instance from now on at a sound check Phally will play a G and Pete, Mick and me will tune up in turn so no one puts anyone else off. Other points are settled and we pool what we've learned so far about audiences on this tour. We also discuss what must be done on the next, and all important, all headline tour.

The other Stan who drives the limo wanders in and we all nip back to the hotel to drop off the stage gear before going to the Zig Zag Club. Perhaps the name of the club's a tribute to my mate Pete's magazine which finds its way slowly round, hand to hand. The best way – word of mouth – the best publicity you can get. The Zig Zag is dark. About forty tables in a low-ceiling square room which has a little alley running off the main room for beer, sandwiches, the gents, and the manager's tiny office. I sit with Mick in a corner and people start wandering over. One in particular knows all about us and plies us with questions. He's a big fat guy with glasses and he offers me a downer which I accept as I don't want to drink too much. Next thing I'm staggering all over the place and a kid who is trying to question me gets me in the tiny manager's office. It's no good. I'm all at sea and start mauling the manager's dog around and it hates me. After two narrow escapes from its eager jaws I think fuck this and lurch back into the main room. My questioner is now my helper and responds to my urgent request by pushing me quite forcibly to the nearest bog. My fly was half-way down when Stan swings through the door, chin jutting dangerously.

'Who's this bloke? Who are you, come on who are you?'
'Take it easy man, I just brought the guy to the john, that's all.'
'Well, I'm watching you, I'm watching you very carefully.'

Stan's nose seems almost to be touching my helper's chin now, and he just stands there gaping back.

'Look man, the guy wants a piss.'
'Then why are you with him?'
' 'Cos he can't fuckin' stand up!'
'Oh, well just remember I'm watching you mate.'

Stan stalks out, Mick's hat on his head, convinced the guy was going to take liberties and my poor helper shakes his head in disbelief.

'Shit man, I'm only trying to help.'
'So's Stan, mate, so's Stan.'

Out through the bog door, and I'm thinking clearly but my body's all wrong and I knock tables all over the place. I can see Mick and Pete fiendishly jamming on stage. It sounds good so I decide to join in. The drummer's good too, whoever he is. Lee's impassively watching and Stan, having downed his fifth beer is now definitely looking for a fight.

I knock about six people over on the way to the stage. Fortunately, they seem to be in the same state as me and just laugh. And now I'm at the organ. Mick's up the other end and it's the inevitable 12-bar in G. It does go on. Jamming bores the arse off me, but it whiles away the hours. I can never understand how the long-suffering public can put up with it, but there must be reasons, there's a lot of people who love it. It's like cricket to me, great to be playing, but boring to watch. We once jammed for five hours at Upsala in Sweden with Fairport just to get our own back on the crowd. Pompous bastards.

We keep messing around. I'm on Hofner Bass now (remem-

100

ber when they called you a capitalist pig if you actually owned a Hofner) and Pete Banks is up there trading solos with Mick.

I warble through *Cadillac*, an old Vince Taylor number and then have a go, and I mean a go, at *Red House*. I can't sing blues in the accepted fashion, but it gives Mick and Pete Banks a chance to turn out some nice notes. A word of praise for Bull Angus's organist who really got it on, and then it was all over and what was left of the crowd stamped and applauded. I must admit it does do you good to get out of the tight arrangements we work within now and again. I dunno, I'll have to think about jamming some more maybe.

Anyway, we must have been dragged out then because the next thing I know I'm in bed and it's 5:30 a.m.

Tuesday, 12 December 1972

These early flights are a bastard. Stan gets up at 11 a.m. for the plane to Detroit. He says it's the only one and I don't believe him, but I can't be bothered to check it so I just sling my gear in the cases and a porter takes them down to a waiting limo. I feel like death on wheels and my breath stinks even though I've brushed my teeth twice today. The trees opposite my first-floor window are covered in snow, the ground a pool of ice. Slush and snow and the other Stan, the driver of the limo, bangs ice off the boot with a wooden stick. He's already got the engine going but it's backfiring bad temperedly and I don't blame it.

Weary heads wander in and out of rooms. Mick's missing. It's only 170 miles to Detroit and he's gratefully taking the advantage of a bus ride instead of the dreaded plane.

We're flying Delta today. The airport's very small (just like the one at Jersey) and we have qualms as we gaze across the hazy runways. A couple of United Airline jets stand forlorn, their engines covered with what look like huge plugs – similar to the caps on Smarties tubes. A petrol tanker with a skirt of icicles and the grey mist shrouding everything.

The airlines, as usual, won't commit themselves but we meet up with Flash again and the singer's saying something like they've been stranded there since 10 a.m. We decide the airport's closed but have breakfast anyway, just in case our plane happens to turn up. Stan gives up and goes off to get the money back, and then to ring the Greyhound station. Looks like we'll be travelling with Mick after all. I nip in the bar and have a drink with Flash. They seem really nice blokes and we talk of this and that. They're on their way to Kentucky and they don't reckon they're going to make it. They're trying to work out if it wouldn't be better to forget about Kentucky and head for Lexington where they play the day after. If they try for Kentucky and get stuck halfway, they might miss both the gigs instead of just the one. This time of year, when the weather is bad, a lot of kids are disappointed as you can't sue anyone because of the weather, an act of God as the saying goes.

Fortunately our gig in Detroit isn't until Wednesday. It's now Tuesday, so the three-hour bus ride is only a minor irritation. Stan comes into the bar and we say our goodbyes to Flash and wish each other luck.

It's 3 p.m. and the bus is due out at 4. A young hairy comes up and says there is a nutter in the next room who says he hates all hairy groups. He's going to do all kinds of things to us so we stick together just in case. American nutters and English nutters are a very common breed, but you never know over here what the silly sod might have under his sweaty little arm-pit.

Seats in the waiting room have arms attached with 6-inch T.V.s; if you have a long wait, you put your bread in and pass the time away (how many times have you sat for hours staring at the walls in your local bus depot). I don't see why this idea hasn't been taken up in England. They must pay for themselves a thousand times over in the long run.

The bus is coming in from Evansville which is the other end of Indiana, and what with the weather being so bad, we're quite relieved when it gets in only 30 minutes late at 4:30. These guys that drive the Greyhounds really know how to get through no matter what. We load up the cases, no porters here, back to reality lads, and it does us all a bit of good. Mick arrives having been able to sleep all the time we sat at the airport and Pete and I still feel like dead ducks. I don't know how Stan's bearing up – he seems to have a second wind. I'm having trouble trying to find my first. We get on the bus and Stan entertains us with his cassette (it has no outside mike and an automatic level). All you have to do is switch it on so you can get impromptu conversation from anybody on tape without them even knowing it. Mick moans about his voice; he never realized he talks so quickly, but Stan's all proud saying his diction is improving and we all agree to keep the lad happy. In point of fact, Buff is the only one who talks really well. The rest of us, me in particular, are very lazy in our speech. I don't see what all the fuss is about anyway. It's dark now and I get a double seat and recline them both. The old afghan is my pillow and I semi-doze all the way, getting up only twice – one to get a candy bar – and once to have a fag in the bogs at the rear of the bus. (You're not supposed to smoke on the bus.)

The bus is nearer 1 hour than 30 minutes late, and it's a very jaded mob who stagger off the other end in downtown Detroit.

Now I don't know if they're colour conscious here but the porters refused to port and the cabbies refused to cab.

'Look here, mate, why won't you take us?'
'That guy will take yuh, man, no sweat.'
'That guy won't take us. Look, you can see the guitars, man. We're musicians, we're not into all this crap.'
'I'm hip to that, man. That man will take you, no sweat.'
'I only just got here – it's not my problem, man, ya hear.'

One spade, a huge old guy who didn't give a fuck, told us he'd take three of us, but refused to look at us. Other cabbies stood and watched and he ignored them as well. I'll swear I saw the world on that man's face. Stan finally got another guy – some Greek or Cypriot – to take the rest of us and an old Negro spat as he passed. A young Negro ran up and showed us watches and rings and then ran off when a patrol car cruised

103

round the corner. You could have cut the atmosphere with a knife – the same in the cab – you could just feel the hate in the air. These fuckers don't care what you do – you are white and that's it. To my knowledge I have never been disrespectful, rude or uncivil in any way to a man of any colour unless he's had a go at me first. I'm English – a visitor in America, and too young to be in any way to blame for any grudges these guys might have. Even if their grudges are justified, and I know many of them are, that is no excuse for a cab driver not giving a traveller a ride who is a visitor to his country. If he's a cabby, that's his job, and I state here and now these guys were ignorant bastards who practised what they've always been against, every chance they got. Fuck 'em, I'd rather walk next time around. I play fucking music, that's universal, it doesn't know barriers and if all the world were musicians, there would be less trouble. These twats aggravate the problem just as much as their equally ignorant white opposites, and I want no part of it!

I write this at 1:30 a.m. Wednesday morning and the hotel is a Hilton. The first I've ever been in, and it's too expensive. We're here because the Holiday Inn will not take our travel agent's credit. Come to that, it's just like a Holiday Inn, same lay-out, only better wallpaper and furniture. As I write, the newsreel tells of a new Boston strangler who strangles hitch-hiking co-eds, and now the attorney of the original killer (who is now serving a life sentence) is trying to get the case re-opened.

Buff's in the next bed, and Stan's across the way with Dick. Dick, Ritchie and Phil got in an hour ago after a hazardous drive in the wagon. Pete lords it in his single room. He's fluked a magnificent room with a bed twice the ordinary double size, a three-piece suite, tables etc.

Three lonely groupies hang around downstairs waiting for a chance to get up here, and my fingers get stiffer and stiffer clutching Buff's biro. I'd better stop now before writer's cramp becomes a reality. Trudy's moaning on the phone because I didn't ring earlier (typical) and I think of Solveig and Saucer, and our little flat in Wembley. I wonder if Bill's fixed my Anglia. In a vain attempt to cease the piss-taking by certain

104

Mustang owners in the group I'm getting it sprayed black and gold and having big tyres fitted. Tara for now.

Wednesday, 13 December 1972

3 p.m. on a freezing Wednesday afternoon and I open the curtain to a city which could easily find a home in mid Germany. Everything in various shades of grey. Smoke-belching chimneys in the distance; even the tiny walk through the park immediately below is turned grey by the dull snow. A dozen lit Christmas trees stand sentry around a small statue of a child. The cinema across the street is showing *Lady Sings the Blues*. Motor City is no longer Motown City, Berry Gordy having moved over to a sunny L.A. to pursue MoWest operations. Mick thinks there may be a few pawned guitars owing to unemployment so we're all ready to go when Stan says a bloke is coming from *Creem* magazine at 3. It's after that now, and he still is not here so Mick's hanging on and if he doesn't get here by 3:30 we'll go out anyway.

Lord Watts wanders in from his palatial suite demanding money with menaces off Stan. Phally sits on the bed impassively munching a bright shiny apple and refusing to do anything.

Well 3:30 comes and still no Ben from *Creem* so Mick, Pete and I climb in a cab and go to a shop called Sams that Mick fished out of the Yellow Pages.

Sams is your typical pawn shop – gaily painted front, cheap guitars in the windows, plus guns, rings (all types of jewellery) radios, T.V.s, generators, garden and engineering tools, huge tool boxes, massive spanners, hammers – up the top end the desk where you pawn is surrounded by mesh to hold off maniacs. In this shop a while ago 16 bullets were fired killing a policeman, a black and injuring others. Just before you reach the mesh, you turn right and up on a high shelf Fenders, Epiphones, Gibson's etc., all the best are there. The man that shows us the stuff is nice, but the mood changes as we haggle for low prices and they keep them too high. Neither side is reasonable and finally the owner says 'Fuck off'.

'Fuck off back to England.'
'Er, we bought a Junior here last time.'
'You offered $15 for that Silvertone?'
[Mick] 'Yes.'
'Fuck off back to England.'

We fucked off back to the cab instead and found another shop down a couple of blocks. The cabby says this place is worse. He gets his hair cut at the barber's next door and his barber says this bloke's the biggest shark in Detroit. Two guitars in the window, a Kalamazoo and a Junior.

[Mick] 'How much for the Junior?'
'A hundred.'
'Can I have a look?'
'If you mean business you can have a look.'
'The back's off the electrics.'
'$80.'
'I'll take it.'
'$83.50 with tax.'

Thus old jammy Ralpher netted a £200 guitar for about £33 plus he'll have to pay half again on the way back, customs duty, but that still only makes it £50 in all. I can see Sid Bishop's little eyes gleaming in Top Gear, but Mick will probably keep it. Pete and I get a good deal too, a couple of acoustic Gibsons, the old type with no cutaways and F holes complete with Les Paul Junior pickup for $75 each. I wonder what Sid will think of these. (Well you know how it is Ian – we can't sell them, they'll hang there for ages – No really, they'll have to be dirt cheap. Bob will tell you isn't that right Bob? They'll hang there, right.) Old Batesly round at Orange is just the same. Money fiends, but they're nice with it. I always promise myself if I get a guitar I don't want I'll sell it privately, but I never can get to do this – I always wind up arguing with Sid!

'MOTT THE HOOPLE HIT DETROIT AND BROUGHT OUT EVERY FUNGOID IN TOWN THROUGH NO FAULT OF THEIR OWN. IT WAS ONE OF THE GREAT

CONCERTS OF THE YEAR. EVEN THE AUDIENCE WAS GREAT, GREAT LINES.' – L.B., Dec. '72.

So said Lester Bangs, the guy who gave us our all-time write up, the review in *Fusion* 1969 on the first Mott the Hoople album. You can think, 'What the fuck, Ian got pissed and didn't write about the Detroit gig,' but I left it to someone more experienced than myself. The room's full of people and I'm listening. The gig was good. I don't want to bullshit, the gig was good – that's it. . . .

Buff just came in with Karen and I'm too pissed to take the hint – sorry Buff. Out of the right corner of my eye I count 210 lights and on my left, a colour T.V. tells me Johnny Carson's got it all together. So Budweisers sit on Buff's bed undrunk, and I'm about to attempt the impossible – groovy baby – I'm drunk, forget it. . . . No that's not true.

In 1969 Mott, among a few others, brought Friars to its feet in Aylesbury and a cult built up around Dave Stopps (Friars promoter), Pete Frame and the light show. An' they were the days. Bowie thinks he started Friars but Friars was years before his time.

Dave Stopps was, and still is, a good promoter. Of course, like Bill Graham he gets his share of criticism from the locals. Capitalist bastard, etc., but I wonder if Dave got done for bankruptcy, would the underground help him out. I doubt it.

1968 and 69 were good years from the British Clubs. New bands like Yes, ELP, Broughton, Free and ourselves were asking reasonable prices and queues formed for miles outside Friars, Cook's Ferry, Marquee, Croydon Greyhound, The Roundhouse, Fishmonger's Arms, waiting to see their particular favourites perform. The buzz was in the air, it was like the early West Coast scene and the kids were eager, happy and alive with anticipation. Mott were underground then. Why I'll never know, we weren't into drugs but somehow the freaks (sane as sane) related to us. We were green as grass, not too good but enthusiastic and Guy Stevens, our aid and mentor drove us on into the happy madness of streetkids making good. It was fun. Nothing to lose. It's different now. We flashed around when it wasn't groovy to flash. The press didn't like us, but what the fuck – we were having a ball. The American press liked us but it was a fluke. We just didn't know what we were and what we had. We know now and spend the majority of our time trying to get back to where we belong. Fuck stardom, but can we afford to? A rock band's life is equivalent to that of a footballer. You've got to take it while it's there. I've dug holes in the road, I know what it's like.

I remember a kindly prospective employer – 'And if you work five years you get this . . . and if you put in 10 years you get that . . . Syd over there (Syd being some kind of factory superstar) has been with us 45 years. Your pension scheme is this, we run a life insurance scheme so when ('when' not 'if') you die your family gets this. . . .'

You ain't having my body and mind mate – they belong to me. I'd rather jump off a fuckin' bridge.

Maybe we're not God's gift to rock and roll bands, but certain people love us, and I appreciate that – I won't ever forget it. This is Budweiser talk. Trudy – where are you. Scratch my back and bring me back to normal! Nancy was here tonight and you'll be angry when I ring you, but I was a good lad. Nancy was sad – I'll always remember her as being the sad one, and she was good, no matter how she fought it. Her mother and father were the last generation of U.S. bread opportunists. The people that said, 'My kids won't have to fight like I did.' That's what fucked them up in the 60s and 70s – not rock and roll – dig?

Thursday, 14 December 1972

Well in the light of day I survey the damage. Buff can't stand up and is packing from a crawling position. I've got the shakes and if this is what an alcoholic feels like first thing in the morning he can keep it. I refuse to read what I wrote last night. The thing that saddens me is that I've no fuckin' will-power. I don't eat for three days to slim and then I drink like a fish for a couple of nights and ruin the whole idea. There's crates of the stuff all over the place – where did it come from? Loads of

Budweiser and we haven't even got room for a can in the cases.

I have got to eat. Downstairs in the coffee bar Buff and I order poached eggs, toast, bacon and very large orange juices. Gradually, my bones start to function and nerves come into being.

Two English pilots sit next to us and talk of gardening and a mate of theirs who's working hard on a little cafe in Surrey. We didn't interrupt the conversation, but it was nice eavesdropping. Good old England. A word about the lobbies in American hotels. There's a few in every party who always have to wait for the remainder to turn up and while you are waiting you are subjected to the same treatment every time. It's so boring and bloody infuriating. What happens is the guy and his wife come in and stare blatantly. They're so intent on looking at you (and, face it, we've been around for years now – hairies). They don't realize you can see them too. The woman (this painted atrocity with bright red lips, stained teeth, beehive lacquered hair job and fake fur) shoves her painted paw somewhere in the direction of that all-American 48-year-old female mouth (trying to cover it – but it's impossible) and whispers in her partner's ear. This happens right in front of you and then our rimless, beglassed, embarrassingly obese lump of pastrami (breath comes too) giggles nervously straight at you. In England they have slightly more tact – I mean they do it behind your back so you don't get narked at what you don't see. But these fuckers have no finesse – they do it right there in front of you. Most of the time, if you are in the mood, you stare back hard and their eyes sort of wander off and away they go. Sometimes, just for fun, I've gone up to them and said something like, 'What are you looking at?' Now you might think this is a yob thing to do but they're yobs, so I say it and their whole bodies change. The guy transforms into what he is officially, 'C'mon Hester, we don't have to talk to this guy.' And all of a sudden he's big and strong and masculine and she's just so right – they're all nobodies.

And now I'm on my way to Texas on a Branif with what has got to be the worst air hostess in the business. I like Branif – they've painted mad colours as if some eccentric billionaire

109

airline-owner just has a bit of fun, but this bird is ruining the whole thing. I was writing a little earlier and she comes up.

'Sir, put your bags under the seat. All these bags must go.'

I carried on writing.

'Sir! Did you hear me?'
'Yes, I heard you.'
'Well you did not say yes or no so I assumed you did not.'

[Thinks, bollocks.] I hate bossy little farts; especially about 2 p.m., it's very early and I don't feel well. Then she comes again and tells some 14-year-old kid off for the same thing. She's right in what she's saying but her attitude is unbelievable. I couldn't help it. 'Fuck off you old bag.' I didn't think she'd heard me, but she must have heard something because she stomped back down the aisle like an enraged dwarf, frustrated by her size.

'What's that you said?'
'Look, what the fuck are you, a school teacher or something? There's no need for this drama.'
'Right!'

Off she goes, maybe to get me slung off or something. We don't see her again so she must have been transferred to another compartment. God help the poor bloke who gets lumbered with that. Birds who come on like that need a good punching. It's the only way to keep them quiet and it knocks some sense into their stupid, thick heads.

Ah, peace at last. Stan's got Mick's hat on again and sits to my right; Buff's in front, Phally and Stu beyond. Pete's behind and I can see Zee too. I like Zee, he said he'll fix my velvet pants (they've gone again). Lee's somewhere around (dirty sod, I couldn't believe him last night), and Tony's sitting in the first-class section. Perhaps he's thinking of how he's going to make us stars. He's got a job. I mean I want to be a star, but I keep thinking we're just ordinary blokes and we don't have the killer instinct. I can't keep myself composed continually like Bowie does. It's like keeping your stomach in – mine flops out occasionally.

I can't see Mick, but he's here somewhere. I saw him in the limo, so unless he escaped at the airport, he must be here.

There's a huge tyre in Detroit which I always remember when I see the MC5. It's on Edsel Ford and you pass it on the freeway to the local airport. Today it had a hole in it and you could see the scaffolding inside. I always wondered how they got it to stand up. The top of it was covered in snow.

They've just given us some food which is bloody awful. Branif aren't as good as they used to be. Still, don't think they're as bad as United.

The gig tonight is dodgy. People keep changing the bill around. Originally the Supremes and Fats Domino were on, but they've disappeared mysteriously and now we're playing with It's a Beautiful Day and Spirit (which Spirit I don't know). Quicksilver have been on and off the bill like a yo-yo, but at the moment they're on too. When you start hearing things like this you almost know it's going to be a farce. So, Tony and the roadies will go and see if it's possible to do a decent gig. Trouble is, it's a lot of bread and we need the money after the long lay off in New York. Maybe it'll turn out flukey great.

There's a grey field below and a grey sky above. We're flying 29,000 feet up and in the distance the clouds build up like mountains and you'd swear it was a different planet if you were here. It was great meeting Lester Bangs. I've always wanted to see him since that *Fusion* write up. That article was so true it's frightening. He doesn't like the new album though. He likes us to rock more, but I tell him this is what we'll do on the next one. Apparently he bores the arse of everybody, raving about the Rolling Stones. I know the feeling Lester, I do the same. To me, the Stones are the best rock 'n roll band in the world. They live it; they are it. Long live the Stones. Nuf said.

That hostess is now chatting away to a guy in first class. Eyebrows raised, hands going – really being the ace hostess to get her little ego back and prove to herself she's not what I said she was; but she is and she knows it and I know it. I wonder

111

what she's saved up to say to me when we get off the plane. She can win if she likes, I'm saying nothing.

Bloody hell, that flight was dodgy. Fog most of the way and you couldn't see where you were going. We landed O.K. though, and another gaudy, rude, bright plane stands next to our equally rude blue one – that's a real bit of Texas for you. They don't mess around with colours, just slap it on as loud as possible.

Texas in the rain is nowhere near Texas in the sun and Dallas looks like any other midwestern city as we weave our way through the traffic to yet another Hilton hotel. It's alright travelling with Tony, all the best places, and these are the mad days, out of proportion. Fuck proportion. It's in league with logic and all those other barbed wire words.

Phally and I sit in the foyer bemused. The ceiling is high and a giant Christmas tree stands right in front of us. Red balls, red swallows, red empty presents and the whole thing sprayed with instant snow.

Room 517, Stan having chased his hat (it doesn't seem to be Mick's anymore) for about 100 yards slightly out of control. He gives me 605 and Phally 517 and tells us we're sharing. That problem is ironed out and here I sit at 6 p.m.

Zee came up and took my velvet pants away to be fixed; he's really nice, goes out of his way to help. Lee comes in to say the gig is officially off. It's total chaos down there and would do us more harm than good. Bit of a drag because the only gig in town is the one we're supposed to be doing, and if we go to watch the other bands, the promoter will probably shoot us for not gigging. Phally lays on the bed listening to a tape of last night. The sound's good; so's the audience.

This is your average hotel room; I won't bother to explain it to you but the hotel has only 10 storeys. Contrary to what you hear, everything ain't all that big in Texas. But Texas to me is America, like the America I always had fantasies about.

So what's Dallas got that anywhere else hasn't got? The first house ever built here is still on display, but it's been 'restored' and is called the Restored John Neely Bryan Cabin and was originally built in November of 1841, and that's about it. Country and western enthusiasts would no doubt call in at the BD Jamboree at Cadz, the Levee 5615 E. Mockingbird or the Longhorn Ballroom on Corinth Street. The main attraction of this town has been the Lee Harvey Oswald shooting of John F. Kennedy outside an old red-brick building across Elm Street as you look from a park. Memorials are everywhere to the man who captivated a nation, but the obvious American lust for the dollar knows no bounds and cards showing the exact spot where it happened have been doing a roaring trade for years now. The first time I was here three years ago I had to buy one to take home, it seemed to demonstrate what a whole book on the American way of life might not. The card's worth 10 cents.

The gig here is off and Houston was too, but that one's been sorted out so it looks like this wasn't a wasted journey after all. Stan's just told us Tony is giving us all a Christmas bonus of £200 each so everybody has a good meal in the restaurant.

Phally's overjoyed, he can pay his electric bill and have the lights on all over Christmas. Buffin's playful and Mick's just coming off the mandies that he takes to help him fly. Pete just sits there pleasantly fucked, and I feel the same. Everywhere you go now, hotels, airports, stations – they all play carols through lousy sound systems. I couldn't decipher which was which in Detroit. Tony says we've sold 1,000 tickets in advance at Houston. It's a 2,000-seater, so it should be about three-quarters full on the night. Incidentally, there were 1,875 last night at Detroit. Bob, the promoter, was pleased and says it will be full next time.

Well it's 12 midnight and in 517 Johnny Carson is doing one of those forgettable shows he sometimes does. I don't wish to slag him, but it does seem to be a plug service. People come on, recite where they are playing, what albums they have out and then tell J.C. how wonderful he is and everyone is happy. To-night Ed Sullivan is a guest. You'll remember his legendary show which ran for 20 years – 24 with the radio show he did before. His future gigs consist of showing the best clips of his old shows and Carson asks questions like, 'Is there anything

113

you feel you missed in life?' and, 'Was there anyone you missed interviewing?' as if the guy's life is finished and he doesn't even twig it. The whole thing stinks a bit. Somebody says talk shows are an art form but all I see is a mutual-admiration society listening to each other's achievements and smiling smugly as the Hollywood audience dutifully applaud. I get sick of it and Dick Cavett's better for me on Channel 8.

Mysterious phone calls come with regularity from the ladies of the lobby, but we're tired from last night's binge. Phally screams. The salad they brought him has got Danish Blue cheese in it, but he tortures himself for the sake of his appetite. For the fourth time this week, I swear never to drink another beer – I didn't touch a drop today. I rang Trudy earlier and she said that Pete Frame was in New York for a concert review and rang her, but he's already gone back – it was a quick job. He said Solveig was in season, but they sprayed her rear with some stuff to kill that sexy smell which brings the male dogs running. (Pete's got two males.) I'm sure she's going to fall though. Trudy, however, insists she's too pure. At least Saucer is a tom.

Friday, 15 December 1972

10 a.m. A bell rings continuously waking me up and my bleary eyes wander round the darkened room just for something to do, chancing on the blinds, and what do I see but strong rays of sun forcing their way through – hurray. I leap knickerless from bed, thrust the glass door aside and stand facing the elements naturally. A beautiful awakening is ruined by an icy, windy Chicago-style blast which nearly knocks me senseless and I write these few words from the safety of my bed – it looks nice though.

It's bloody awful sharing a room with Phally. You have to sit all quiet and not put the telly on or he moans at you for waking him up and making him 'ill' for the rest of the day. This group amazes me. We go out and get pissed all night, get in about six in the morning and they all wake up about three saying they're ill. Anyone else would ruefully rub their head or guts and complain of a hangover, but this lot are 'ill' thereby disclaiming any responsibility for their own condition. Stan always says flatly his legs have 'gone'. When asked where and why he either can't or won't elaborate – they've just 'gone' and that's it. Ah well, the Houston flight is at one. The phone will ring at 12; it's now 11 so another hour before I can legally switch the T.V. on. Perhaps I'll have a quiet shit or something. Pity we don't have more time. There's some good pawn shops here and in Fort Worth, not far away.

Speaking of pawn shops. Did I ever tell you about the time in San Francisco I bought the Maltese Cross, since immortalized in *Disc*, *Melody Maker*, *Sounds*, *NME*, etc. Trouble was they didn't bother to take photos of me – just the cross. It was funny that day in the pawn shop.

MICK: 'Look at that fuckin' guitar.'

ME: 'What is it?'

MICK: 'I don't know, but it's amazing.'

ME: 'I've got to have it.'

MICK: 'You've got to have it.'

ME: 'How much do you reckon?'

MICK: 'Could be anything between $100 and $250.'

ME: 'I'll go to 300. I've got to have it.'

MICK: 'Yeah.'

ME: 'Eh, excuse me, can I have a look at the white cross guitàr?'

MAN: 'No.'

ME: 'Er, why not?'

MAN: 'Cos I'm busy.'

ME: 'But is it for sale?'

MAN: 'Yeah.'

ME: 'Well can I have a look at that cross guitar?'

MAN: [He's on the phone.] 'Look you get that fuckin' stuff through the fuckin' customs or I'll bust your fuckin' head, I don't care. . . . You get it. . . . Look you sly son of a bitch . . . you get your ass down here with that fuckin' stuff. . . .'

ME: 'Ahem – cough.'

MAN: 'Look, will you come back some other time, I'm busy.'

ME: 'But I want to have a look.'

MAN: 'Have you got any fuckin' money?'

ME: 'Enough.'

MAN: 'You wanna pay $100 and I'll get it off the wall?'

ME: 'Yes.'

MAN: 'O.K. then.'

He waddled round the thin corridor between counters and hanging merchandise, pulled the cross down and laid it on the counter. I couldn't believe it. It was well made, the neck being the only problem. It needed ironing, there just wasn't enough holding it on.

MAN: 'You wannit?'

ME: 'Does it work?'

MAN: 'Of course it fuckin' works, whaddaya think I got here, a junk shop?'

ME: 'Got an amp to try it on?'

MAN: 'No, trust me; it's O.K. Look, you wanna guitar right? I give you the thing for nothin'.'

ME: 'Give it me for nothing?'

MAN: '$75, that's fuckin' nothin'. Look, I thought you were bums. O.K., I feel bad, got trouble with the Canadian customs. Give me the money. I'll give you a case, you won't believe it, it shouldn't be allowed this case it's so good. C'mon, 75 cash 3 tax. You're pros, you know, it's a good deal.'

Mick and me think, well the shape of it is good and it looks good and he's a conning bastard but we'll take a chance – I've got to have it.

ME: 'O.K.'

MAN: 'O.K., O.K., where you guys from, Australia? . . . oh, London, you in a band? What's the name of the band? . . . Mouser Hoop— Hell, I can't say that thing. What's that again? Hey, that's a fuckin' name man. Hey Laura, these guys from England. I was there in '43. Peterborough – you know Peterborough?'

And that was that. I took it to try at the Fillmore that

evening and it worked – not well – but encouragingly enough to know I would eventually get a sound. Albert King was intrigued:

'Where d'ya git that son of a bitch?'

'In a pawn shop.'

'That's a mean guitar man, that's a mean son of a bitch – how much did ya pay for it?'

'$75.'

'How much do ya want for it?'

'Got to keep it Albert.'

'Yeah, that's a mean evil son of a bitch.'

Of course there's more to San Francisco than the Fillmore West, which was never as good as I had imagined and nowhere near the Fillmore East. Across the bay there's Sausalito, and the mountains; Alcatraz, the former prison is there too. When I was there some Indians were squatting in it – mainly for publicity in their fight for a well-deserved better deal. It stands to the left of Sausalito, and Angel Island to the right – heaven and hell within seeing distance. Angel Island is a sanctuary for birds and the like.

The drive to the airport is short and sweet. We glide down Mockingbird Lane and houses that looked sad yesterday come alive today under a clear blue sky. Terminal 64 is really a funny sight. All-American boys stare at us in amazement – you'd have thought they'd seen something resembling a hairy by now, but apparently they haven't so we stare back. Alien creatures from the same planet – pathetic.

Straight on the plane. This time Branif do a superb two-tone blue job paintwork and I'm quite put out by the tastefulness. I like 'em horrible. Stuey sits to my left, Buff, Phal and Stan behind, Zee and Lee together. (Zee bought 12 of the Kennedy postcards I told you about – he can't believe them.) Pete sits on his own, one seat back. He's still 'ill'. Mick brings up the rear. Today he's taken nothing and looks much better for it. Mind you, the journey is only 40 minutes. Dallas lies about 250 miles north of Houston, which itself almost makes the coast. We should arrive about 3:30/3:45 p.m. so we'll have most of the day to mess around. The days have gone really quickly for me, what with the gigs, the travelling, and this book, serial, article or whatever it is. Pawn-shop day today. The gig doesn't start until midnight and the sound check's at 11:30 p.m. so that gives us until the shops close. I've been farting about with my trusted Echo too, got to get some songs together soon. Another single and album should be in the pipe line around February. The thing I really miss is my old upright piano in my flat at home. Run downs are easier to find on a piano and bass lines can change the sound of a chord. One thing about the States, it kicks you up the arse and you can usually get inspiration for songs here – one way or another.

Songs – now they're something else. You don't have to just write them, you've got to arrange them, produce them, mix them, cut them and process them. The chances of getting exactly what you want are virtually nil but let's start from the beginning.

I write a song on maybe the guitar or the piano. The first thing is to convince the band that it's good. My way is to piss about with the song at a practice or a sound check – if it's good someone will pick up on it. Usually Buff or Pete will say 'What's that?' and lean over the piano and then nod approval. If this doesn't happen I usually chuck it out unless I'm certain sure and then I push. Having got the band's approval I hang on to it until we get some time in the studio.

Now the studio can make or break the song. Some twat engineer reading *Reveille* can put you off your stroke and he may not even try for a good sound on bass and drums – that pisses Pete and Buff off for a start. Having bumbled through this drama we then endeavour to get a back track down. This is usually bass/drums/rhythm guitar and forms a kind of musical skeleton on which to build the song. Most studios have 16-track machines. We use six tracks for drums (six mikes on the kit) and one or two on the bass, the rhythm is usually one track and can be taken out. It's only in to keep the song rolling in it's early stages. I then take a $7\frac{1}{2}$-inch tape off the back-track home and listen to it for a few days on my Revox tape recorder. This way I can work out arrangement, what further instruments I wish to dub on, etc.

Then we go back in and finish it off to the best of our ability. Various amps are used to get the right guitar sounds and Verden can experiment on organ sounds. I've never yet experimented on vocal sounds but I mean to in the future. The various echoes can enhance your voice. David used a first repeat echo on *All The Young Dudes* and it made my voice sound infinitely better.

Finally you get all the instruments down on the 16 tracks and then you have to mix. The producer, in our case Bowie, tries to get the best of everything on the tapes together so the song sounds at its best. He and the engineer then record the combination and we sit back and listen to see if it could be made even better. Sometimes the first mix is *the* one, other times you might remix 10 or 20 times before getting it how you want it. Unfortunately studio and mixing time are expensive and so you nearly always have to compromise a bit and you feel the song slip away owing to the limited time. The better companies like C.B.S. try to make it as easy as possible for you time-wise but even they have one eye on the clock unless it's Dylan or Simon and Garfunkel. They know they'll get their money back off these people.

Having got the mix you then have to cut the song. This means converting the tape on to disc. It might sound easy but more than one group have lost the crispness and presence of an album on the cut. Again it's down to the engineers involved. You have to hope for the best and again it costs a lot of bread. They talk about frequencies being too high or low, of limiters and other technical contraptions of which I have no knowledge. I wish to fuck I had. See you sometimes get albums that jump on various tracks. This can mean the cut was done too high and it can really mess an album up.

O.K., so you've recorded, mixed and cut. Next stop the processing department of the record company you work for. An average working guy who doesn't even know you doctors up the final master disc and sticks it into the press. This master is the gear that makes the ruts in the record and a bit of shit or some other technical hassle can fuck up 5,000 albums before you even know it. All the group press is geared to a certain date line. Adverts in the musical papers, interviews, radio plugs, T.V. appearances, etc., so the company have to let those 5,000 shitty copies into the shops. Hence the irate letters from album buyers you see in the *Melody Maker*. I remember on our first album a number called *The Road To Birmingham* was put on the album instead of *Rock 'n Roll Queen*. We didn't even know about it until after the release. They changed it after the first 5,000 copies.

Ah well, a little info to while away the hours. There's a million other hassles but it would be draggy to list them all. This has been just a brief outline. Any would-be recording stars reading this – good luck lads – you'll fucking need it!

It's about 6 p.m. now. We left Dallas an hour late and got right down, straight in and bumps all the way. Even the pilot said he shouldn't have done it but he was behind schedule so he thought he'd give it a bash – charming. We loaded our trembling bodies into the limos and paraded into Houston. It's a clean town, and apart from downtown, it's a low town. I don't like high towns, low ones suit me better. The limo driver, a huge lad, boasts about the new Continental Hyatt. To me it looks like a dark brown German concrete fortress left over from the last war. Heroes have travelled to the moon after living near here and they no doubt got pissed on the sly in downtown Houston bars, trying to forget all about it. It's a particularly revolting thing to be a hero in America.

Our hotel is a Sheraton and we don't mess around when we arrive. Cases into the rooms and then downstairs and into a cab. Unfortunately we have to sit and wait for twenty minutes. Stan kept saying he was coming and when he did finally make it we only had 30 minutes pawning time left. A mad rush to the Market Street area revealed a couple of good Gibsons and a Strat, but all were too expensive when taking the customs into consideration. We missed half the shops anyway (because of you know who) and on top of that we wound up with fuck all and Stan bought a suitcase – just what he wanted. The case being the cheapest he could possibly buy, it will bust as quick as the last one did.

120

Stan and Buff get a cab back and Stuey, Mick, Pete and I decide to walk. The wind blows fiercely and we pass a sign on a dilapidated mission hall which says, 'Man, come visit us and thou shalt verily learn to dig.' Down the street a little way, two giant searchlights beam alternately across the sky. A lot of traffic, but the air's still clean and we get back to the hotel feeling quite breezy except for Pete who says the wind has blown right through his head and his eardrums and throat hurt. We split up, Pete preferring room service, Mick and Stuey to a coffee shop across the street and me to room 214. I just stripped off and weighed myself – 162 pounds it says. That's one pound more than when I got here. Some bloody slimmer I turned out to be.

Texas is bigger than Britain by the way, and this is where they say 'all' even if there's only one of you. The view from the window is just as it is in Manchester or Sheffield, your average light show. Perhaps if I have a hot bath I'll get rid of that pound.

Saturday, 16 December 1972

I'm now sitting on a Delta 707 heading for Chicago. The weather forecast for Chicago is 6 degrees and 25-miles-per-hour winds – far out.

I never will understand why they put so much ice in a glass of Coke. Actually it could be they don't like giving too much of the stuff away. My top lip's numb and that's what happens everytime – it's like going to the dentist.

Zee and I sit like two bibbed babies, trays binding us to the seat and napkins all over the place. Because of a flight mix-up we're flying first class (my first time kids) and there's a bit more room. Me and Zee are sitting in the front seat and I'm having pilot fantasies. Mick's flattened out across the corridor mandied to the hilt and Phal sits behind. It's just occurred to me that a lot of you don't know about mandies. As I've said before they're rock 'n roll sleeping pills. Certain doctors – some quacks, some progressive – know that a musician's life ain't exactly 9 till 5. They also realize the pressures involved. They will give out prescriptions only after examining you and determining that the tablets aren't doing you in. Me and Mick get ours on prescription from a guy in Harley Street who knows we need instant sleep now and again and he also knows we're intelligent with them. Mandies can be dangerous if taken in large amounts with alcohol and have caused deaths in the past. In short I take them when it's late and I'm not tired owing to awkward flying schedules and I also take them to calm my adrenalin down. Adrenalin can keep you up all night prior to an important gig. Mick's different, you know by now how he hates the planes and so he takes a couple to make him doze off and forget about the flight. You want to get high? Take a couple of mandies, or even one, with a bottle of Hirondelle, but take a bit of advice, I've been through it. It's a fucking mug's game. Use your loaf. Nobody ever made it stoned. They might have looked stoned but don't kid yourself. They were together enough when it came to making it.

I may sound a bit like Malcolm Muggeridge here but life's to be lived, not avoided. Get yourself out on the street, mate!

We didn't play last night. This is getting ridiculous. The promoter was clueless. We got there at the designated time and slipped in the back door (The Metropolitan). Stan says a quick sound check and out in the car again to a hotel next door where the promoter is laying on food and wine. We got on the stage and kids were running everywhere, about 200 of them. Already 1,200 tickets have been sold and there's more queuing up. They break a glass door and surge in. Stewards try to hold them at the gate but one by one they're slipping through. Stuey and Stan go out to lend a hand and we start tuning up. The entrances are bulging with heads and someone says over the P.A. if they don't calm down there'll be no show. NO USE. They continue to fight to get in and Stuey brings us off stage. There's no one supporting us except two local lads who look very scared folk singers. Phil says if we don't go on they are going to riot and wreck the gear. A chick comes up.

'Jeez, I'm high – I know you from the park last time. Gee your band is fantastic, what's your name? You remember you told me to be quiet.'

'Oh yeah, how's it going?'

'Fine man, fiiiinnnnee! You all stayin' at the Holiday Inn?'

'I don't know, ask Stan, with the hat on.'

Stan told her to get out before he knocked her out and another bloke gave Pete a cloak he'd made and we made for the back door. Blokes blocked the exit and a foot and arm came through. Stuey pushed the arm and kicked the foot and four guys shoved us into the car. Tony said, 'Off you go lads,' and back we came to the Sheraton. Stuey said they might come looking for us so we all stayed in Mick's and my room and Mick and I gave birth to a song called *I Can't Git No Breakfast in Texas* which may or may not ferment. We mucked around watching T.V. It was about 1 a.m. and no room service so it was pretty boring as we know each other well. We'd seen John and Yoko earlier, also Stevie Wonder, Roberta Flack and Sha Na Na. We discussed the merits and faults. Presently people wandered in. Stan, Stu, and Tony returned from the hall with expenses paid by the promoter in accordance with the contract. Lee had walked from the gig losing Zee and Richard Cromelin (a reporter) somewhere on the way. They eventually came and the room was pretty crowded. Two extremely large ladies one white and one black, the latter with the hugest tits I've ever seen, sat at the bottom of my bed, and two very suspect young gentlemen with dyed hair and more than a touch of colour in their cheeks, sat quietly – content to be there.

Mick had a clothes sale as is his wont now and again. All of a sudden he'll empty a huge pile of stuff onto the bed and the bidding commences. Richard Cromelin buys a top, Lee buys a jacket, and a pair of snakeskin boots and Zee also buys a jacket. I get a shirt and a pair of good pants off him and Zee gives me a pair of clogs with laces that I've had my eye on for a little while. He won't take any bread at all and I'm embarrassed but grateful.

We discuss promoters with Tony. You see, over here everybody is given a contract of the conditions under which we will play. They stipulate the size of stage, piano and organ in tune, time for the roadies to set up the gear and the all important sound check. Well, they always sign the contracts but a large majority of them don't even bother to check the clauses therein and they get you there by bullshitting how wonderful you are, how people are really waiting to see your band, how great the clubs he'll take you to after are, and how expert the groupies are. You get there and usually the piano and organ will be there but maybe one Leslie cabinet instead of two. The stages are usually good but because of bad organization somewhere along the line the sound system isn't even up and by the time it is up it's time to let the kids in. Now this guy has broken the contract and he knows it and he's known it all along, but he's sure you'll go on: (a) because you'd seen the kids and you can't let them down; (b) because he can be very nasty if you don't go on.

Tony's policy now is: (a) the band don't even go to the city unless pretty sure of the gig and if they do get there they still mustn't gig unless everything's arranged down to the last five minutes for a sound check. In this way the band doesn't see the kids and feel rotten and (b) if people want to get nasty with Tony, then he gets nasty back and has ample help to do it.

This evens the whole thing up, making the band as hard as the promoter. Obviously you suffer on a few gigs. One hears lurid tales of promoters announcing the group have ripped off the kids and he's innocent of the whole thing. The band is always the mug and we've been trying to alleviate this situation. We want to play to audiences, we love to play anywhere, anytime, but the audience and us must have the best sound possible so's they can get into it and we can too. It may seem hard to walk out as we did last night, but those kids would not have known of the problems involved and would have judged us on a very bad sound. The Rainbow comes to mind. My God the sound was so bad I nearly fainted with embarrassment. So fuck it, I hope it gets around soon that if the rider isn't fulfilled we don't work. The sooner the better for everyone.

By the way, all we got for those two days wasted in Texas was $1,000. That's about a third of what it cost to get us there, back and hotels, etc. See what I mean – mugs.

The green has left us far behind and Michigan is ready for a white Christmas. I hope Mayor Daley doesn't cancel this gig as he did the last time we were here with Johnny Winter. The engines are quiet so we cruise inwards and downwards to Chicago. O'Hare Airport is one of those. You can wait an hour, sometimes more just to land.

I'll admit it, I don't like Chicago. A guy can say good evening here and make it sound like an invitation to duel. It looks so innocent and cute down there, but that's just a snowy façade. I never walk the streets in Chicago. Maybe it's my paranoia, but you can stick it. The sooner I'm in Cleveland, the better.

We're on with The New Riders of the Purple Sage tonight, and I've never seen them so that's something to look forward to. We're going down. A pilot missed the runway last week killing a fair few people on board. Ice on the runway – solid ice everywhere, but the sky's blue. How can the sky be blue when it's six degrees out? Pass other airline buildings – Northwest, Continental, Eastern, United, one small Ozark (sorry, three small Ozarks), T.W.A., A.A., and finally into Delta. No ice here and up goes a Jumbo like a huge bullet headed eagle after its prey. The portable gangway concertinas into the front left side of the plane and people stand in a row like sheep and try to read what I'm writing. Up the gangway and through the sea of ever-staring straights. Turn right and head down the gangway for the baggage – one hell of a walk (I eye a wheelchair but as usual I daren't) and then I rip into the news-stand but they've no music papers and nothing particularly horny either. Back down the main corridor and left again down an escalator and a short walk to the Delta baggage area. I'm writing this and watching for my gear on the rollers. My desk is a Chicago newspaper stand sporting copies of the *Chicago Sun Times*, and *Chicago Today* in their ovens, 10 cents for dailies and 30 cents for Sundays. This baggage area's like any other and I can see my bags.

Bloody hell, it's enough to freeze your balls off! Icy cold darts through jeans, through your legs and out the other side. The limo isn't allowed to stand, wait, stop, load or unload or anything else so he's gone round the back and we amuse ourselves daring the cold. Some loader cocked my suitcase right up. The handle's gone and the hinges too. It's 4 p.m. already and I've got to get another one from somewhere before the shops shut. American baggage loaders are notorious. I complain to the Delta man. He more or less says it's a wreck anyway, but gives me a bit of tape which proves hopelessly inadequate. Here's the car and on into Chicago. The Holiday Inn, at the side of the lake next to the lake tower where we stayed the last time. I remember having a row with a bird at the side of the lake and watching dead fish float by – that was 18 months ago. We're all on the 18th floor. I've got the single today, 1802; it overlooks the lake which is undecided as to whether it should ice over or not. At the moment it's half and half. Lighthouses flash in the distance and in the foreground a modern low block is outlined in a square of yellow lights.

Phally and I ring Trudy and Elaine. They go back on Wednesday and I make arrangements for her to pick me up at the airport on the night of the 23rd. Mainman's having a small party with David, the Spiders and us, everybody who's made the latter part of '72 successful. That'll start to happen as soon as we get into London on the 9:45 flight. Then everyone will split for a well deserved holiday before the New Year and (we hope) *the* year.

Tiredness is beginning to show. The soap spews its suds all over bottles in my toilet bag instead of sitting neatly in its box. Dirty socks get stuffed in with clean ones and one tends to wear one's underpants another day longer. Bags appear under my eyes and it becomes more of an effort to do anything. My dreams tend to be more evil of late. I've always killed someone and am on the run and I always wake up before I'm shot, but I dream of a murderer and it's pretty bloody awful. Drama.

Drama too, at the sound check. New Riders said if we sound checked more than two numbers they were going home and the promoter said he'd cancel the gig if they did. We conceded and then they tried to get us to go on before the folk singer, Eric Anderson, who would get the mood going for their quiet C.W. approach. This we wouldn't agree to and that was O.K.

126

in the end. The two numbers sounded bad and we all came back to the hotel somewhat jaded. Talcum powder had spilt all over my brown leathers and the arse was split so I spent half of the three quarters of an hour we had to get back to the theatre doing them up. Quick hairwash and shave and Stan was banging on the door: 7:45, time to go.

Eric Anderson was on when we got there and I liked him, but it's going to be difficult for him. James Taylor, Cat Stevens, the syndrome is saturated and it's difficult for a folk singer to captivate. He did well, however, and got an encore.

The promoter laid on wine and sandwiches and the hospitality was good. The Chicago Auditorium is a beautiful place and the feeling is good, but somewhere between an encored folk singer and the New Riders I think we might die. My doubts proved groundless though, and apart from the high hat-stand freaking Buff, things turned out well. We did a long and lusty encore – went back on but just felt like rocking and we didn't do *Dudes* just *Honky Tonk* and the audience was great. We worked with the crowd at the end . . . 'Give me, give me, give me the honky tonk blues'. It was a gas of a gig overall. Thank you.

Chicago don't forget us. We left during New Riders' act and the slide player was absolutely great. I turned from the stage to leave, Stuey was hustling, and I'll swear I saw Jeff Beck; in fact I know I saw Jeff Beck but he was engrossed in the slide player too so I left it at that. Mick got a standing ovation for his solo in *Ready for Love* and under the circumstances we couldn't have done better.

The film *White Christmas* is on with Bing Crosby, Danny Kaye and Rosemary Clooney. Tony enthuses about a building here where people apparently live and die. It's the largest apartment building in the world and it is totally self-sufficient. Entertainment, shops, all services, you never have to leave the building all your life. Salute the first generation of battery hens and, of course, Defries would like some of the action. As we drove back that evening we saw it. A frightening monster which sways three feet from side to side in the north wind. 50-storey office blocks mathematically leave their numbered office lights on to effect huge Christmas crosses, even our own Holiday Inn sports a huge cross. I never dug Christmas much. I only wish I could get into it like the commercial picture it is supposed to be. Poor old self-pitying me – an envious agnostic. To me it's just hassle but to some it's really beautiful, relaxed, quiet family time and I'm jealous as hell for not naturally feeling this way. I think it's mainly because I have two children whom I don't see very often and T.V. makes Christmas a kid's day and I feel such a bastard. Still, I suppose it's soon over. Sorry to drag reader, but I'm writing what I'm thinking at the time, and red wine takes its toll and it's valid because everyone gets pissed now and again. It's a release from this shithouse game we're in. See you tomorrow.

Sunday, 17 December 1972

Another foot of snow fell last night. Somebody said it was zero and the Cleveland area is reported to be getting between three and seven inches of snow. The Cleveland airport has in fact been shut now for two days. United Airlines having already spent $60,000 keeping passengers in Chicago hotels. There is a waiting list of God knows how many people and they're all in pretty bad moods. The check-in desk resembles a dole office. The occasional shaking fist and loud words being exchanged between harassed businessmen and earnest young men on behalf of their flying machines.

I'm sitting on the plane now and I don't know how it happened but we're in first class again. Stan shepherded us to the second class compartment and then stated dramatically that there were no seats and it was all over. A dainty young fellow (we were surrounded by the buggers) who serves the drinks heads us back again and owing to some mix-up on the company's part, we're first class. Far out, as long as they don't charge us the extra. The plane slowly reverses out and the young man is making me a bloody mary, I ask for a tomato juice and that's the nearest he's got – the little devil.

The hostess goes through the routine, 'These are your magazines, please take them with you.' A chick goes through a fictional air hazard – fasten your seatbelts, don't smoke, if we crash bend forward with your head on a cushion between your legs. (You'll go quicker that way.)

The engines build and the young fellow has now changed from his grey suit to a dashing tartan type affair – a flashing smile from even teeth – silly twit. Out along the length of runways leading to the big one – it looks like Siberia through the porthole.

I'm wondering if Ritchie, Phil and Dick are going to make it in one piece. If they broke down in this weather in a secluded spot there's no telling what could happen. I just can't see tonight's gig happening, but we'll all try for it. Already we've lost Bob the light man, Zee, Lee and Stuey. Tony's here and Stan and the band. Buffin was naughty last night and we're all ashamed of him, he's apprehensive about the outcome. An Aztec Hereford baby would be really something special. Still like the young 'uns to have a good time now and again. Oh ar, long as they keep the noise down.

In Cleveland we're staying at a Hotel Sheraton again, and I fluke a single room owing to a balls-up at the desk – my lucky day. Mick, Buff and Phally go down to eat. I follow for something to do even though I'm not hungry and we bump into a couple of guys from Dr Hook who are supporting us tonight. I congratulate the singer on his incredible vocal on *Sylvia's Mother* and Mick tells them about their film which we saw on *Top of the Pops*. They'd never seen it and they didn't know they got to no. 2 in the charts either. They said they're coming to England and Europe late February/March and we say we'll see them later. Nice easy-going guys. I have a feeling they'll be good on stage. Mick says Phil told him that the New Riders had a bad time last night in Chicago. C.W. isn't exactly the ace music in that city anyway but I won't forget that steel player in a hurry. I'm a bit tired. It's 3:30 p.m. and a black guy is on T.V. saying how the Cleveland police bully and maltreat blacks. He says Cleveland's east side is one of the worst criminal areas in the country. That's nice, we're right in the middle of it. It's rumoured that Columbia Records are going

129

to wine and dine us this evening, but I'll believe it when I see it. Still, Dr Hook are Columbia's too, so it would make sense. The sound check was late, but the roadies did a hell of a job getting through from Chicago when lorries lay strewn all over the place on the way along the roughly 250-300 miles journey. Dr Hook have already had a sound check and apparently they're a bit like the New Riders. The titles of their songs are somewhat rude, one's called *Let's Ball* and another is worse, but I forget it now. Stan, my informant, is inclined to exaggerate anyway, and I wouldn't wish to credit them with titles hyperbolized in Stanley's wonderful but mangled head.

We had about an hour at the gig – only rehearsed two numbers, the rest was getting little things fixed. Dee Dee and Daria turned up, our earliest fans from the first tour. We met them in Cincinnati on the day Iggy walked on the people's hands. They both look just the same. Daria is slightly heavier owing to the recent appearance of a baby called Justin who's now six weeks old and thriving. She didn't want to know the father, she just wanted the baby, and she's 20 now so I suppose she knows what she's doing. Anyway, we only had an hour 20 minutes so we scooted back to the Sheraton for our respective toiletries.

8:15 saw us shining in the lobby and a real buzz was on – the place is a sell out and Tony even sent down his own tickets to help out. By the time we got there they'd sent 200 away on top of that so at last we're playing – like an English gig – where everybody knows us. Wine and beer but no food, the tight sod. We arse about the dressing room in good spirit. The current game being who can photograph Stuey, who has an aversion to cameras. We're getting changed and Pete brings in his leopard-skin boots, the first reserve. I get a fit of the shakes. They're expecting a lot tonight and I hope we can live up to it. Stan comes down for us; up a few stairs and we hear the roar as the lights go down and the intro music plays. We'll have to get rid of this intro thing altogether, it's too long.

Here we are, sea of faces. My bloody mike's not working – run over to Mick's, first fuckin' number and my mike's off! I feel big – *Sucker* moves along great, Mick painfully twists notes through his solo. Everybody's happy. Biffo threshing away and

Phally quietly smiling. Pete's got his eyes shut under that mane of blue silver hair and Mick, as always, looks slightly perplexed with the whole procedure. They stand up when I announce *Ready for Love* and applaud again when Mick starts to sing. I can't believe 'em, and they give me encouragement too as we start *Sea Diver*. Mick's and my voices are both a bit rough. Constant changes of climate and time irregularities have left us slightly weak and vulnerable to sore throats, colds, etc. Mick gets through *Ready for Love* O.K. but I fluff on a note in *Sea Diver*. I do a little semi-scream and a laugh to get myself out of it, hoping the crowd understands. *Angeline* wasn't as good as usual, but *One of the Boys* was great – about the best we've ever done it. Goodnight everybody, thanks for comin' and up went the roar as we trooped off. We're all jumpin'. It was definitely about the best we could have possibly done and it sounds like it was good enough. Grab a quick beer. Stan says don't do *Dudes* but we feel we have to.

I walk back out, get my guitar in the darkness and turn to a sea of lit matches and lighters – it looked incredible from the stage. They did it in the big 10,000 seater for Bowie and God knows what that must have looked like, I can't remember ever doing a gig, apart from a festival, where the crowd did this. An old campaigner, nothing can shock me, but I must admit, I had a lump in my throat. It looked great.

Dudes was done well and they loved it and then *Honky Tonk* and it was all over. All I can say is I'll never forget that night. It reminded me of Croydon a lot, sort of kids – eager and keen. I think Cleveland is the best city in America for rock 'n roll music at the moment, but that's only in my short experience. Bill, a local radio DJ here who can claim a large part of the credit for bringing our records into the public eye in Cleveland says the city swings and we agree that it should be kept a secret so as the Cleveland kids don't get bogged down with too much media and too many bands becoming apathetic like perhaps New York or San Francisco.

We all retire to a restaurant somewhere (I was too tired to find out where). The C.B.S. party is now tomorrow night so tonight Mainman treats us handsomely. Tony taking the captain's place at the top of the table and looking not unlike Blue-beard with his recently acquired frizz. His crew is generally getting pissed in a relaxed atmosphere. Back to bed, the hall-way on the sixth floor is like Piccadilly Circus. I courteously avoid the attentions from both a black lady with red hair and a young man whose dreamy eyes caressed my genital area. Pissed out of his brain, his eyes two short cuts and I wished Lee was here – he's so good at handling this kind of an attack. Finally abed, I put a quarter in the bed vibrator and pass out having only used 10 cents' worth.

Monday, 18 December 1972

I have that rich feeling you get when you've had a good gig the night before; if you've had a bad one, it's very hard to live with.

Some bloody bird woke me at 8 a.m. (I forgot to put the 'Do not disturb' sign on the door) and since then a road has disappeared and my ears are singing to the song of the drills. It's about midday and the drills are on one side, drama sob on the T.V. in the middle, chambermaids banging around on the right. The noise is almost claustrophobic. I might as well have slept in the lobby. I ring up Tru and tell her the latest and she's well pleased. I can hear bloody Christmas carols now on top of the other noises, this is unbelievable. Well, it's later than I thought, 2:45 and Tony wants a Godfather meeting at 3, then he'll go to New York to see Mellie who's flying in today from San Francisco. Stan is already in a state of panic about Memphis. The last gig, a week away or less and Clair Bros, the usual P.A. people we use have now closed down for Christmas leaving us in the hands of some company Dick hasn't heard of and if their sound equipment isn't up to it, it's a long way to go for a bum gig. On another gig in Scranton we're supporting Edgar Winter, and I don't like the look of that one myself. We'll just have to wait and see.

I scramble around and get down to the second floor, Parlour C, which is a small conference room in which we're about to have a small conference.

Lee sends down for coffee and we're all here except for Mick who's disappeared. Mainly the discussion involves efficiency. How the crew can work even quicker than they are working, too much time wasted between numbers, notes are taken down. We need a ramp for orchestra pits. A better system of communication between P.A. and stage. Clothes to be changed, slicker. Guitar changes (if need be). Rehearsals are discussed too. See the tour we're on is really a last-minute affair and

133

we'd have liked at least three weeks to improve the act for the States. Normally before a tour of this nature you know exactly when you're flying out and arrange accordingly.

It's really best to rehearse in England. It means you're not away so long and it's a hell of a lot cheaper too. Fees for rehearsal rooms here are astronomical, not to mention the extra money that would be spent in hotels. Remember when you're touring you've got to keep your place in London paid up as well.

Normally we'll rehearse a couple of weeks in a small studio like A.C.M. in Kings Road, this costs about £1 an hour. The third week we like to use a proper stage, somewhere like the Sundown at Edmonton. This runs us about £40 a day. It's a lot of bread but if you get your set off really good and you're really confident in the performance of the numbers then it's worth the bread.

We really must have more warning next time. It's good to do the job as painstakingly as we can. If the show's well rehearsed you can really work at putting it across. The 'putting it across' bit being almost as important as the music these days.

All in all the meeting takes two hours and proved everybody's really concerned in a concentrated effort for the next tour. Momentum is really picking up. We are now trying to make it and everybody in the group's got to pull together on that final run home, and with a bit of luck, we just might do it at that.

Tony's flight for New York comes increasingly closer so we pack up and Mick, who's just got back, takes us all round to Sam's Pawn shop on 29th and Prospect. The Columbia guy here is really nice and offers Ritchie his car. Me, Buff, Mick, Peter, Phally and Ritchie all pile in and wander down there. Prices are again a little high, but Phally and Pete both buy solid Epiphones for $110 – which is a good price if you want a good guitar to practice on at home.

I vaguely look for something for Trudy, but all I can find are golf appliances, film apparatus, fishing tackle, guns, swords, and she wouldn't really appreciate a set of drills.

Anyway, it's 7:30 and we're back at the hotel, with time to

kill. I wander into the restaurant and decide to eat with Phil, Ritchie and Dick. I meet Dennis, Ray and Jay from Dr Hook briefly too while I'm waiting in the restaurant. 45 minutes later, I'm still waiting and the soup still hasn't appeared. If this bird wants a tip she's going about it the wrong way. She's German, hardly speaks English and most of the ordering is done in that pidgin English one uses when in Europe if one doesn't know how to speak the local lingo.

A few birds are hanging around. One's got ostrich feathers hanging out of her sweater making her look like an almost plucked scrawny chicken.

In all, the meal takes 90 minutes and I don't leave a tip. A tip here is 10 to 15 per cent of the bill. In this case the bill is $5.10 (approx. £2) but I'm not leaving bugger all. When it did come it was very average. A small piece of steak, a baked potato and a salad which consisted of one-eighth of a tomato and a load of lettuce with cheese dressing. Forget it, Sheratons are on the way down.

9 p.m. it's party time, but nobody is ready. Phally thrashes chords out on his new guitar and Mick plays around on a little Silvertone he got for $20. Pete assumes an almost acrobatic angle in the sink to gargle, Buff's wandering and Stan's bustling nowhere. Finally at 10 the first load departs. Lee, Zee and Stu are already there. Buff, Pete, Stan, Dick, Ritchie, Phil and myself make up the first lot. John the limo driver will go back for Phall and Mick.

The place is called the Grog Shop. We walk through a large club room. A small band is playing and I try to say hello to the R.M.I. player but get blown out. Fuck you. If this is it I'm off back to the hotel! It's half empty and piss-takers abound. Then Lee appears from somewhere and directs us up some stairs – along and into a crowded room, full of inquiring glances. We bravely walk the gauntlet. I do polite flashy-teethed hellos and cop a brandy and a huge onion in case I have to talk to somebody – this is mostly a businessman's excuse for a piss up.

Record people, promotion, distribution, press, local radio, that type of thing and the proof of the pudding was when Dr Hook got up to do a small but excellent set and were drowned by the babble of voices. Birds everywhere, moving, on the make continuously – what the fuck am I doing here? 'Stan, let's go!' Stan has the light of a merryman in his eyes and is on the way as they say. Stuey's smoked too much and he's past it. Zee runs around and eventually Lee, Zee, Buff, Mick, Phally and me are ready to go. Out the front door to the limo which has conveniently disappeared and we are left standing there like lemons for 25 minutes waiting for a cab. That fucking limo service wants to get stuffing. The money they charge, and the bloke's not there when you want him!

My guts have that empty feeling; a bad taste is in my mouth and wind is caught inside me, and I wish it would come out – either end will do. I take a mandy, sip a beer and fade away to a Tom Courtney film which looks good.

Tuesday, 19 December 1972

Well, I'm sitting on a Vista-something engine-prop plane, there's fog outside. I've got my chin out, and I don't like it. Thirty-five minutes of 'don't like' taking us from Cleveland to Pittsburg. Then a two-hour wait before another short flight to Scranton. This morning was as normal, the only unusual thing that happened was that while Dick was making a phone call Mick walked in with a pair of scissors and cut the flex. This was quite odd, nobody said much about it and he sellotaped it back together again. Mick, by the way, is travelling by lorry today with Phil and Ritchie, and we have the pleasure of sound man Dick, an excellent lad, who takes his place on the plane.

I'm still not liking this flight.

Scranton's a definite now. Rico the promoter's been on the phone quite a bit, we seem to have jumped in popularity there. Stan couldn't get limos so the guy (who is also a second-hand car dealer) loaned us three of his free of charge. Bloody hell – let's get down and out of this thing. Stan's reading *Playboy* (we always wait for Buffin to buy it, then borrow it). Buffin's reading the airline magazine, as is Phally; Dick's behind with Pete and I can't see Zee or Stuey.

I just found out that Stuey went back to England early this

morning. No wonder he was so stoned last night. Lee has nipped to New York, but he'll be back tomorrow for the gig. Tony's sitting Scranton out and we'll see him in Memphis for the last gig. It's been a great little tour, so much better than I expected.

Well, here we are, Pittsburg Airport – grey, miserable usual type of place and we decide to eat in the airport's V.I.P. restaurant for once. Now the restaurant is a different scene altogether. All the waiters are dressed to kill and the head waiter is hip to any language you want to talk. I wade my way through liver and bacon (Phal's current obsession) and half a bottle of Chianti (my dad's all-time favourite). We become increasingly aware of a group of women at a table across the empty bar opposite who are talking in exceedingly loud voices. O.K., it's Christmas soon, some office must have just broken up for the holidays, but then they start to make rude observations about Pete's hair and eventually one of them, a peroxide blonde who no doubt has left her long-suffering spouse at home, staggers across.

'How d'you git yer hair that way?'
'Same way you got yours.'
'I wouldn't be seen out on the street like that!'
'You're ugly.'
'Now young man, no need for rudeness.'
'Go away.'

Back at the table the blonde has a spate of giggling and rams the table cloth in her mouth. We find American women from 35-45 exceedingly loud-mouthed, stupid and coarse. No Englishman would stand for them. Insults are exchanged between them and Pete and Buff; and Pete and Buff leave with Phally and Dick. Zee and I are a little behind.

WAITER: Your meal O.K. sir?
ZEE: Your whores have big mouths.
WAITER: Those 'whores' just spent $400 on food, sir. I suggest you check your dime tips and then pick them up and take them back to England with you.
ME: Wait a minute now, wait! How much of a tip on $8?

137

WAITER: About 1.40.

ME: Well I left 1.25 because I was told that was correct.

WAITER: Well we don't want it. Take it away.

ME: Listen you fuckin' midget (a lighted cig hits him) if you
want to fuck those slags it's your affair – let 'em wash you in
dollars. We see bastards like you every day. Why don't you
go and marry a fuckin' dotte?

CASHIER: I think you should apologize.

ZEE: Apologize for what? To whores? Fuck off.

ME: You're all a load of fuckin' twats.

By the time we're half way down the hall, an irate waiter
shouts, 'They're not whores. They're not whores.' I scream to
the contrary. You'll never know how much these loud house-
wives are whores. They're unbelievable, absolutely sickeners
and a good laugh was had by all.

Into the chemist for vitamin E and some Revlon makeup,
purchased to hide our masculine shaving blue. A chemist with a
huge cigar stares accusingly (take the cigar out of your mouth
you cunt – you're a chemist).

By this time the Chianti has taken hold and I've got to stay
awake. If I sleep now, I won't be tired this evening and Scranton doesn't exactly sound like Las Vagas. I'm on a second plane,
but owing to the wine I don't know what type it is. I have to
finish now as the hostess wants my table up.

That was the roughest landing yet. He came in too soon and
had to spurt up again before landing bumpily, but it's O.K.
now. We're not in Scranton exactly but half way between
Scranton and Wilks Barry.

Wednesday, 20 December 1972

First a couple of things I forgot to tell you before about the
Columbia party. Stanley got slightly merry and according to
Buff walked right up to the plucked chicken and put his face
about two inches from hers. Stan has a kind of questioning
belligerent look that transfixes you and she just stood there not
knowing what to do. Apparently they were in this static position for about 45 seconds then Stan screamed, 'onions', and
walked off.

We can't think of a security bloke for the next tour as Stu will be with Bowie. We need a hard man just in case of trouble. Actually it's not only punch up trouble you encounter on these tours – it's more people who pester the life out of you. The fans are great. They're polite and realize you've only got so much time on hand but these fuckers who continually harass you are a real pain in the arse.

They'll follow you from city to city, they'll ring you hourly. Sometimes they plead with you to see them, sometimes they're nasty because you won't and threaten you and the daft thing is they're mainly blokes. Not only faggots either. There's a breed of guy who just loves being with musicians. He's usually sadly lacking and hangs on to you for a bit of reflected light. He'll never take no for an answer – you can explain till you're blue in the face and ten minutes later he's forgotten. He tells everyone he knows you. Tries to lay chicks on the group name. Never has bread and the horrible thing is you feel such a twat having to blow him out all the time. He trades on your pity and uses 'loyalty' to cover up for anything he can get on your back. Open your door, he's there. Go for a swim and you meet him three feet under. Go to a club and there he sits pretending he's with you and making you look and feel an idiot. Brings some slag up to be introduced and you play his game because again you feel sorry for him. 'Fore you know it he's running your fucking life. Dylan had it with Weberman. A guy called Wayne was my shadow. Oh for a heavy man. A few well chosen words and that would have been it.

Try keeping stray kids out of a sound check. You can't unless old muscles is there. He doesn't have to do anything he just has to stare. Nip in a red-neck bar after a gig in Texas or New Mexico you won't last five minutes without your heavy. You'd be amazed at the amount of people who still hate long hair. Especially if there's bread attached. Jealousy still abounds too. No bloke likes his bird eyeing other fellas and musicians don't have lilywhite reputations. No, taken all in all, you need a heavy man, no doubt about it. Promoters can be bastards too, remember the St Louis gig?

Stan can't think of anybody with brains, because brains are

needed more than brawn, and I can think of a couple of guys but they've settled down now, their long-suffering wives finally having gotten the upper hand, and I don't want to upset any families. Jimmy Taylor, for instance, from Northampton was a wild man and very clever with it too. He never turned on me once, but I saw him at a gig with his wife not long back and he's got a house now and she's a gas. The gigs are only for five weeks anyway, and he might just get excited enough to get restless again but I wouldn't want that for him or her. There's not much family fun in this type of life. It takes a special kind of woman to put up with it. There are very few of them around, and even when you've got a good one – the very nature of the job, and the time you are away, last-minute alterations, the obvious temptations, the odd hours and the ups and downs, can cause endless arguments which are usually pointless and end up in stalemates. The very things that attracted the girl to you in the first place become threatening to her when she's your old lady. They used to call them skiffle widows – I don't know what they call them in this trade, and I take each day as it comes. I find women a necessary evil. I've had more trouble in my short life because of women than anything else and I'm sure they suffered even more; but I'm a ladies' man, I have to have a good woman and even though Trudy can be a huge pain in the arse at times – I'm fucked if she's not there. She fills my gaps in and I like to think I do the same for her. I'll probably get into a row for writing this.

It's about 1 p.m. and the maid just gave me towels and Buff's still asleep. Stan and Dick seem busy next door, and soon I'll venture out into Scranton. The town was once the whorehouse of America or so I'm unreliably informed, but somehow it seems peaceful now. There's a little square outside over the window. The grass is covered in snow, covered in footprints. The umbrellas are up and one memorial is dedicated to the soldiers and sailors of 1861-5. Another memorial just as austere, says MEN, and the whole town looks like Germany which is what it is I suppose, a mainly German settlement.

I must get Tru some earrings for those ridiculous tribal holes some idiot stabbed through her ears when she was a child. She insists on keeping them open. Perhaps she believes them to be some sign of fertility or something. We live in the Middle Ages. People will laugh in 100 years time.

Rico the promoter amazes; he's really been good what with loaning us cars gratis and seeing we were generally O.K. We load into three of his cars and head for a boys' club building – used more for basket ball than gigs. The place holds about 4,000 and he's already sold 2,000 in advance, so it should be good.

The stage is a wood and scaffolding affair. Edgar Winter's lights shoot up out of their travelling crates at the back and both sides of the stage being about head high. Another band called Eggs Over Easy are opening, but as far as I can see, we're the only ones sound checking. I've never known echo like it. The whole place rattles on half volume and my voice comes back after about three seconds. Guys wander round with T-shirts, the word 'FANG' inscribed, presumably either the P.A. people or the security, and it all seems quite together. We try three numbers and then call it a day. The crowd will deaden the echo and we'll just have to adjust as it happens.

Back to the hotel in an ancient Plymouth Fury and we have one and a half hours to get ready. Mick wanders off then rings Stan to say he's found cheap guitars in a shop up the road and I'm off like a bullet. I arrive to find him holding an immaculate Melody Maker which he just bought for $70. Some blokes. Fanatically foraging around I find an old Epiphone Melody Maker and also one of the newer Gibsons, two pick up Melody Makers. I get these for $60 each. Incredible.

The guy can see we're interested and he pulls out a wooden fitted coffin-type case from the back of the shop. It's covered in dust and built of wood with an old Wells Fargo label on it. Opening it we see an immaculate Martin and have a guess what's on the mahogany block inside? 'C. F. Martin—*New York*'. That makes the guitar at least 130 years old and it's immaculate! He won't sell it but if he did sell it he said he'd charge about $325. To the right person that guitar would now be worth up to £1,000 or more. Bloody hell, we sweated – the serial number of the case had '20' on it, and for all we know that might have been the 20th model of that Martin ever made. Excuse me while I dream.

Time was flying by. The guy that ran the shop was eccentric to say the least. I even had to go down to his cellar to find cases for the guitars. He wouldn't. He threw in a couple of leads and packets of strings as well, so I got a great deal. Forty minutes left before the gig and I hurriedly washed, shaved, and rubbed my flowing locks with Knights Castile, I've run out of shampoo.

We go like madmen getting ready in time so Stan won't shout, and finally make it only to be met by super-cool Stan saying, 'Take it easy, the gig's running late. You've got 30 minutes.' I ring room service for a beer and a bacon and lettuce sandwich. The T.V. show is the new *Bonanza*. Little Joe magically becoming big Joe and small brothers appearing in mysterious fashion.

At the gig it is packed. They're chanting, 'Mott.' Thank Christ, they know us. Eggs Over Easy have just come off and as we change the stamping becomes louder and louder. It's great to listen to. You know they're determined to have a good time and they want to see you. A roar goes up as we enter the backstage area and Dick shoves on the Jupiter tape. (Pete recorded Jupiter on a cassette once. We played it over the P.A. at a rehearsal and it sounded so good we've used it as an introduction ever since.) Bang, and in, Bob working the lights industriously and no major problems. The whole gig is great in a sweat rock sort of way and Mick's volume switch on the Esquire is the only thing that causes any trouble. He swops to the new Fender Strat he's just bought and it all goes off great. We finish on *Angeline* and a healthy old din keeps going until we saunter back on. They've all stood up, what a feeling. I hope I never become immune to scenes like this. Dick told us after the gig that the sound wasn't too good, but I think the people couldn't have dug it more than they did anyway. It was a bit like a school gymnasium gig – that's about the nearest I could get.

Peter, Buff and Phally want to go straight back to the hotel, but Mick and I prefer to stay and see Edgar Winter. Lee and Zee kick up a bit and they're right, but I just feel like loosening up and Buff and my room is in a bit of a state, and I don't feel like facing it yet. A young kid gets through the security net and gives me a couple of photos he took at the Tower Theatre in Philadelphia and it turns out he's been a fan of ours for two years and we enjoy him enjoying us. I wish press had been there to see the light shining in this kid's eyes. O.K. we're not big yet, but we are his heroes, and no one, including the press, have the right to reduce us in the eyes of a kid who's as happy as he is. We made his day and he made ours.

I slipped out to wish the Winter group a good set, and the guitar player said he dug our set (pause for piss-take by readers). A roar told us they were on and it was flat out rock 'n roll all the way. Edgar still extending his vocal chords to ridiculous heights in *Tobacco Road*. I don't believe how thin Edgar Winter is. He and his brother, you can almost see through them on a clear day.

Unfortunately, I was happy, and when I'm happy I want to relax, and then I drink. Mick had wandered off somewhere, Lee was arguing with a radio station rep who wanted an interview:

'I'm sorry, the boys would love to do interviews, but Mr Defries will not allow it.'
'Who's Defries?'
'Don't you know Tony Defries?'
'No.'
'You will.'

Meanwhile I sink my sixth beer and feel at ease with the world. I wander out and sneak to the back of the hall and watch Edgar Winter scat singing with the guitar player. They certainly know how to move. I wander back into the dressing room and ladies hang around. When will they ever learn?

By the time Mick, Zee, Lee and me get back to the Hilton it would be reasonable to say that I'd gone completely. All I can remember is rowing with Mick and then making up. Smashing Stan's door in because he wouldn't answer, and generally making a complete prat of myself. I must have finally shut my big trap about four and dozed off. The next thing I knew it was

1 p.m. today, and Buff is shouting, '50 minutes to get ready', into my brain.

Thursday, 21 December 1972

There's only one thing to do, straight into the bogs and turn on the cold shower. Well, it probably weakened my heart but it woke me up. One multivitamin, one vitamin-E pill, one Alka Seltzer of Lee's and one Winston fag and I was ready to pile my dirty clothes into the over-loaded suitcase and head for the lobby.

Buff's already been out and bought some records. He finally got the L.P. of old rock hits he wanted and he even bought our single. A tribute to Columbia – even we buy our own fuckin' records. Phal seems quiet, Mick O.K. and Pete a little depressed. He sees a saga developing over the gig in Memphis. There's been too much trouble over flights and it's too near Christmas. All the airlines are in chaos and if we miss Christmas at home the natives are going to be restless – not to mention the girls and relatives.

Scranton looked beautiful this morning. The bare trees, and the snow on the grass reminds me of Dr Zhivago when Omar Sharif was on that train. Small houses and you feel you could handle Scranton, it's small and doesn't overwhelm you.

They're very proud of the airport too. It's being renovated to accommodate the larger planes. A huge board in the tiny terminal building tells exactly where the bread is coming from. It's a DC-9 and the weather is bloody awful. One of those blind flights through the fog en route to Allentown, 25 minutes away. I feel uncomfortable and pull the little blinds down over the two windows to my left preferring to pretend I'm not here. My previous night's folly has left me muggy and I try to sleep, but I'm too hot and apprehensive. Although it was a short little flight and the takeoff and landing were good, I didn't feel safe somehow. A man reading a newspaper saying, '11 killed in Chicago air crash', didn't help either.

We landed in Allentown and Mick's off like a shot. Phally

follows and Zee and Stan take off in pursuit. We're supposed to sit tight and take off again for Washington D.C., but it looks like Mick's had enough, the fog's done him in, and Phal for that matter. They won't come back on. Mick's nerves are shattered completely, and we just sit there not knowing what to do.

Stan makes us stay on and we take off for Washington minus Zee, Mick and Phally. The same again; fog all the way. Things are getting a bit chaotic now. Ritchie and Phil get a message to Stan that they've broken down as well, and the plan now is for them to team up with Zee and Co and try to drive, bus or train it down to Memphis.

They've got about 30 hours and Memphis is 1,500 miles away.

Safely down again at Washington and Stan starts to ring again. First the office; Zee rang in and said they met up with Ritchie and are in some garage somewhere in Pennsylvania and what should they do?

Tony says carry on to Memphis. If Mick knows we're there he may still fly so's not to let us down, but I don't think it's a question of letting us down anymore. If the bloke's that bad, and he can't fly, that's it. He has our sympathy.

Pete's all for going home and then we find out Zee, Mick and Phal are heading for New York. The chances of doing Memphis become even slimmer. Mick is probably already thinking if he can just manage that last flight he'll be home. If he comes to Memphis that means three more flights and he knows he may not make it. Still, perhaps Tony can talk to him when they get to New York, even bring them down himself. Tony's extremely calm, never panics and he might quieten him down a bit.

If that bloody plane had gone straight to Memphis today that would have been it, we'd have made it. It's such a shame. We're really big in Memphis, bigger than in Cleveland. They've even got a police escort to go with the limos at the airport. Either that or there's trouble there, one of the two.

So there you are reader, you know as much as I do – rock 'n roll labourers after the golden fleece. We've got the same chances of making the gig as winning the bloody pools, and you can win the pools on a Wednesday night in the safety of your own home. Still, rock's like a drug and I'm an addict. I'll still be here when I get my pension, if anyone will have me. Mug!

On the bright side, Memphis is Memphis. Elvis's famous house is here somewhere with the notes on the railings. You never know, we might just possibly get to see it, but I doubt it. My life-long ambition, to meet Dylan, was set back again too. I'd probably freeze if I ever did anyway, so what's the point. By the way, I missed a free meal writing this last lot down. My scribblings are written all over sundry pieces of paper all stuffed in a little black bag. I hope Tru can decipher it all when she comes to type it. I can't even read my own writing three days after.

A hat looms two seats in front and English football results show Stan how his beloved Hereford United are faring. Outside it's beautiful, the wing a navy blue against the slightly lighter blue of the sky and then the dusty blue of the clouds beneath. Little patches of vague yellow where they are at their thinnest signifies lights underneath and then we sink down into the clouds themselves. How I hate this racing through blindly. Ah, the clear light of Memphis below, thank Christ. It's been a long day; I didn't think we'd make it.

Through the terminal and sailors call us gay as usual. I hesitate to do one of our repertoire of standard answers to idiots because there are about 40 of them and we're in the South now.

Two guys meet us, one has a girl and I'm sure I'll get to know their names as they're running the gig. Stan supervises the baggage (it's all here, Phal's and Mick's as well) and then out to the limos. Three of them and Memphis City Police to boot. I just couldn't believe it. Stereo blaring in the limo, an old black guy singin' along in the driving seat. Two police motor bikes out front, sirens going and lights flashing. One bike draws back to the second limo, takes a bottle of wine offered, has a huge swig and gives it back – the other motor-cyclist has a bottle of bourbon stuck in his belt. Through the lights, one bike blocks the traffic and the other speeds us through on down into the centre of Memphis. All I can tell you is that it's 8:30 p.m. now and dark, it looks a bit like Texas. Sirens still wailing we swerve into the forecourt of the Downtown Motor Inn. If only Mick and Phally had've been here, what a welcome. Posters shoved in our hands and the *Dudes* commercial comes appropriately over the radio. I wonder if old Elvis is listening. They promise to show us his house sometime. It's on the other side of Memphis. On guess where? Elvis Presley Boulevard. Wonder if they'll ever have Hunter Terrace or something like that in Wembley.

They insist that we go to a party now at the promoter's house and they're so nice we agree, but God knows what it'll be like and I'm totally knackered. Pete seems to have woken up though, and Buff's happier. Stan loved the police riders and he's wide awake and in a silly mood. His hat at a jaunty angle and he's gone. Lee's grinning away too, so we might as well relax and enjoy a bit of that southern hospitality. Don't ask me what my room number is – they're all the same now. I've got fifty minutes to become a dude.

And southern hospitality it was. Bourbon on the rocks and a few smokes too; me playing the piano dreamily at five in the morning in a beautiful house belonging to Mike, one of the organizers. The house had a dark blue light plus fairy lights from a Christmas tree, and outside a candelabra's lights reflect in the window and a small statue of Christ is just visible from the garden. A bar in one corner of another room and the limo driver transformed to barman – the police motor-cyclists were relaxing now. Various ladies drifted around and when I asked one for an ashtray she pointed to the obvious place. Too obvious for me. I settled for a chat with a young guy and a lady, they were really nice. Rock was there; he plays for Joe Walsh's group, Barnstorm, and is a character straight from the Colorado Hills outside Boulder. He told me Walsh has been studying karate and broke a foot so he's not due in until later. Earlier Stan got in touch with Mick and things look slightly better. Mick was feeling more together and they had booked stand-by flights for the 8:40 in the morning. This means they can only get on if there are cancellations. It looks better, but it's still distinctly dodgy. One thing, if Mick does get on the plane he can't get off. It's non stop to Memphis. We'll see anyway. We're all back safely. Bed now and Dick Cavett is having one of his better shows with Jack Lemmon and Bobby Fischer the chess champion who turns out to be a real entertainer and very down to earth. I've heard great things about Beale Street so I'll investigate and find out tomorrow. Meanwhile – sleep. Oh, I'll just go and get an ice-cold Coke. (Take note all you shit English hotels who pride yourselves on service.)

·Friday, 22 December 1972

Well it's 11:30 on this Memphis morning, the date of our last gig on this tour and my writing is almost done. A visit to Stan's room reveals no new information on the whereabouts of Mick, Phal, Zee, Ritchie, Phil and Dick. It's asking too much to imagine they'll make it, but miracles do happen. We decide to go Christmas shopping and Stan, Pete, Buff and me stride out on a brisk Tennessee winter morning. Straight down about three blocks – Beale Street. The street blues songs were written about, and it's rumoured the street where Chuck Berry bought his first guitar. It's a tumbledown affair. Pawn shop after pawn shop, cheap jewellers, hardware stores and barbers. Most of the pawns shops have the Japanese copy guitars in and very few Gibsons are around. When you do find them, they're expensive and I saw only one bargain, an old Gibson acoustic bass with the pegs coming out the back and a four figure serial number. It's immaculate, but it's too much trouble. I've already got four plus my own and I can't really afford the $150.

Back to Union Street and left up to Main Street and we're the only whites on the block and I've never been so relaxed in all my life. We split up and I wander into Goldsmiths (Memphis' greatest store) and find a model of the Santa Maria galleon on the top floor. I decide to buy it for my Mum and Dad, and ask the woman to pack it well – it's got to go a long way. While I'm waiting a young girl comes up.

'Gee, it's great to see a *real* person.'

'Sorry?'

'It's great to see a *real* person man. I mean I feel like crawling up foetal.'

'Really?'

'Yeah, you know all these freaks buying all this trash. Wad'r'ya gettin'?'

'A galleon.'

'A what?'

'A galleon! A ship.'

'Oh, great.'

'Yeah.'

'You really did me man. You wanna know something? I'm gettin' married – ain't that something.'

'Great. How old are you?'

'21.'

'You look younger.'

'I know. I'm not younger, I'm 21. You playin' at the concert tonight?'

'Yeah.'

'What's the name of your group?'

'Mott the Hoople.'

'Gee, I'd really like to go but I gotta work in this store until midnight. It would be real nice if I could see you later – am I imposin' on ya?'

'Well the thing is we've been invited out after the gig so we'll be pretty busy. Anyway, I don't think you should be seeing me. Your boyfriend will get angry if you're getting married soon.'

'Oh, that's cool. See that's what we do round here once in a while to get the presents together, make some good money.'

'Oh.'

'Well, I gotta serve now. The lady's got your stuff ready.'

'Oh yeah, right. Merry Christmas.'

Grabbing the galleon, which has now grown to the size of a tea chest, I scramble out of Goldsmiths and stagger down Main Street. Black dudes stare at my boots. Some of the guys look incredible, and I never saw more beautiful women. It's all clothes and music here. Older women scurry by, shopping bags full of toy guitars and dolls for the little ones. I curse the zealousness of the packers, the bloody box weighs a ton and I'm sweating in my old afghan. (It's not old actually, it's new.) Back to the hotel and dump the box. Stan's going to hate me for the size of this thing. He's got to carry it.

The miracle has happened, Stan's got everybody here once again under his wing. After a mad six o'clock dash to N.Y. La Guardia Airport this morning, they all got told to go to Newark, and finally because of the chaos as much as anything else, got here complete with the gear. Amazing!

I run down and hug old Ralpher, the hero. Phal looks pale and we've lost his guitar so he's upset as well. No sweat, Zee shoots off to the airport to get it from Lost Property. Phal still thinks we forgot it though and a tired row breaks out. End-of-tour strain can make you think you'll never gig again, and we're all starting to get a little annoyed with each other. It's happened before and it'll happen again.

I really am knocked out to see Mick. He's eating and I nip off to a jeweller's I saw before to get Tru a little gold bracelet with a little heart and tassle attached. It doesn't cost all that much, but she said not to get her much as we've got other gifts to buy. When I get back I bump into Mick and we go out again – me showing him where I've been. He finds one guitar shop we'd missed before, but there's nothing in there so we content ourselves wandering round a couple of cheap discount stores. Lighters are bought, Zippo style for 99 cents and I get a T-shirt which everybody has since laughed at. I don't know why; I think it looks good.

Mick buys a Tennessee T-shirt and odds and sods he always likes to decorate his Shepherd's Bush flat with. He'll really be looking forward to seeing his girl Nina now, it's been five long weeks and he's a faithful old bugger. Pete's the same; God help Pam.

Saw this huge cop in one store; he must have weighed at least 20 stone, and his voice, I wish we'd have had a tape recorder. It was like gravel and deeper than anything I've ever heard before. Zee's knocked twice now, and is starting to panic on the sound check. I must go now.

Christ. What a sound check. The P.A.'s weak and only one

150

guy seems to know how to run it. The guy on the monitors doesn't know his arse from his elbow. We're all pretty down. A bad P.A. can really mess up a whole gig, and we're all knackered, especially Phal and Mick who've had about six hours sleep in the last 48 hours. Bob's frantically (as usual) gesticulating all over the stage trying to get the lights together and union men take their time. Ten minutes to lower a back cloth.

There's about 100 ushers out front staring – I hate that. Nobody should watch a sound check. You start bad and try to get it better. It should be done in private. Lee and Zee have disappeared, and Stan's only concern is us playing the numbers. So we do them messily and there's no spark. It'll be better to-night, but I don't know how much. I still haven't finally checked the piano sound; that's something I hate to leave to chance. Saw Joe Walsh wobbling around – the offended foot stuck in a large sock. He likes Mick's Esquire a lot. Rock was saying last night they used to do *Thunderbuck Ram* and they have a tape of them performing it in front of 9,000 people. We'd love to hear it, but it's back home in Colorado. From the way they describe where they come from, it must be great.

Well that's great; that's fucking great. Here I've been telling you how nice people are and we've been done over.

Mick's had $270 and his Panasonic tape nicked and Lee's had a case taken full of camera equipment and his passport too. One wonders what more can happen to Ralpher. What a great way to do a gig. The police are on their way now. He's saved up the whole tour to take a bit of money back home. Lee's tickets gone too now – he can't fly to his parents for Christmas; he doesn't even have identification and you can't do anything without some kind of I.D. in America.

The police arrive. One big, one little and take down what little they can take down. They check the trash cans, etc. and we remember three young guys, two white and one black, who sat watching us in the lobby as we left. Lee and Zee got back about 6:30, so they must have gotten in between 6 and 6:15. Quick work.

The police are nice, but really don't seem all that bothered.

The bigger of the two getting our autographs on an album. Christ, it gets worse. The hall's only half full – who was that prat who told us we were big here? We're on a percentage and the Christmas bonus is supposed to come out of that. Looks like when expenses are paid we'll be left with fuck all. I've got $3.

Twenty minutes later – hold on – Phil just rang and said it's three-quarters full and there's still a large queue to get in. Apparently the box office is very slow and a lot of people are complaining they can't get in quick enough to see Barnstorm.

Now you're not going to believe this, I'm pissed but you just aren't going to believe it. The gig was TREMENDOUS. We went down a storm; 3,700 people, and Joe Walsh went mad with us on the encores. Pissed and brilliant he was. Mick and him talking on stage. The only communication. Unbelievable – an amazing gig. Easily as good as Cleveland. The crowd were up all the way through and I can hardly write for the excitement.

Saturday, 23 December 1972

In the light of the following morning I still can only echo what I said last night – an amazing way to end a tour. There were actually 3,700 in and they went – they really went. So did Trudy's present. I deliberately took it to the gig so as to avoid having it thieved at the hotel, but somehow it went, what a downer. They all tell you how wonderful and all the bullshit, and somebody nicks your case. Then people wonder why we don't like people backstage. Still it's a drag, but I won't let it spoil my mood. Everybody was knocked out and exhilarated including Ike and Rich the limo drivers. Lee jumps around and Stan's all excited drinking a bottle of champagne and refusing to give anyone a swig. Bob going wow and the promoters smile and talk about the next one confidently. Apparently the people don't go mad very often now but when they do it's a night to behold – believe me! Kathy from the Mainman office flies in to be on the last gig and loves it. Needless to say, the band's happy. It's all over, next stop LONDON.

By the time we left the gig it must have been 12:30 a.m. and by this time we're all a little stoned and I beg Ike to take us over to Elvis's place. Ike nods and we fly on through the night until we reach the legendary Gracelands, home of the king himself (his dad lives next door).

We get out at the gate (the one with the notes) and survey total unreality in the cool Memphis night air. One of his many cousins comes out and we ask boldly if we can drive up the little road to his place, but the guy's not having any. Elvis is in. He's been here two or three days, and he's just got back from the pictures an hour and a half ago so they won't let anybody near the place. The best he can do is open the gate so we can all get a clear view and he gives us a picture postcard. In my drunken state I decide this ain't enough.

This guy who's in the limo with us draws the guard's attention, putting his arm around him and pleading with him to let us in. Meanwhile, another guy pushes me in the back and I'm off up the left-hand walk, sliding behind trees, casually walking expecting any minute to be pulled back. Miraculously, the guards didn't notice, and I was wearing an afghan, so they must have been bloody blind and I just went on. A huge nativity scene stood on the grounds to the right of the house lit up. Blue bulbs outlined the driveway, and outside the front of the house were red, yellow, blue and green Christmas trees either side of the main door. It's not really a huge house, in fact quite modest for the size of the grounds. There seem to be columns by the front door and two huge flashy chrome cars stood outside.

A T.V. eye stands out sharply against the uneven bark on the trees and I keep to the wall, bending down to stuff my pockets with a few leaves for the lads who are probably getting fed up waiting for me. On at the back with four or five older cars, and a multi-coloured fun jalopy looking thing. I hear dogs barking, but you know what it's like when you're pissed.

I walk across under the patio and there's a back door. I turn the knob and it opens. Fuckin' hell! Am I dreaming? I'm in the dude's house; he's somewhere within 50 feet of me now, but I really daren't go further. Inside the door there's two more doors – one on the right looks like a sports room, but I'm a bit too far gone to tell properly, and the one on the left looks more like where he'd be – plush carpeting, a short hall and what looks like a staircase. I'll never know if these doors opened or not because I didn't try them. Instead, I knocked loudly. No answer. I knocked again and a black lady, very nicely dressed, peered at me through the window. I've since found out that it was probably Alberta, Presley's maid. She fits the description I gave to a couple of guys that went to his parties.

'I came 4½ thousand miles to see Elvis Presley – is it possible to see him?'

'I'm sorry, but Mr Presley's tired and he ain't seein' anybody.'

'Are you sure I can't see him?'

'Yes, I'm definitely sure.'

'Well I'm sorry for the inconvenience, and I'll go back to the gate. Don't worry, I'm knocked out to have gotten this far. Thanks anyway.'

'You're welcome. Good night.'

I felt elated. I didn't really want to meet the guy – he'd have only gotten angry at me staggering in in the middle of the night and invading his privacy. I felt like a 14-year-old groupie – but I'd done it for the buzz, and it had been great! To tell you the truth, I'd get a bigger buzz out of Jerry Lee Lewis, but there I'd been, in the king's house, and fooled the entire army. Actually I hadn't fooled them that well because as I wandered round the front a wagon was waiting.

I told the exceedingly worried looking guard it was all over and that I was sorry I'd caused him trouble and that all I wanted to do was walk down the drive and out. He motioned me on and I walked straight down the middle of Elvis Presley's driveway with a wagon slowly following me. It was a gas of an experience, and I won't ever forget it.

Even in my obvious state, plus the fact I broke the rules, everybody had been extremely courteous, and I whooped my way back into the car. Phally piles in and it turns out he went right when I went left and he wound up at the front door where he was nabbed, so Phally keeps a memory too. What a high, just like kids who'd been scrumping and got away with it. Thank Christ they knew we were harmless, or those Dobermans would have torn us to shreds. I feel sorry for the poor bugger though, he can't have much of a life if idiots like me are pulling stunts like that and they probably do. Never mind El, count your royalty checks and forget all about it.

Back to the Downtown Motor Inn or the thieves' kitchen as we've now dubbed it, and we're well into the morning.

The eighth floor looks like Rome. All of Barnstorm are there, Rock playing harp stridently and Joe Walsh, completely out of his head playing beautiful bottleneck. I sat with him a while and backed him on my old Echo – he was playing Pete's Martin. People I've never seen asleep on beds and myself and a bird roll a couple of guys off Buff's bed onto the floor and drag Buff in from where he collapsed in the hallway undressing him and shoving him into bed. Stan, the eternal shepherd, was drunk, but still watchful. Bob Goddard naked but for gaily painted knickers talks earnestly to two young people on the floor. Champagne and bourbon bottles, 7-Up, Coke, a million cigarette butts, unknown faces, my hand aches from the shaking it's done, and I finally slam my door – happier than I've been. A great night to end a real breakthrough tour; I'll suffer for this tomorrow. I'll ring Trudy and then go to sleep.

Sunday, 24 December 1972

Today is the 24th and Mott are homeward bound. Twenty-seven guitar cases and 12 suitcases are wearily packed for the last time, aching heads soothed by Veganin. Stan looks half dead, but it's going-home day, and the mood is good. I find a bullet in bed with me. Larry, one of the cycle cops, gave it to me last night to remember him by. A live .32 for a bed mate! Oh shit, my achin' head. I give Zee my brown high-heeled boots because he gave me his clogs and Lee comes in and gives me *The Hobbit*. I know I should have read it, but I haven't, so I will. Rich and Ike are genuinely sad to see us leave, and we all have our pictures taken outside the Inn.

155

Into the limos and up to the airport. I've got that 'driven like mad from Germany and missed the ferry' feeling. Death. I buy Tru a replacement Christmas present at the airport, a tiny pair of jade earrings with money I borrowed from Ritchie, and we hang around a while and have sandwiches and juice to get rid of the fag taste in our mouths.

Onto a DC-9 and I'm just being welcomed to Chicago, having written this last bit all the way through.

First class, and I appreciate the room to spread my aching limbs in. I feel about 90, but we're here and there's one to go and that gets us all the way to Heathrow, Trudy, Solveig, Saucer, the Anglia and Wembley and Christmas Eve.

O'Hare is as grey as ever, full of grim faces. It really is a down place, Chicago. We wander round the gift shops and wind up waiting 30 minutes for a glass of milk in one of the drug stores. We're all tired, but still not nasty. I find a piece of wood and on it a metal plate which sums up flying so much better than I can. It's a poem by John G. Magee, Jr, and it goes like this:

O, I have slipped the surly bonds of earth
    And danced the skies on laughter silvered wings;
Sunward I've climbed and joined the tumbling mirth
    Of sun split clouds – and done a hundred things
You have not dreamed of – wheeled and soared and swung
    High in the sunlit silence. Hov'ring there,
I've chased the shouting wind along and flung
    My eager craft through footless halls of air,
Up, up the long delirious, burning blue
    I've topped the wind-swept heights with easy grace,
Where never lark, or even eagle, flew;
    And, while with silent, lifting mind I've trod
The high untrespassed sanctity of space
    Put out my hand, and touched the face of God.

A good poem, a poem you want to learn.

6:15 p.m. and it's time to wander down to the G-11 gate for the last big one. Phil and I moan about the distance, but eventually make it. Three security police unzip baggage and check thoroughly for guns, knives, etc., and we walk through the

156

doorway. The light flashes on alarm and my Zippo lighter catches me. The guy holds them, and money and my cigarettes (silver foil) and a few hotel keys picked up accidently on the way. Through again, and this time I'm clear. Everybody's O.K. There's green, red, gold and blue boarding passes and the plane's a T.W.A. Jumbo and they're letting them on one colour at a time. We're the second lot on and I'm sitting next to a hard-looking individual and as there's not too many on board I move over to the centre row. On a Jumbo there's three seats on the left, then a carriageway, then four seats then a carriageway then another three. I'm sitting in red D-325; it's quite complicated really.

Still there is a good view for the film and as I'm dead centre (nearly) nobody's in front. I've put the seat in front of me down and put the old legs up. A menu's shoved in front of me entitled 'The Madrid'. There is a choice of three meals – Charbroiled Filet Mignon, Loin of Pork Fermier or Barbecued Breast of Chicken. Looks like the chicken, that's the only one I understand. Oh, perhaps a little wine to go with it. There's cheese and biscuits too. Phal loves cheese and biscuits, oh the beer's 50 cents. Must get some money off Stan. I want fags and a bottle of something for Christmas too.

I've taken a mandy too, so the flight should be quite painless. The end of this flight will be the end of this book and it makes me sad. I've lived with it through so many moods and it's been an exercise in self-discipline; something I needed to do for a long time. A little girl plays peek-a-boo with me and the engines jet and die as the pilot runs through his routine tests.

Soon we'll be off the gound, that is America, flying contrary to time and my three in the morning will be nine tomorrow morning when I arrive in England, I still can't work out if I'll stay awake or asleep. Take it as it comes. I'll tell you something about American tours, I was almost a zombie before I left England – no real buzz, but I feel like I've lived a lot over the last five weeks and surely that is what it's all about.

Already the next tour is semi-planned. We open in L.A. the first week in March. It's O.K. That's the only way I can live. The guy just said the flying time is 6 hours 40 minutes to Lon-

don and he's now going through the safety routine. The two
hostesses demonstrating as the steward talks look like bizarre
plastic-clad go-go girls – they've got it down to a fine art. Now
he repeats the routine in Italian – perhaps the Mafia dig English
Christmases. I'm writing along alone; all the rest sit together at
the back, but I've had enough. A bit of peace is what is called
for.

We're moving, the giant nose swings to the right and we start
to taxi slowly out onto the maze of runways that web O'Hare
and occasionally drive ground-control people mad. Soothing
music plays, putting me in mind of *The Star Gazers are on the
Air* when I was a kid. Now we stop again and engines begin
to roar – but die and I think we're in one of those queues
O'Hare is so famous for. Outside it's dark, and masses of lights
which mean nothing to me aid the pilot towards the big runway. I see the last American light show outside the edge of
Chicago and the word extravagance comes to mind.

Here we go. No we don't. Still the wheels hug American
concrete. The bloody trouble with queues is you can't smoke
when you're on the ground, and after a while it becomes a
drag. I had some gum, but I lost it. A baby's crying and the
captain says we're now number three for take off in five minutes
over Flint Michigan, Ottawa, Canada, across the Atlantic,
over Shannon and on into London. The weather's supposed to
be good all the way. Number one now and the captain tells the
crew to strap themselves in. Well if we're next the plane in
front of us must be crawling down on its hands and knees, it's
taking so long.

Here we go. A new urgency in the engines. A sweeping left
turn and the big ones start to roar. My back presses the back of
my seat; we are off American soil. Straight up at a 30 degree
angle (that's what it seems to be) and I wait for the 'No
Smoking' signal to go off – C'mon you bastard. Yippee! They're
off, fags out. I sit like a lord, feet out, headphones, menu and
writing tools on my seat, the piece of wood with the Magee
poem on it, Winston fags, a Chesterfield Zippo lighter and *The
Hobbit* book on my left. I think I'll order a beer.

In fact, I ordered two beers and had what I found out to be

steak and not the chicken. There's about an hour to go and we cruise into an Irish dawn at a leisurely 600 miles per hour. It's a rainbow. The clouds are still black, then the sky deep red through lighter shades into old gold, yellow, pale green and finally royal blue. The lights go on in the plane and I raise my weary head and decide to shave and wake myself up. The film was *Ginger in the Morning*, I went to sleep half way through even though it looked pretty good.

Hostesses appear again and morning orange juice is served. I get 200 Winstons for $3. The ride's been smooth so far, apart from a couple of bumpy spots, and Mick's faring well. Ritchie, Phil and Dick are on the flight with us so it's the old gang all on the way home. The sky gets brighter as you watch it and everybody awakes now. Sunday, the 24th of December – England, football and chips. I feel like it was years since I've been here.

Through the clouds and there's London; no messing – straight down and into Heathrow. Nothing quite like the feeling you get when the wheels touch old England. I've felt it every time I've been away. We 'deplane' and straight away it's quiet, even in the tunnel it's quiet. None of the mad jiving rush, shouting voices, general melee of a hundred mixed bloods that there are in America.

Which is best? You've got to do the one to appreciate the other, and right now England feels like a private bedroom. I'm through the customs easily – a miracle for a musician! – and only Phal and Buff are detained, and not for long at that.

Trudy waves, Nina's there and I can see Sue, Elaine, and Pam. Hugh's there from the office and me old mate Miller has been hauled from his bed to give us a lift home. It's 9 a.m. English time and the old ladies are having morning tea and lightly boiled eggs, and working men are checking the Sunday papers and nursing hangovers, and I've got to check the bills and pay the rent, and Trudy's got to fix my pants. Colin York's got to pick me up for Christmas and I've got to write some songs. But this tour's over now and me thinks the 'times they are a-changin' again',

See you later . . ▪

159

NOW AVAILABLE - IAN HUNTER'S BRAND NEW ALBUM

'THE ARTFUL DODGER'

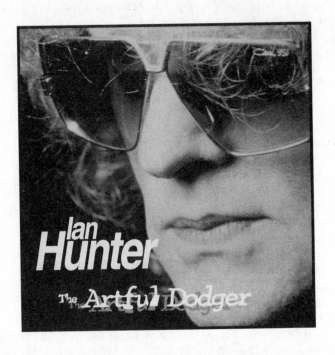

ON CITADEL RECORDS (CIT1CD)
DISTRIBUTED THROUGH BMG RECORDS
AT ALL GOOD RECORD SHOPS
OR BY MAIL ORDER FROM CITADEL RECORDS LTD
FOR £13.99 INC P&P

Citadel Records, P.O. Box 1275, Bulford Barracks. Wiltshire SP4 8RW

PRAISE & ACCOLADES FOR THE
INTERNET GIRLS SERIES

New York Times bestselling series
San Francisco Chronicle bestselling series
Publishers Weekly bestselling series

School Library Journal:
★ Both revealing and innovative, this novel will inspire
teens to pass it to their friends . . . nonnarrative
communication can be a great way to tell a story.

Publishers Weekly:
Myracle's approach is creative . . . an engaging
quick read . . . readers will cheer.

Booklist:
Myracle cleverly manages to build rich characters
and narrative tension without ever taking the story
outside of an IM box.

Kirkus Reviews:
A surprisingly poignant tale of friendship, change,
and growth. Perfectly contemporary. ROTFL.

Teen magazine:
Changing the way you read.

OTHER BOOKS BY
LAUREN MYRACLE

ttyl

l8r, g8r

bff

The Infinite Moment of Us

Shine

Bliss

Rhymes with Witches

Luv Ya Bunches

Violet in Bloom

Oopsy Daisy

Awesome Blossom

Eleven

Twelve

Thirteen

Thirteen Plus One

Peace, Love, and Baby Ducks

Let It Snow: Three Holiday Romances
(with John Green and Maureen Johnson)

How to Be Bad (with E. Lockhart and Sarah Mylnowski)

LAUREN MYRACLE

ttfn

AMULET BOOKS · NEW YORK

Cataloging-in-Publication Data has been applied for and may be obtained from the Library of Congress.

ISBN: 978-1-4197-1141-1

Printed and bound in U.S.A.
10 9 8 7 6 5 4 3 2 1

Amulet Books are available at special discounts when purchased in quantity for premiums and promotions as well as fundraising or educational use. Special editions can also be created to specification. For details, contact specialsales@abramsbooks.com or the address below.

ABRAMS

THE ART OF BOOKS SINCE 1949

115 West 18th Street
New York, NY 10011
www.abramsbooks.com

To all the girlies—and yes! even a few guys!—
who shared their IMs with me or emailed me
about life in general. Yahootie!!!

❤

SnowAngel: hey there, zoe-cakes. r we studs or what? 😃

zoegirl: yahootie!

SnowAngel: i have a total adrenaline buzz going, even tho i am completely and thoroughly exhausted. my muscles r gonna be crazy sore tomorrow.

zoegirl: i hear you. can you imagine how in shape we'd be if we did that every day?

SnowAngel: we could call it the winsome-threesome workout-of-the-century. we cld make an exercise video and rake in oodles of cash.

zoegirl: even my toenails are tired

SnowAngel: *flops onto pretend bed and groans*

SnowAngel: i told chrissy what we did, and she was like, "u ran up the escalator at peachtree center? that super-duper long one?"

zoegirl: okay yes, but the critical point is that we ran up the *down* escalator. you did explain that to her, didn't u?

zoegirl: that's gotta be the longest escalator in the world. seriously, it's as long as a football field.

SnowAngel: i nearly lost it when maddie stopped for a breather and the escalator took her down, down, down. she was all, "noooo! i'm losing ground!"

zoegirl: hee hee

SnowAngel: but in the end we conquered it, cuz we can do ANYTHING, baby.

SnowAngel: it's like in "the cave" by my buds Mumford & Sons. "but i will hold on hope . . . and i'll find strength in pain!"

zoegirl: god, i love Mumford & Sons.

SnowAngel: i know. and that one particular song—it's like therapy every time i listen to it.

zoegirl:	i like the line about wanting to live life as it's meant to be lived.
SnowAngel:	i do too, and how even when things are hard, we just keep going.
SnowAngel:	and do u know HOW we keep going? or at least how "i" keep going?
zoegirl:	how?
SnowAngel:	cuz of u and mads. 😊 😊 😊
zoegirl:	awwwww
SnowAngel:	it's true. true blue, me and u, and don't forget to add maddie 2.
SnowAngel:	do u like my rhyme?
zoegirl:	very impressive
SnowAngel:	wait, there's more! er, let's c . . . since 7th grade they did not part, they stayed connected in their hearts. zoe's the good girl, maddie's wild, and sweet darling angela is meek and mild.
zoegirl:	meek? hahahahaha! mild? hahahahaha!
SnowAngel:	fine, miss brainiac. U find something to rhyme with wild.
zoegirl:	"and sweet goofy angela tends to act like a child"?
SnowAngel:	hey now!
zoegirl:	just teasing. you know i love you.
zoegirl:	i've just got kid-type people on my brain, because guess what? i got the job at Kidding Around!
SnowAngel:	wh-hoo! *happy dance, happy dance*
zoegirl:	there was a message waiting for me when i got home. i'm psyched.
SnowAngel:	ah, what joy, to be wiping noses and chasing toddlers. when do u start?
zoegirl:	um, don't freak, okay?
SnowAngel:	why would i freak? ur not gonna say something to make me freak, r u?
SnowAngel:	wait a minute. don't u DARE tell me u have to start tonight.

zoegirl:	the thing is . . . i do.
SnowAngel:	zoe! noooo!
zoegirl:	saturday night's their busiest night! the director wants me to come in for training.
SnowAngel:	but we were gonna watch "Bridesmaids" again! and eat ugly carrots!
zoegirl:	i know, and i will miss eating my ugly carrot very much. but we can watch "Bridesmaids" tomorrow. that'll be even better, because that way maddie can join us.
SnowAngel:	the point being that she has plans tonight too? yeah, rub it in. u've got yr job and maddie has her cousin's wedding and i have a big old pile of poop. thanks a lot.
zoegirl:	angela, you are such a drama queen. and you don't have a big old pile of 💩. you have a delicious bag of carrots! with hopefully at least one ugly one mixed in for luck!
SnowAngel:	😮
zoegirl:	you're not really mad, are you?
SnowAngel:	of course i'm mad! *flames shoot from ears*
SnowAngel:	only not really, cuz this way i can watch as many episodes of "extreme makeover: home edition" as i want, and i will cry and it will be very emotional, if u would just TRY the show then u would c what i mean.
zoegirl:	umm . . . no
zoegirl:	but you know what's weird? and i mean this in the nicest way ever. last year you would have been totally upset if i'd changed our plans at the last minute. i mean, truly upset, with all kinds of wounded hurt feelings. but this year, you're so much more chill. why is that, do you think?
SnowAngel:	cuz i'm a junior, that's why. *struts around in funky

junior-ness* cuz i can drive, even tho i don't have a car. cuz i choose to live my life the way it's meant to be lived, even tho i will be all alone on a saturday night, and even tho there is seriously something up with my parents, not that they'll admit it.

zoegirl:	there's something up with your parents? explain.
SnowAngel:	it's just this feeling i've been getting.
zoegirl:	like what? and for how long?
SnowAngel:	i dunno, maybe a week?
zoegirl:	a week?! why are you just now telling me???
SnowAngel:	it's like they're hiding something. i can't explain it better than that. i keep thinking that maybe i'm making it up, but then i think that i'm not.
zoegirl:	hmm
zoegirl:	maybe it's a *good* thing they're hiding—like that they're taking you to hawaii
SnowAngel:	i dunno, that somehow doesn't seem very likely.
SnowAngel:	but, whatever. i'm not gonna worry about it, cuz i'm the new and improved Chill Angela. u think they wld name a Barbie after me?
zoegirl:	definitely. for her accessory, she could have a tiny iPhone.
SnowAngel:	no, her accessory would be a tiny picture of u, me, and mads, cuz that's why i'm chill for real. cuz no matter what, i've got u guys giving me my me-ness.
zoegirl:	maddie and i don't give you your you-ness. you give yourself your you-ness.
SnowAngel:	"you-ness." now there's a word for ya.
SnowAngel:	my granddad's name was eunice, btw
zoegirl:	your granddad? don't you mean your grandmom?
SnowAngel:	nope, my granddad. only he spelled it "unus."
zoegirl:	ugh. what were his parents trying to do to him?
SnowAngel:	his full name was unus faye. he went by U.F.
zoegirl:	i am so sorry to hear that.

SnowAngel:	yep
zoegirl:	well, on that note, gtg. wish me luck on my first day, which is really my first night!
SnowAngel:	good luck on yr first day which is really ur first night!
SnowAngel:	ta ta for now!

Sat, Nov 20, 5:16 PM E.S.T.

SnowAngel:	hey, maderoo. getting all dolled up for yr cousin's wedding?
mad maddie:	my dear, the dolling is done. and fyi, i look fab.
mad maddie:	the pops, however, has hit a new low
SnowAngel:	ooo, do tell
mad maddie:	ahem. he bought this self-hair-cutter thing, right? cuz he's such a cheapskate that he didn't wanna fork over 10 bucks at lloyd's barbershop. and of course he decides that today, the day of donovan's wedding, is the perfect day for a trim. so i get home to find dad in the bathroom, hair-cutter aloft, and as i walk to my room, i hear the buzzing begin. bzzzzzzzzzzzzzz.
SnowAngel:	what'd he do, give himself a mohawk?
mad maddie:	if only. so then the buzzing stops, and he goes, "oops." "what happened?" i yell. and he says, "i put on the wrong attachment. huh. guess my hair will be a little shorter than usual."
SnowAngel:	uh oh
mad maddie:	and then for some reason he starts asking if i have a safety pin or a needle or anything pokey. i think he was taking the whole thing apart. but no, i did not have anything pokey, so after a while he puts it back together and the buzzing starts again. and then it shuts off. and he starts LAUGHING.
SnowAngel:	oh crap. what happened?

mad maddie: my idiot father forgot to put ANY attachment back on, which meant that when he started up again, he took off an entire strip of hair down to his scalp. as in, bald. and then once he'd done that, he figured there was nothing to do but complete the scalping.

mad maddie: my father is a cue ball, angela.

SnowAngel: oh no!

SnowAngel: that cracks me up that he would laugh, tho. that's so yr dad.

mad maddie: he was all, "what? it's just hair." the moms is massively annoyed.

SnowAngel: if my dad went bald on the day of a wedding, my mom would jump out a window. or push HIM out a window.

mad maddie: ah, well. we'll go to the reception and drink away our troubles, cuz that's what my family does. shld be a good time.

SnowAngel: that blows my mind that u can drink right there with them.

mad maddie: it's cuz we're irish. it's the law.

SnowAngel: my parents would be like, "you are underage. go sit at the kiddie table." but yours are like, "here, have another beer!"

mad maddie: well, they won't be the ones actually giving me beers. they'll leave that to my crazy aunts and uncles. and it won't be beer, it'll be champagne.

SnowAngel: la di da 🍸

mad maddie: and before long uncle duncan will be ranting about the middle east and aunt teresa will be doing the line dance she learned in 8th grade to michael jackson's "beat it."

mad maddie: i'm telling u, donovan's fiancee has noooooo idea what she's in for.

SnowAngel:	sounds fun
mad maddie:	**it definitely won't be boring**
SnowAngel:	do u wish—even just a little—that u and ian were still going out, so he could go with u?
mad maddie:	**not at all. ian is a fleck and i am a plane, high in the sky. that's how over him i am.**
SnowAngel:	swear?
mad maddie:	**ok, maybe not a plane. maybe just a . . . telephone pole.**
SnowAngel:	meaning what?
mad maddie:	**meaning that maybe i do miss him, but what's the point? if ian had wanted to come to donovan's wedding with me, then he shouldn't have broken up with me.**
SnowAngel:	he didn't break up with u. u broke up with him.
mad maddie:	**but only cuz i knew that he was going to. he called me a ball and chain, if u don't recall.**
SnowAngel:	WHAT?!!
SnowAngel:	he did NOT call u a ball and chain. he made that ONE comment about wanting to hang out with his friends more, and u did your porcupine thing where u bristle up over nothing.
mad maddie:	**there was more to it than that one comment. it was obvious i was cramping his style.**
SnowAngel:	omg. only u wld interpret it like that.
SnowAngel:	it's ok to have feelings, u know. it's even ok to miss ian.
mad maddie:	**thx, Dr. Phil.**
SnowAngel:	he adored you, mads. or rather ADORES you, present tense. he would take you back in a heartbeat.
mad maddie:	**well, that boat's already sailed.**
mad maddie:	**nice of u to say, tho. yr so good to me.**
SnowAngel:	yup, cuz i luv ya

SnowAngel:	anyway, who knows? maybe tonight you'll meet someone new. maybe you'll meet your future husband!
mad maddie:	**or maybe NOT. i'm not looking for a husband, angela—sheesh!**
SnowAngel:	u never know . . .
SnowAngel:	so zoe got that job at Kidding Around, did u hear?
mad maddie:	**such a dorky name, Kidding Around. it's like, "hiya, buddy, watcha up to?" "not much—just kidding around." with everyone slugging each other on the shoulder.**
SnowAngel:	cuz it's a childcare place, for when parents don't have a babysitter or whatever. KIDDING around. get it?
mad maddie:	**der, angela. not getting it was never the problem.**
mad maddie:	**yikes, time to motor. old baldie's calling my name.**
SnowAngel:	have fun at the wedding! tell donovan congrats for me! OH, and you and zoe are both coming over tomorrow, ok? we're having Sunday Afternoon Movie Madness.
mad maddie:	**that sounds awesome—only not "Bridesmaids." i know it's supposed to be funny—and it is—but it's oddly depressing too.**
SnowAngel:	we will take a vote
mad maddie:	**fine, we'll take a vote**
SnowAngel:	and my vote counts double since it's my house. 😊 buh-bye!

Sat, Nov 20, 10:32 PM E.S.T.

mad maddie:	**dude! future hubby alert!**
SnowAngel:	for real???
mad maddie:	**no. cute boy, tho. very very cute.**
SnowAngel:	where r u? is the wedding over?
mad maddie:	**reception. boy's name = clive.**

SnowAngel:	CLIVE?
mad maddie:	**but i call him chive, cuz i is witty. friend of donovan.**
SnowAngel:	cool—i wanna hear more! call me!
mad maddie:	**can't. lurking behind dessert table.**
SnowAngel:	yr lurking behind the . . . ?
SnowAngel:	maddie. go somewhere and call me, cuz guess what? i think i figged out why my parents are being so weird.
mad maddie:	**spill**
SnowAngel:	short version: when i told zoe, she was all, "maybe what they're hiding is a GOOD thing, angela," and i think maybe she's right. i think they're buying me a car!
mad maddie:	**holy shit!**
SnowAngel:	i know!!! they keep talking in these hush-hush quiet voices, and then they clam up whenever i come in the room. seriously, call me and we can analyze every last nuance—it'll be awesome!
mad maddie:	**can't, sorry. it's bunny hop time!**

Sun, Nov 21, 11:01 AM E.S.T.

zoegirl:	maddie! how was the wedding?
mad maddie:	**it was awesome, altho i'm kinda hungover. not terrible, tho.**
zoegirl:	more, please
mad maddie:	**it was mainly family, so the ceremony wasn't huge, but with my family that's probably a good thing. donovan looked great in his tux, and lisa looked drop-dead gorgeous.**
zoegirl:	what was her dress like?
mad maddie:	**her dress? i don't know. it was . . . white. NOT froufrou. for lisa it was perfect, especially cuz she's so tiny. but, like, naturally tiny. healthy tiny.**

zoegirl: did she seem happy? was she glowing? when i fall in love, it's gonna be with someone who makes me glow.

mad maddie: ok, excuse me while i barf

zoegirl: whoa, you really are hungover

mad maddie: uh, no, i was barfing cuz somehow ur channeling angela with this "glowing" shit. why does everyone have to get all mushy when it comes to love?

zoegirl: i am *not* channeling angela. you cannot compare me to angela, that is so unfair.

mad maddie: i don't know if lisa was glowing, but she smiled a lot, and at the reception she gave me a big hug, which surprised me. i used to think she was snobby, but now i'm wondering if she's just shy.

mad maddie: she's not, like, the coolest girl in the world, but she's the coolest girl for donovan, if that makes sense. i think they're good together.

zoegirl: well, that's awesome. you can be cynical maddie if you have to be, but i want that someday. i want to fall in love for real.

mad maddie: u don't consider mr. h for real?

zoegirl: don't, maddie. i don't even like to joke about that.

mad maddie: about what? the fact that u almost had an affair with your horny english teacher?

zoegirl: i am covering my ears now. la la la.

mad maddie: how about his whole christianity kick, can i joke about that? ya gotta admit, it's great material. it's not very often that a guy uses God to try and lure in the girls.

zoegirl: please stop

mad maddie: zo, it happened over a year ago. it's ancient history. when WILL i be allowed to joke about it?

zoegirl:	changing the subject. i talked to angela this morning, and she said you met some guy named after a seasoning. cilantro? paprika?
mad maddie:	ha ha. it's clive. i just call him chive. he goes to northside.
zoegirl:	what grade's he in?
mad maddie:	he's a junior like us. he loves music, which is why he goes to n'side, since they have such a good performing arts department. i told him how i wanna major in music AND advertising and then be the person who makes album art.
mad maddie:	we talked forever—he's got GORGEOUS eyes—and then we kinda ended up getting down and dirty-ish in the corner. the moms totally caught us, which was completely embarrassing.
zoegirl:	oh god
mad maddie:	but she was wasted too, so she didn't care. she got all teary and started saying stuff like, "u and clive! it's meant to be!" and i was like, "mom, no. i love being single." and she goes, "r u telling me ur a slut?"
zoegirl:	nuh uh
mad maddie:	then she calls out to all my aunts and uncles in this really loud voice, "someone bring me another drink—my little girl's a slut!"
zoegirl:	i swear, maddie, your family is so incredibly different from mine. there is no way i would ever have a conversation like that with my mother.
mad maddie:	cuz your family is normal
mad maddie:	she was just joking, tho. she was just being wild.
zoegirl:	was chive around for all that? did he hear your mom call u a slut?
mad maddie:	yeah, and he laughed. that's the cool thing about him.

zoegirl: huh

mad maddie: i had FUN, zo. the whole night was fun. i know it's not your style, but i had a blast.

zoegirl: are you going to see him again?

mad maddie: who, chive? i hope so, but not in a date-y way if that's what ur asking.

zoegirl: why not in a date-y way?

mad maddie: cuz i'm not looking for that. we don't all have to GLOW, zo. we really don't.

mad maddie: hey, how was your first night at Kidding Around?

zoegirl: i *love* it. the kids are so cute. there was this one little boy, he was maybe 3, and he had all these fake tattoos on his arm. i would point to one and say, "so what's that?" and he'd say, "a snake, but not a *real* snake." or "a bat, but not a *real* bat." or "a lightning, but not a *real* lightning, because if it was real lightning, there would be thunder. only not here. somewhere else. where the indians are."

mad maddie: what indians?

zoegirl: i do not know, to tell you the truth.

zoegirl: oh—and guess who works there with me?!

mad maddie: who?

zoegirl: doug schmidt!

mad maddie: doug? as in angela's doug?

zoegirl: he's not really angela's doug, seeing as how she's not the slightest bit interested. but yeah. i was like, "doug! wow!"

mad maddie: he's gonna be all over u, i can c it now. he's gonna use u as an inside link. angela may not be interested, but it's a sure bet HE is.

zoegirl: maybe. i just think it's cool that a guy would take a job there in the first place.

mad maddie: what'd angela say?

zoegirl: we didn't talk about it much, because she was kind of distracted. she thinks her parents are buying her a car.

mad maddie: oh yeah, that's right—and she says U planted the idea.

zoegirl: i did not! i just said she shouldn't assume that whatever's going on with her parents is bad.

zoegirl: although i may have to revise that opinion based on a new and not-so-good development. *don't* tell angela.

mad maddie: don't tell angela what?

zoegirl: well . . . i saw her dad at starbucks this morning. i was getting cappuccinos for my parents because i'm such a good daughter, and there was mr. silver. and he wasn't alone.

mad maddie: who was he with?

zoegirl: a woman. a woman wearing a tailored skirt and blouse. the kind of woman who actually uses lip liner.

mad maddie: lip liner, that's hardcore.

mad maddie: so what r u saying?

zoegirl: nothing, i'm not saying anything

mad maddie: u don't think he's having an affair, do u???

zoegirl: no no no, i'm sure he's not.

zoegirl: i just got a weird vibe, that's all.

mad maddie: weird how?

zoegirl: you know how normally mr. silver's so friendly and buddy-buddy? well, today when i went over to say hi, he looked really uncomfortable. all brusque and at the same time blushing, like he'd been caught in the act.

mad maddie: WHAT act?

zoegirl: i don't know. and he didn't introduce me to lip liner woman, even though she was smiling very pleasantly like "oh, and who's your little friend?" it was one of those moments where he *should* have introduced us, but he didn't.

zoegirl: there was something suspicious about it. it made me worry that

zoegirl: never mind

mad maddie: what?

zoegirl: it's stupid. it's superstitious. but, like, things are going *so well* for us. you're happy, angela's happy, i'm happy. and then i think, crap, when's the bad thing gonna happen, you know?

mad maddie: and u think the bad thing has to do with angela's dad and lip liner woman?

zoegirl: i didn't say that

mad maddie: anywayz, ur crazy. enough bad stuff happened to us last year to last a lifetime.

zoegirl: tell me about it. let's see, first there was me and mr. h, then angela and her boy problems, and then as if that wasn't enough, you went all psycho with your wrong and terribly misguided jana obsession.

mad maddie: "obsession"? that's a bit of an exaggeration, wldn't u say?

zoegirl: no. you were like her clone, mads. you started to talk like her, dress like her . . .

zoegirl: i am *so* glad you're over that.

mad maddie: listen, pal. if i'm not allowed to mention mr. h, then ur not allowed to bring up jana.

zoegirl: fine, then you know how i feel.

zoegirl: but don't you see the pattern? it was last year right around thanksgiving that all that bad stuff

	happened, and now here we are, right around thanksgiving again.
mad maddie:	**nooooo, zoe. it was BEFORE last thanksgiving that all hell broke loose, cuz over thanksgiving itself, we were blissing out on cumberland island. or have u forgotten?**
zoegirl:	of course i haven't forgotten!
zoegirl:	why didn't we plan a trip for this year? weren't we going to make it a tradition?
mad maddie:	**oops, too late now**
zoegirl:	see! that's what's making me feel this way. we're too complacent, just going along like everything's fine.
mad maddie:	**yeahhhh, cuz everything IS fine.**
mad maddie:	**don't worry, zo. life is good, and ain't nothin gonna change. see ya at angela's!**

Sun, Nov 21, 7:42 PM E.S.T.

SnowAngel:	zoe! it's been so long since i saw u—almost a whole hour! u left your sweatshirt at my house, dumb-dumb head. 😊
zoegirl:	oops, sorry. would you bring it to me tomorrow?
zoegirl:	is maddie still there?
SnowAngel:	she just left, *after* patching the butt of her jeans with duct tape cuz she realized they were ripped. it cracks me up, this "i'm such a crazy-ass" stage she's in.
zoegirl:	crazy like at donovan's wedding?
zoegirl:	it blows my mind that her mom would call her . . . what she called her . . . and she would think it's funny.
SnowAngel:	but her mom was drunk. she didn't MEAN it.
zoegirl:	yeah, but that makes it even more mind-blowing. do YOU get drunk with YOUR mom?

SnowAngel: hahaha. my mom would be the one marching around and slapping drinks out of people's hands.

zoegirl: i like maddie's mom a lot. and of course i love maddie. i just worry about her sometimes.

SnowAngel: oh, she knows what she's doing. probably.

SnowAngel: what'd u think about chive?

zoegirl: i don't know. i need to meet him before i decide.

SnowAngel: i wish she was still going out with ian.

zoegirl: agreed. ian is such a good guy.

zoegirl: you think they'll ever get back together?

SnowAngel: no, cuz u know how maddie is. when she gets hurt, that's it. there's no looking back. and ian really hurt her, even tho he didn't mean to.

zoegirl: and even though she'll never admit it out loud. she's so funny that way, always having to be so tough.

SnowAngel: like with chive and the whole smooch-and-run incident, u mean?

zoegirl: exactly. i know maddie thinks that's fine—it's her typical maddie no-big-deal approach—but sometimes i think she's putting up a front. i mean, when you fool around with somebody, it has to mean *something* doesn't it?

SnowAngel: u would think so, yeah

zoegirl: she and i talked about that at your house, actually. it was while you were downstairs searching for the dvd. i think i maybe said some things i shouldn't have.

SnowAngel: ooo, like what?

zoegirl: like that i don't agree with the whole friends-with-benefits philosophy. like i think that works out great for guys, but not so much for girls.

SnowAngel: i don't think that's a bad thing to say. why is that a bad thing to say?

zoegirl:	i'm just worried i came off a little harsh. i kept talking and talking, and all these words came out of my mouth, like . . . word-vomit. somehow being with maddie just brings that out in me.
SnowAngel:	word-vomit. lovely. it's pretty hard to offend maddie, tho. i'm sure it was fine.
SnowAngel:	so did u notice my parents and how freaky-deaky they're being? they're thoroughly hiding something. it is so obvious.
zoegirl:	huh
zoegirl:	well, whatever it is, i wouldn't worry about it.
SnowAngel:	???
SnowAngel:	what happened to "i'm sure it's something good" and "maybe they're taking u to hawaii!"
zoegirl:	nothing, it's just
SnowAngel:	just WHAT?
zoegirl:	ok, fine. your dad *did* seem a little off.
SnowAngel:	how so? tell me, tell me, tell me.
zoegirl:	i don't know. he didn't stick around and tease us the way he usually does.
zoegirl:	i guess he just seemed strung out.
SnowAngel:	cuz it is no doubt very exhausting doing price comparisons b/w PT Cruisers and VW bugs. omigod—do u think he's getting me a bug?!!
zoegirl:	er . . . i'm not sure that was the vibe i was picking up.
SnowAngel:	if i got a bug, i could put a daisy in that little flower-holder thing. i think that is so cute, how they come with their own little vases.
SnowAngel:	but a used car would be ok 2. ANY car would be ok. then i wouldn't have to rely on u and maddie all the time.
zoegirl:	i know i said to stay positive, but what if it's not a car?

SnowAngel:	what, now u think it's something bad after all? like that my parents r getting a divorce, or that my dad's got cancer?
zoegirl:	angela, no! i'm sure it's not that!
SnowAngel:	it's not like those thoughts haven't crossed my mind. i overheard my mom talking to my aunt sadie on the phone, and she was saying things like "i'm completely overwhelmed" and "don't know how we'll tell the girls."
zoegirl:	oh crap, angela
zoegirl:	did she mention anything about . . . anything else?
SnowAngel:	anything else like what?
zoegirl:	hold on—just got a text from mads. be right back.
SnowAngel:	zoe!!! u r supposed to be talking to ME, not maddie!
SnowAngel:	get back here this instant!!!!

Sun, Nov 21, 7:59 PM E.S.T.

zoegirl:	angela's all freaked about her parents—she brought it up, not me—and i feel really weird about the whole starbucks encounter. should i tell her about seeing her dad with the lip liner woman?
mad maddie:	**shit, don't ask me**
zoegirl:	i'm sure it's nothing, but at the same time i don't want to be the one to bring it up.
mad maddie:	**then don't**
zoegirl:	but if it was *my* dad, i'd want to know.
zoegirl:	i think.
mad maddie:	**u think 2 much, zoe. that's your problem.**
zoegirl:	you're right, you're right. no need to worry angela over something that could be nothing until we find out for sure!

Sun, Nov 21, 8:04 PM E.S.T.

zoegirl:	hey there, i'm back

SnowAngel: yr on my bad list *glowers fiercely*

SnowAngel: abandoning me like that when my father could very well have a deadly disease!

zoegirl: i'm 99 percent sure your dad doesn't have a deadly disease. really, i am.

SnowAngel: so what's going on with maddie, who's apparently so much more important than me?

zoegirl: please. she had a biology question.

SnowAngel: ???

SnowAngel: u guys aren't in the same class.

zoegirl: i know, but mr. mack uses the same exact lesson plans. boring boring.

SnowAngel: oka-a-a-ay, but i'm taking bio too. why didn't she ask ME her question?

zoegirl: you poor thing! you're having a hard day, aren't you?

SnowAngel: yes *sniff, sniff*

zoegirl: oh, angela. you better go have some chocolate, or better yet some ben & jerry's. or both.

SnowAngel: perhaps i will. in bed with my bunny slippers on and a drop of lavender oil on my pulse points for relaxation.

zoegirl:

SnowAngel: *takes deep calming breath. takes deep calming breath again*

Sun, Nov 21, 8:10 PM E.S.T.

SnowAngel: it CLD still be a car. my dad cld be strung out about car payments . . . cldn't he?

zoegirl: angela, put it out of your mind. you're going to drive yourself crazy. now go get that new york super fudge chunk!

SnowAngel: ok, ok. good night!

SnowAngel: *stomps into room and plops down on bed*

SnowAngel: am i a happy camper? no, i am not. care to hazard a guess at why?

zoegirl: er . . . did something happen when you got home from school?

SnowAngel: i caught my mom talking to my aunt sadie AGAIN, and in front of her on the coffee table was an empty container of maple pecans, which she only eats when she's stressed. so i confronted her, and she finally admitted that something IS going on.

zoegirl: she did? whoa.

zoegirl: did she say it has to do with . . . life changes?

SnowAngel: life changes?

SnowAngel: omg, do u think my mom's going thru MENOPAUSE?

zoegirl: menopause?! no, i was talking more about . . . life changes in general. when people, u know, change.

zoegirl: but that doesn't matter. just tell me what she said!

SnowAngel: *groans*

SnowAngel: what she SAID is that she didn't wanna talk about it w/o my dad and chrissy. so we're going to dinner tomorrow night, and they'll tell us then. chrissy and i get to pick the place—anywhere we want.

zoegirl: anywhere you want to go? oh no!

SnowAngel: what?

zoegirl: nothing, it's just that it's so Lifetime Movie of the Week. parents *always* let the kids pick the restaurant when they're about to give bad news.

zoegirl: i remember one about a girl whose parents were getting divorced, and her friend was like, "don't pick mcdonald's, because then you'll never wanna go there again. pick some place you really hate." so she picked a chinese restaurant and ended up getting sick all over the table.

SnowAngel: i'm not picking mcdonald's, and i'm not picking
              chinese. i'm sorry, but i'm picking some place
              really good, cuz if they're gonna give us bad news,
              they're gonna have to do it over a super-nice meal.

zoegirl: and then there's that strategy, which is equally
              good.

SnowAngel: oh god

SnowAngel: i'm probably not getting a car, am i? 😞

zoegirl: well . . .

SnowAngel: i'm gonna call maddie. i have to tell her what's
              going on.

zoegirl: chin up, angela. just remember: everyone loves
              you no matter what!

Tues, Nov 23, 7:31 PM E.S.T.

mad maddie: hola, zo. ever since i got home from school i've
              been thinking about angela. u figure she's left for
              her big family dinner?

zoegirl: she's probably in the middle of it this very
              second.

zoegirl: i'm worried.

mad maddie: i had the craziest thought about what might be
              going on. forget the mr. silver's-having-an-affair
              theory: what if angela's mom is preggers?!!

zoegirl: what???

mad maddie: she's not THAT old, u know. she could have some
              eggs left. and maybe the woman mr. silver was
              talking to was just a friend, someone he could
              spill his guts to. and that's why he looked so
              nervous, cuz he didn't know what u'd overheard.

zoegirl: oh man, angela would *freak* if her mom's
              pregnant.

mad maddie: it would explain all the hush-hush-ness

zoegirl: you're right, it would

mad maddie: and i really don't think mr. silver's the type to have an affair, do u?

zoegirl: i'd be so sad if he was.

mad maddie: we'll know soon enough, i guess

mad maddie: in other news, i may be crippled for life. u may have to call me gimpy. or the gimpster.

zoegirl: huh?

mad maddie: i was taking a shower and the conditioner was all at the bottom of the bottle, so i turned it upside down and shook it and it flew out of my hand and hit my foot. it totally cut my toe open. blood was, like, swirling down the drain.

zoegirl: owww!

mad maddie: "death by conditioner." i can c the obituary now.

zoegirl: "instead of flowers, the family has requested donations to aveda."

mad maddie: ha. only i'm a paul mitchell girl.

zoegirl: paul mitchell doesn't lather

mad maddie: it does if ur not afraid to slab it on. u gotta be fearless, girl.

mad maddie: lemme know if u hear anything from angela!

Tues, Nov 23, 8:03 PM E.S.T.

SnowAngel: call me! now!

zoegirl: are you at the restaurant?

SnowAngel: yes. call me!!!

Tues, Nov 23, 8:25 PM E.S.T.

zoegirl: maddie, you're not going to believe this

mad maddie: believe what? did u talk to angela?

zoegirl: just now. she is beyond upset.

zoegirl: maddie, her dad's not having an affair—he lost his job.

mad maddie: he what?

zoegirl:	he was fired. isn't that terrible?
mad maddie:	**WHY?**
zoegirl:	i don't know. "downsizing" is what her dad told her.
mad maddie:	**omg**
zoegirl:	and get this: it happened over a month ago. i mean, mrs. silver knew, but not angela and chrissy.
mad maddie:	**he's been hiding it this whole time?**
mad maddie:	**it's so dumb when grown-ups do that. don't they know it always makes things worse?**
zoegirl:	tell me about it.
mad maddie:	**so who was the mystery woman at starbucks?**
zoegirl:	well, i asked angela that—although i didn't mention the affair part, so don't you either. and angela said it was probably his career counselor. he's, like, got to start his life all over again.
mad maddie:	**whoa**
mad maddie:	**what's he gonna do?**
zoegirl:	i don't know. angela couldn't talk long because she had to get back to the table, but she said she'll tell us more when she gets home.
mad maddie:	**man oh man**
zoegirl:	i *told* u something bad was gonna happen. i told you things couldn't go on being so great forever.
mad maddie:	**jesus. i guess u were right!**

Tues, Nov 23, 9:20 PM E.S.T.

SnowAngel:	my life is hell—complete and utter hell!!!!
mad maddie:	**i know, angela. i'm so sorry.**
SnowAngel:	no, u DON'T know. it's so much worse. i can't even talk, cuz i'm crying so hard. i can't even make my thumbs punch in the right letters!
zoegirl:	angela! what's going on? WHAT'S worse?

23

mad maddie: CALL ME, YOU BIG DUMMY! call me and i'll add zoe in. then you can tell us instead of bad-thumb-typing us.

SnowAngel: if i cld talk, i wld. but i can't. all you'd hear is me bawling. plus if i heard your voices i'd break down even more.

zoegirl: angela? you're kind of scaring me. please tell us what's wrong. please?

SnowAngel: fine. there's no other way to say it, so i just will.

SnowAngel: my dad's making us move to california!!!

zoegirl: *what*?

SnowAngel: i hate my parents. i hate everyone! why is this happening?!!!

mad maddie: ur moving to CALIFORNIA???

mad maddie: NOOOOOO. angela, that's crazy!

zoegirl: you *can't* move! you . . . you can't!

SnowAngel: well, apparently i can, cuz i'm a TEENAGER and i have no control over my life! i have to do what my stupid PARENTS say, even if it's the most horrible thing in the entire world!

zoegirl: wait—slow down

zoegirl: your dad lost his job, and that majorly majorly sucks. but how did we get from there to california???

SnowAngel: cuz all this time when my dad's SUPPOSEDLY been at work, he's actually been meeting with his career counselor and filling out online applications. that's how!

mad maddie: zoe thought your dad was having an affair, btw

SnowAngel: WHAT???

mad maddie: she did. she thought the career counselor was his lover.

zoegirl: maddie!!!

SnowAngel: i don't care. i wish the career counselor WAS his

	lover, cuz believe me, that would be better than the truth.
SnowAngel:	he applied to this one company in el cerrito, and they offered him a position. they want him to start right away!
zoegirl:	el cerrito? where's el cerrito?
mad maddie:	**angela, listen to me. forget el cerrito, forget your dad's career counselor lover. U R NOT ALLOWED TO MOVE.**
mad maddie:	**your dad hasn't said yes, has he?**
SnowAngel:	he hasn't accepted the job YET, but he's flying us out to look at housing. he's trying to make it sound "fun." we're going over thanksgiving!
mad maddie:	**THANKSGIVING?!!**
zoegirl:	angela, please tell me you're kidding. thanksgiving is this thursday!
SnowAngel:	we're having turkey at my aunt sadie's at 11:00, and then we're catching a 3:30 flight to california. our meal won't even be digested by then! it's insane!!!
zoegirl:	i can't believe they just *sprung* this on you. this is so awful!
SnowAngel:	i know! dad was all, "we didn't want to worry u w/o reason, we wanted to work out the details." and i was like, "were u EVER gonna tell us, or were u just gonna stick us on a plane and be like, 'good-bye, old life. hello, el cerrito!'"
SnowAngel:	crap, i can't do this. my hands are shaking. my whole body is shaking.
mad maddie:	**want us to come over?**
SnowAngel:	will u?
mad maddie:	**of course, and we'll figure out how to beat this. we will, angela. CUZ U R NOT MOVING TO CALIFORNIA.**

SnowAngel: what about u, zoe? will your mom let u out of the
               house this late?
zoegirl: i'll lie to her if i have to. i'll tell her i have to go
               buy new highlighters.
SnowAngel: plz come quick
mad maddie: we're on the way!!!

Wed, Nov 24, 4:30 PM E.S.T.

mad maddie: god, zoe, poor angela. she was like a zombie
               today, wandering around school with that beat-
               up expression on her face.
zoegirl: i know. i feel terrible. 😞
mad maddie: yeah, i could tell. every time i saw u, u gave me a
               death look.
zoegirl: that wasn't because of angela. that's because i'm
               still mad at you about the whole mr. silver thing.
               i can't believe you told her i thought her dad was
               having an affair!
mad maddie: i'm sorry i'm sorry i'm sorry. how many times
               must i apologize?
mad maddie: but c'mon, angela knew not to take it seriously.
               she's good that way.
zoegirl: she's good *every* way
zoegirl: i can't live without her, mads. i can't even
               imagine it.
mad maddie: i can't either. but i thought about it on my way
               home, and i have an idea. the silvers will fly to
               california tomorrow, and angela will tell her dad
               she hates el cerrito, and that'll be the end of it.
               cuz mr. silver can't say no to angela, right?
zoegirl: i don't know. he's said no to her before. like when
               she wanted to build a fire pit in their backyard,
               remember?

mad maddie: just so we could roast marshmallows, which is such an angela kind of thing to wanna do.

zoegirl: and then we roasted them anyway in the oven, and the pot holder caught on fire and mr. silver had a fit. poor angela!

mad maddie: AAARGH, my head hurts. we have to talk about something else or i'm gonna explode.

mad maddie: did i tell u i almost found a googlewhack?

zoegirl: ???

mad maddie: it's distraction therapy. u type 2 words into google. the goal is to get only 1 hit. for example, "toking marsupials."

zoegirl: toking marsupials?

mad maddie: or "phlegmatic weepies" or "crampy dailiness." or my fave, "crapulent porker."

mad maddie: those aren't mine, tho. i can't take credit for them.

zoegirl: huh. pity.

mad maddie: it's extremely hard to find a true googlewhack, but i came close. "flatulent madigan" got 60 hits, while "absorbent madigan" got 636. but "madigan's pantaloons" only got 3.

zoegirl: distraction therapy, you say?

mad maddie: 3, i tell u! this is muy impressive!

zoegirl: i'm not sure i'm grasping the point of all this . . .

mad maddie: the point is that there IS no point. it keeps me from thinking about angela, that's all.

mad maddie: but since U made me think about her again— thanks a lot—do u think she's coming to dylan's party tonight?

zoegirl: i don't know. she's pretty depressed.

mad maddie: which is exactly why she needs to come.

mad maddie: what about u? are u coming?

zoegirl: i have to work first—i picked up a shift since we have tomorrow off. but i'll swing by after.

mad maddie:	ooo, you picked up a shift at Kidding Around? nudge-nudge, know what i mean, know what i mean?
zoegirl:	maddie? you're trying to make a sex joke about a childcare facility.
mad maddie:	it's a stupid name. i can't help it.
mad maddie:	so shld i invite chive to dylan's? i wanna invite him to do SOMETHING, only i don't want it to be boring, which i'm fairly sure dylan's won't be. do you follow dylan on twitter?
zoegirl:	i did, but it made me want to buy him "hooked on phonics." HIS SPELLING MAKES ME CRINGE! so i muted him.
mad maddie:	HA. well, apparently there will be copious amounts of beer.
zoegirl:	dylan's an idiot to tweet that. what if his parents see it?
zoegirl:	tonnie wyndham's in my english class, and last week she said on facebook how she'd plagiarized her book review. only ms. griffith found out, because ms. griffith surfs the net and types in her students' names.
mad maddie:	that girl needs to change her privacy settings.
mad maddie:	she doesn't seem to have much interest in privacy—or shld i say boundaries—in the first place, tho. today in health, she asked how many calories r in a tablespoon of sperm.
zoegirl:	ewww!
mad maddie:	wanna know the answer? 9.
zoegirl:	that is revolting. mrs. wayker actually knew?
mad maddie:	guess it's not the first time it's come up.
mad maddie:	ha—come up, get it?
zoegirl:	i am *never* giving anyone a blow job, not even my husband.

mad maddie: bullshit. u totally will.

zoegirl: why would you say that? it's disgusting!

mad maddie: prude, prude, prude. when u find the person who makes u GLOW, u'll go down on him quick as a wink. and then HE'LL glow. you'll blow; he'll glow.

mad maddie: god, i'm on a roll. this stuff just comes out of me—i don't even have to try.

zoegirl: maddie, there's nothing here for you to be proud of. hate to break it to you.

mad maddie: blah blah blah. i'm gonna make the bold move and call chive, and then i'll text angela and tell her that she's required to go too.

Wed, Nov 24, 5:41 PM E.S.T.

mad maddie: hey, girl. ready for dylan's party?

SnowAngel: dylan's party? that's tonight?

mad maddie: yeah, and newsflash: you're coming. and so is chive! wh-hoo! so u'll get to meet him, which u claim u've been wanting to do.

mad maddie: more importantly, it'll get u out of yr funk. u've been moping about in your room ever since u got home from school, haven't u?

SnowAngel: yes and no. i was moping for a while, but it wasn't helping, and all i could think about was how terrible everything is. so i rode my bike to little five points to clear my head.

mad maddie: huh. exercise. not familiar with the concept.

mad maddie: did it work?

SnowAngel: well, it's not like i'm leaping up and down for joy, but i don't feel QUITE so suicidal anymore.

SnowAngel: wanna know why?

mad maddie: er . . . why?

SnowAngel: cuz of what happened when i got back home, which i am calling my GREAT BRACELET

BREAKTHROUGH. *strikes a tragically romantic pose* even in these darkest of times, i found a light at the end of the tunnel.

mad maddie: **angela, what the hell r u talking about?**

SnowAngel: i parked my bike when i got to little five points, and i did a little window shopping. and i found a bracelet that i love sooooo much. it's made out of brown leather, and the ends connect with a silver clasp, and on the front there's a slender silver rectangle with the word "believe" etched onto it.

SnowAngel: i know ur gonna say it's corny, but it's like fate was jumping out at me and telling me that everything's gonna be all right. telling me to BELIEVE.

mad maddie: **oh, angela, ur not gonna start carrying around little pewter angels, r u? or those stones that say "joy" or "happiness" or—god help us—"believe"?**

SnowAngel: don't u WANT me to believe?

SnowAngel: why r u making fun of me when i'm actually feeling the tiniest bit better?

mad maddie: **i'm not making fun of U. i'm making fun of those dorky stones.**

SnowAngel: back to my bracelet. in order to look right, it has to be fastened nice and snug, cuz otherwise the "believe" part rotates around where it's not supposed to. i was able to get it PRETTY tight, but not just-right tight, cuz it kept slipping out of place just when i thought i had it.

mad maddie: **why didn't u get chrissy to fasten it for u? or me? u could have brought it to the party and i would have fastened it for u.**

SnowAngel: cuz it became this big thing. cuz in my head i was like, "am i the kind of person who gives up? no. am i the kind of person who fights to the end? yes."

mad maddie: **over a bracelet?**

SnowAngel: here is what i finally did, and i think i should get a medal cuz it was so brilliant. i hooked one of my necklaces to the end of the bracelet to make the bracelet longer, sort of. and then i used my teeth to pull the necklace tight, which in turn pulled the bracelet tight. then i used my free hand to reach around and fasten the clasp—effortlessly, i tell u!— and voila, my bracelet is on and gorgeous. and every time i look at it, i just think about how things CAN work out if u make them. isn't that good? 😃

mad maddie: well, lord love a duck

SnowAngel: i know i have to get on that stupid plane tomorrow, but we haven't moved YET. i just have to believe.

mad maddie: does this mean u'll come to the party?

SnowAngel: can u give me a ride?

mad maddie: hells yeah—i'll pick u up in an hour!

Wed, Nov 24, 6:30 PM E.S.T.

zoegirl: hey, angela. i'm texting from work, so i've got to be quick.

SnowAngel: hey, girl. wassup? ur coming to dylan's, right?

zoegirl: eventually, just not till after work.

zoegirl: listen, i just wanted to say . . . well, i'm sorry i thought your dad was having an affair.

SnowAngel: oh yeahhhhhh. THAT.

zoegirl: i don't know why i even thought that. pretty stupid, huh?

SnowAngel: don't worry about it. i told my dad, tho.

zoegirl: you told your *dad*?

zoegirl: omigosh. did you tell him it was me who said it?

SnowAngel: of course. i said it to get back at him for all the crap he's putting me thru, but it backfired cuz he just laughed. my mom thought it was pretty funny too.

zoegirl: angela!

SnowAngel: they said to tell u they have a very fulfilling sex life. aren't u glad u brought it up?

zoegirl: this is so embarrassing! i can't believe you *told* them!!!

SnowAngel: oh well

SnowAngel: c ya at dylan's!

Thu, Nov 25, 11:45 AM E.S.T.

mad maddie: good morning to u on this lovely day of giving thanks, which we americans call thanksgiving, and which wld be far lovelier if not for the taste of sour beer wafting about my tonsils.

mad maddie: can anyone say cottonmouth?

zoegirl: hi, mads. i see you're still recovering from last night.

mad maddie: that was so much fun. i kissed chive on the washing machine, did i tell u?

zoegirl: yes, maddie. you called me from your cell phone even though i was 20 feet away having a very nice conversation with doug, which you interrupted. you were all, "i'm kissing chive on the washing machine! hahaha, isn't that hilarious? i'm kissing chive on the washing machine!"

mad maddie: cuz u r my friend. cuz i wanna share my life with u.

zoegirl: and then you gave your phone to chive and made him talk to me. it was very random and unnecessary.

mad maddie: i did not make chive talk to u.

mad maddie: did i?

zoegirl: you don't remember? afterward, doug and i talked about how much we hate it when people do that. "here, talk to my great-aunt zelda." "here, talk to my buddy from camp whom you've never met and never will."

mad maddie:	weird. well, what did u say to chive on the phone? what did HE say?
zoegirl:	he was nice, i guess. he was like, "let's see, you're the shy one, right?"
zoegirl:	maddie, did u tell him i was shy?
mad maddie:	i dunno, i might have
zoegirl:	why?
mad maddie:	what do u mean, why? cuz ur my bud.
mad maddie:	i told him all about angela too
zoegirl:	well, that's sweet, but please don't go around telling people i'm shy.
mad maddie:	but u R shy
zoegirl:	a little, maybe. with some people. but it made me feel dumb.
mad maddie:	chive made u feel dumb?
zoegirl:	noooo, not chive. he must have realized i was embarrassed, because he said, "hey now, nothing wrong with being shy. just don't be afraid to let loose, okay? you can't always stand around with your hands in your pockets. sometimes you've got to bust a move!"
mad maddie:	ha. bust a move. not sure how that relates to being shy . . .
mad maddie:	so did u like him? don't u think he's awesome?
zoegirl:	i did like him. he had that drunk-and-sincere thing going on, but he was kind of charming.
mad maddie:	he's cute too. more like gorgeous.
zoegirl:	if you say so. but what's going on here? i thought you and chive were just friends.
mad maddie:	we r!
mad maddie:	what, u think i wanna be his girlfriend?
zoegirl:	doug assumed you were. he saw the two of you together, and he said it looked like you were really into each other.

mad maddie:	that's just chive. he does this deep-gaze thing when ur talking to him, as if ur the only person in the whole world that matters.
zoegirl:	well, like i said, doug thought you were a couple.
mad maddie:	doug, doug, doug. why the obsession with doug? anyway, the two of u hung out for the whole party, but that doesn't make YOU a couple, now does it?
zoegirl:	hanging out versus hanging all over . . .
zoegirl:	kidding!
mad maddie:	i'm gonna let that slide, cuz at least i'm getting some.
zoegirl:	ick! maddie!!!
mad maddie:	it was cool that doug came to dylan's, though. i don't usually see him at those parties.
zoegirl:	we were chatting at work, and i told him about it. i thought it was cool that he came too. i was glad.
mad maddie:	i liked his shirt
zoegirl:	"tough guys wear pink"? he wore it on purpose for the kids at Kidding Around. graham especially. (graham's that adorable three-year-old i told you about.)
zoegirl:	last week graham wore pink socks, and a girl named ashleigh told him that only girls are allowed to wear pink.
mad maddie:	alas, it starts so young
zoegirl:	but graham didn't seem phased. i call him graham cracker.
mad maddie:	bet he's never heard that in all his 3 yrs
zoegirl:	last night i played candyland with him, and i let him land on queen frostine even though that wasn't the card he drew. he said, "you're the best, zoe." he kept saying it over and over. "you're the best."

mad maddie:	**awwww**
mad maddie:	**so i thought angela did pretty well with the whole party thing, didn't u?**
zoegirl:	freakily well, given all that's going on.
mad maddie:	**no doubt cuz of THE BRACELET**
zoegirl:	ah, yes, *the bracelet*
mad maddie:	**but now she's having her thanksgiving dinner at eleven in the frickin morning and preparing to jet off to california. isn't that just wrong?**
zoegirl:	i hate that. it makes me so worried for her.
mad maddie:	**worrying won't do anything. it'll only stress u out.**
zoegirl:	yeah, but *not* worrying about it is like . . . denial. i mean, there's a very real chance that she'll have to move.
mad maddie:	**and there's even a realer chance that she won't. stop being a negative nelly.**
mad maddie:	**and now the googlewhack attempt of the day. let's c, how about "graham's hero" . . .**
zoegirl:	you're changing the subject!
mad maddie:	**i'm sorry to report that graham's hero got 876,000 hits. guess ur not as special as u thought u were, zo.**
zoegirl:	maddie, this is what denial *is*! doing everything you can to deny that something's happening!
mad maddie:	**no, this is called having fun on the computer searching for the perfect 1.**
mad maddie:	**i know, i'll try "sudsy canoodle," in honor of chive.**
mad maddie:	**good lord—4,820 hits. what is wrong with the world?!**
zoegirl:	um, hate to burst your bubble, but i just tried "inchoate despot" and got only one hit. then I tried "insouciant lavalier" and got ZERO hits!
mad maddie:	**what? no. impossible. hold on . . .**
mad maddie:	**phew, i am right and you are wrong. *i* just tried "insouciant lavalier" and got 15,200 hits.**

zoegirl:	but . . .
zoegirl:	huh???
mad maddie:	zoe, hate to burst *your* bubble, but u can't use quote marks when u google yr two words. u know that, right?
zoegirl:	oh.
mad maddie:	yes. oh. which reaffirms my point: the world is OUT THERE, and it is wild and woolly and filled with things both possible AND impossible. so until we know which category angela's move falls into—don't worry!!!

Thu, Nov 25, 2:45 PM E.S.T.

SnowAngel:	hey, mads. i'm at one of those airport newstands. it sucks. i told my parents i needed gum, but really i needed to get away from them.
mad maddie:	hey, girl! sorry about the suck, but i'm so glad to hear from u! when does your plane take off?
SnowAngel:	too soon, that's all i know. let's talk about something else. let's talk about the party.
mad maddie:	i'm totally with u.
mad maddie:	what'd u think of chive?
SnowAngel:	oh, he's CUTE, maddie! he's thoroughly cute, in a stoner boy kinda way.
mad maddie:	chive is SO not a stoner boy. u just think that cuz he likes to party.
SnowAngel:	no, i think that cuz of the way he acts, cuz of the way he looks at u all lazy and slow and appreciative. u know, like, "it's cool, dude." that's his vibe.
mad maddie:	that's his VIBE?
SnowAngel:	u know who he reminds me of? Matthew McConaughey, with that sexy smile of his.
mad maddie:	i'll take that. matthew m. is hot.
mad maddie:	and i'm very impressed u can spell his name.

SnowAngel: cuz i read "People"

mad maddie: but chive is so much more than "it's cool, dude." he's really into philosophy, and he's taking all these literature classes. did u hear him quoting charles bukowski while dylan funneled a beer?

SnowAngel: who's charles bukowski?

mad maddie: and that whole story about his dog, napoleon, and how he's gonna pimp him out by putting a gold chain around his neck. that cracked me up.

SnowAngel: i liked the fact that he went to the keg and got u refills. that was very gentlemanly.

mad maddie: a few too many refills, unfortunately

SnowAngel: well, i wasn't gonna say anything . . .

mad maddie: i was so wasted i fell off the toilet seat. it was hysterical.

SnowAngel: yes, it sounds hysterical *looks extremely suspiciously at friend*

mad maddie: oh, don't go all zoe on me. i didn't tell her about that little incident, btw.

SnowAngel: fine, but i DO worry about u. just a little.

mad maddie: u don't need to. sometimes i get kinda psycho, but it's all fun and games.

mad maddie: so were u surprised to see doug?

SnowAngel: that was so awesome that he came! i'm so proud of zoe for inviting him.

SnowAngel: and for the record, she looked adorable in her embroidered jeans and that soft white shirt that actually shows off the fact that she's a girl. i was like, "wow, did she dress up for the party?"

mad maddie: nah, not our zo. sez she came straight from work.

SnowAngel: with doug. i know. i made a point of talking to him, cuz he seemed so shell-shocked at being at a real live party.

mad maddie: oh no, teenagers on the loose! oh no, underage drinking!

SnowAngel: do u think he seemed different somehow? last night he kinda seemed cuter to me than usual.

mad maddie: u r so funny. u just think that cuz for the first time in recorded history, he wasn't slobbering all over u. all of a sudden he's unattainable, so u miraculously think he's cute.

SnowAngel: unattainable? who says he's unattainable?

SnowAngel: not that i WANT to attain him . . .

mad maddie: no, u just want him to lust after u in a constant state of angela-worship, like he did all last year. admit it!

SnowAngel: maybe he's gotten taller. maybe that's what it is.

SnowAngel: anyway, i kinda ended up flirting with him a bit too much—i don't even know why. but that's ok, i'm sure he'd rather be flirted with than not flirted with.

mad maddie: a pity flirt. yr too kind.

SnowAngel: aren't i? i should give lessons to zoe. when i interrupted the two of them, she just stood there like a doormat. i was like, "liven up, zo! ur never gonna catch a guy like that!"

mad maddie: from where i stood, i'd say zoe was doing just fine.

SnowAngel: with DOUG? 😊

SnowAngel: they're just friends. anyway, u were drunk, so yr judgment doesn't count.

mad maddie: ugh, don't remind me

SnowAngel: crudballs, they announced that it's time to board the plane.

mad maddie: wait, don't go!

SnowAngel: i have to, i have no choice

mad maddie: well, call me from california—i want to hear how everything goes.

SnowAngel: i'll try, but my battery's low and i forgot my stupid
              charger.
SnowAngel: real quick—did u like my "believe" bracelet?
mad maddie: i did, oddly enough. i liked it very much.
SnowAngel: i keep touching it and looking down to admire it. i
              know it's stupid, but it gives me strength.
mad maddie: power to the bracelet! all bow down and chant
              "believe"!

              Thu, Nov 25, 7:06 PM E.S.T.
mad maddie: the Kinnick Family Dinner of Thanksgiving
              has mercifully ended, and now i'm at java joe's
              escaping the hellhole that is my house.
zoegirl: why is your house a hellhole?
mad maddie: cuz the moms is on her third glass of chardonnay,
              and the dishes are stacked to the ceiling. my
              brother's girlfriend has taken it upon herself to
              wash them, only she insists on doing it au naturel
              cuz its better for the environment. she sent me
              out for dish soap—that's what i'm supposedly
              doing.
zoegirl: mark's still going strong with pelt-woman, huh?
zoegirl: omg. i just realized something horrible. we've
              been calling her pelt-woman for so long that i
              can't remember her real name!
mad maddie: her armpit hair is long enough to braid, zoe. her
              name IS pelt-woman.
mad maddie: hey, have u talked to angela?
zoegirl: i did, but not for long because her phone died.
              short version: she's not having fun.
mad maddie: well, that's the surprise of the century.
mad maddie: holidays suck. there's so much pressure.
zoegirl: i like holidays
mad maddie: that's cuz ur zoe and u've got the perfect family.

	that's cuz your mom and dad aren't gonna end up throwing beer cans at each other.
zoegirl:	maddie, your parents are not gonna throw beer cans at each other.
zoegirl:	are they?
mad maddie:	fine, wine bottles. and chumley the psycho kitty will attack the remains of the turkey, and before the night is over, pelt-woman will insist that we write something in her gratitude journal. and i will write, "i am grateful that the moms' empty chardonnay bottle only dislocated my shoulder and not my brain."
zoegirl:	you are so full of it
zoegirl:	who's chumley the psycho kitty?
mad maddie:	don't ask
zoegirl:	i just did
mad maddie:	oh. right.
mad maddie:	chumley is mark and pelt-woman's new cat. he's living with us until mark finds a place of his own.
zoegirl:	and when will that be?
mad maddie:	never, cuz he's a loser. he's 22 yrs old and the moms still tucks him in at night.
zoegirl:	lol
mad maddie:	and ppl wonder why i have issues? exhibit a: my family.
zoegirl:	aw, mads, *we're* your real family. me and angela.
mad maddie:	believe me, i'd much rather be giving thanx with u guys. last year at this time, we were all sleeping under the stars on cumberland island. man, that was awesome.
zoegirl:	hold on. *i* was sleeping under the stars, and i froze my booty off. *you* were hogging the tent.

mad maddie:	the stars were pretty, tho. admit it.
mad maddie:	uh oh, there's a goatee boy hovering behind me. he's saying, "um, excuse me, but the sign says tables are 'for paying customers only'?"
zoegirl:	he can't see what you're texting, can he?
mad maddie:	hell if i care. r u, goatee boy? r u reading what i'm writing?
mad maddie:	HA. he's pretending not to, but i can c from over my shoulder that he is. he looks all pinched and constipated.
mad maddie:	alas, i must away to the grocery store. the dish soap is calling my name.
zoegirl:	goatee boy will be so happy
mad maddie:	nah, i'm giving my table to a girl on my other side. she has been waiting very patiently. she gets five gold stars! ⭐ ⭐ ⭐ ⭐ ⭐

Fri, Nov 26, 11:00 AM P.S.T.

SnowAngel:	hiya, zo! hiya, mads! 😋
SnowAngel:	i'm txting from our crudballs hotel. well, at least they let me borrow a phone charger from the front desk. but still. crudballs. you both there?
zoegirl:	angela!!!!! hellooooo!
mad maddie:	maddie kinnick, checking in for duty. angela: how goes it??? did u convince your dad that california sucks?
SnowAngel:	yeah, right. my dad doesn't CARE what i think.
SnowAngel:	guys . . . he took the job! he's starting in december!!!
mad maddie:	WHAT?
SnowAngel:	we're moving to california. we're frickin moving to california!
zoegirl:	omg, angela. in december???
SnowAngel:	dad's leaving in december. the rest of us r staying in atlanta until our house gets sold.

SnowAngel:	after that, we're gone!
mad maddie:	**nooooo, u can't move! u belong here with us!**
SnowAngel:	u think i don't know that?
SnowAngel:	and to add to the suckiness, my dad's boss has an awful daughter WHOM I DETEST. her name's glendy, if that doesn't say enough!
mad maddie:	**glendy? sounds like a brand of toilet paper.**
SnowAngel:	she IS a brand of toilet paper. she's horrible.
zoegirl:	when did you meet her?
SnowAngel:	last night, cuz we ended up having thanksgiving dinner at mr. boss's house instead of the hotel restaurant. aren't i lucky?
SnowAngel:	glendy was a freak, all big-eyed and blinky and burble-laffing every time i said anything, which was ridiculous cuz believe me i wasn't being remotely funny. she acts as if she's been homeschooled.
mad maddie:	**how old is she?**
SnowAngel:	she's 16 like us—not that u'd guess it cuz she's CLUELESS. she wanted to know where i got my glitter eyeshadow, and i was like, "at the store, u idiot." i was like, "don't u know your dad is an evil selfish pig? don't u know he's stealing my life away?"
zoegirl:	oh, poor angela!
SnowAngel:	and later she was all, "after u move here, we can have sleepovers! we can give each other beauty treatments!!!" *slits wrists*
mad maddie:	**so when r u coming back?**
SnowAngel:	sunday. i can't wait. my mom thinks i'm being a brat cuz i'm not "appreciating this rare chance to c california," but i could care less. 😞
SnowAngel:	she's all, "consider this an opportunity," but i don't want an opportunity! i just wanna be with u guys!!!
zoegirl:	okay, so you're coming back on sunday . . . and then what?

SnowAngel: the whole fam is flying back to atlanta together, and then dad's gonna pack his stuff and fly out again in a week. mr. boss is gonna find him a place. after that, who knows?

SnowAngel: oh great—chrissy's poking my shoulder and she won't stop. stupid mom told her to tell me to stop texting and get off my butt, cuz it's time to go sightseeing today with mr. boss and glendy. *holds dagger over heart*

mad maddie: **shit, angela. i'm so sorry.**

zoegirl: me too

SnowAngel: me three!!

Sat, Nov 27, 10:38 AM E.S.T.

zoegirl: hey, mads. i can't believe it—angela is actually moving! i hoped i'd wake up this morning and realize it was all a big mistake . . . but i didn't.

mad maddie: **maybe her dad will change his mind. maybe he'll come to his senses.**

zoegirl: i don't think so, maddie.

zoegirl: god, i miss her already, and she's not even officially gone.

mad maddie: **zoe, don't**

mad maddie: **just . . . don't.**

zoegirl: i thought maybe you'd wanna talk about it, that's all.

zoegirl: guess i was wrong.

Sun, Nov 28, 4:05 PM E.S.T.

mad maddie: **hi, zo. i'm bored.**

zoegirl: me too

mad maddie: **wanna go meet angela at the airport?**

zoegirl: omigosh, what a great idea. she'd be so surprised!

zoegirl: only we can't. you can't go through security unless you're a ticketed passenger.

mad maddie: we could wait at the welcome area. wanna? we could bring flowers and candy and a balloon shaped like a unicorn.

zoegirl: aw, mads, don't *ever* tell me you're not a big sap at heart.

zoegirl: but yeah! let's do it!!!

Mon, Nov 29, 5:15 PM E.S.T.

SnowAngel: k, it's official. my mother is driving me crazy. ever since we got back, she's been in a cleaning frenzy. i caught her trying to throw out a whole bag of old toys, including my complete set of My Pretty Ponies (!!!!), and all she said was, "this house is a junk heap. if i could, i'd throw it ALL away!"

mad maddie: even the beautiful Barbie balloon your two bestest buds gave you at the airport? 🎈

SnowAngel: well, no, not that. she thought that was very sweet, as did i.

SnowAngel: but maddie? why did u give me a Barbie balloon?

mad maddie: cuz the gift store was out of unicorns. anywayz, zoe said u always wanted a Barbie named after u.

mad maddie: is your mom making u get rid of your Barbies too?

SnowAngel: yes. AND my pound puppies.

mad maddie: i loved those pound puppies

SnowAngel: me 2, except for the 1 with the crusty ear from when chrissy threw up on it.

mad maddie: wait a sec, a.

SnowAngel: yes?

mad maddie: something has just occurred to me, and now i'm a little disturbed. u and zoe and i started hanging out in the 7th grade . . . why were u still playing with Barbies and pound puppies in the 7th grade?

SnowAngel: why were U? ur the 1 who just admitted to missing them!

mad maddie:	hmm, ya got me there
mad maddie:	not the Barbies, tho. i could give a rat's ass about Barbie—except when she's big and shiny and made of mylar.
SnowAngel:	aargh. i HATE cleaning. i would actually rather be back at school than at home right now. how sad is that?
mad maddie:	ugh, not me. every single teacher was like, "now that we've returned from thanksgiving vacation, it's time to knuckle down. only two more weeks until final exams!"
SnowAngel:	noooo, i can't handle it! too much pressure! *rips hair from head in clumps*
mad maddie:	u need a glass of nestle quik to calm u down. have u ever noticed with nestle quik how u can actually crunch the chocolatey part? u swish a sip around in your mouth, and the chocolatey crystals just beg to be crunched. it's like at the dentist's, when he says, "ok, now lightly tap your teeth together for me." it's the exact same motion.
SnowAngel:	oh great, my MOTHER is txting me from downstairs. hold on while i see what she wants.
mad maddie:	crunch, crunch, crunch. crunch, crunch, crunch. i'm singing a little song that goes crunch, crunch, crunch.
SnowAngel:	i'm back—sorry about that.
mad maddie:	what'd your mom say?
SnowAngel:	she's such a dweeb. she's like, "hey, sweetie. i know this is stressful, but u've got to remember that it's stressful for all of us. i won't throw away any more of your junk, i promise. love ya, precious!"
mad maddie:	that's so funny that she txts u
SnowAngel:	i know

mad maddie: it's not a bad idea, tho. hey, maybe i should suggest it to my parents. if they texted me—or better, if they texted each other—maybe they wouldn't yell so much.

SnowAngel: i don't wanna be here. come rescue me.

mad maddie: where do u wanna go?

SnowAngel: i don't care. just come get me!

Mon, Nov 29, 9:33 PM E.S.T.

SnowAngel: hey, zo-ster. i saw u talking to doug today. r u guys becoming better friends?

zoegirl: i guess so, yeah

zoegirl: at work on saturday, this one little girl kept hugging him and telling him she loved him. it was so cute.

SnowAngel: doug IS pretty lovable, i must admit. sometimes i think, "why in the world don't i just decide to like him?" in some ways it would be so easy—and i know he'd make the perfect boyfriend.

zoegirl: except i don't think a person just "decides" things like that.

zoegirl: anyway, there's the small and horrible fact that you're moving to california . . .

SnowAngel: but maybe if i had a boyfriend, that would make it better. like, he could pine for me and send me flowers. 🌷

zoegirl: *i'll* pine for u, angela. i'll pine for u like crazy!

SnowAngel: i know, i know. just . . .

zoegirl: just what?

SnowAngel: well, u pining for me is good. i thoroughly expect absurd amounts of pining. but do me a favor and don't pine for anyone else, ok?

zoegirl: huh?

SnowAngel: doug, i mean. as in u and doug.

zoegirl:	you're telling me not to pine for doug???
zoegirl:	where in the world did *this* come from?
SnowAngel:	omg, it's insane, isn't it? it's just that i saw the way he was looking at u in the hall today, and i got this very weird feeling about it.
zoegirl:	what do u mean, the way he was looking at me? do u think maybe . . . ?
zoegirl:	never mind
SnowAngel:	oh, zoe, forget i said anything. i'm just fragile cuz of everything that's going on with me. it's like, i can't handle any more rejection!
zoegirl:	but angela, you've never been the slightest bit interested in doug. anyway, you had your chance with him last year.
SnowAngel:	but he wasn't as cute back then
zoegirl:	anyway, even if i *did* like doug—not that i do, because like you said that's insane—but in what way would that equal rejection?
SnowAngel:	like i said, forget it
SnowAngel:	i'm gonna go before i say anything else stupid. bye!

Tues, Nov 30, 10:18 PM E.S.T.

SnowAngel:	maddie, a realtor came to our house today.
mad maddie:	**oh god. what'd she say?**
SnowAngel:	that our house is lovely. i hate her.
SnowAngel:	she's gonna send over a "stager" to put in fake plants and stuff, and we're supposed to pop popcorn before any showings so that the house will smell buttery.
mad maddie:	**man, that's nuts**
SnowAngel:	she also said that altho sales are usually slow in the winter, there's a small peak in december. i wanted to stab her eyeballs.

mad maddie:	well . . . maybe there won't be a peak in december. try not to think about it.
SnowAngel:	maddie, my dad flies out TOMORROW. how am i supposed to not think about it?
SnowAngel:	i'm so furious at him, but at the same time i don't want him to leave.
mad maddie:	he is a very bad man. i'm furious at him too.
SnowAngel:	i'm exhausted. i wanna talk more, but first i wanna lie down. power nap. i'll call you in a while!

Wed, Dec 1, 4:33 PM E.S.T.

SnowAngel:	my dad's officially in california. tonight he'll sleep in the new apartment, and tomorrow he'll wake up and drive on new streets to get to his new job. how wrong is that?
zoegirl:	i'm so sorry, angela. i know how you must feel.
SnowAngel:	no u don't. u would never be in this situation, cuz your dad's, like, the CEO of his company. he's the one who would be doing the firing, not the one who would ever get fired.
zoegirl:	well, he *could* get fired if the stockholders voted him out.
SnowAngel:	yeah, fat chance
zoegirl:	angela . . . what's going on? do you *want* my dad to get fired?
SnowAngel:	aaargh *bonks head on desk*
SnowAngel:	no, i don't want your dad to get fired. but i don't wanna move, either. i told mom that i'd rather live in a box outside the mall. i told her i wanna stay here and live with my aunt sadie.
zoegirl:	that's a brilliant idea! could you do that—you know, for real?
SnowAngel:	mom wouldn't even consider it. she was just, "angela, don't be silly."

zoegirl:	that sucks
SnowAngel:	i know, especially since aunt sadie's the only person in my family who's been the least bit supportive thru all this. i talked to her tonight, and she was like, "don't tell your mom, but i think it's too bad jeff took that job without even considering the other options. a girl shouldn't be uprooted from her friends during her junior year of high school."
zoegirl:	so so so so true
SnowAngel:	yeah
SnowAngel:	that's all i wanted to say, really.

Thu, Dec 2, 7:17 PM E.S.T.

SnowAngel:	maddie, i've got something terrible to confess. i went shopping today cuz i was super depressed, and—er—i seem to have bought a shirt-on-shirt. please don't hate me!
mad maddie:	**huh?**
SnowAngel:	it's sooooo tacky, i know. *ducks for cover*
mad maddie:	**what, pray tell, is a shirt-on-shirt?**
SnowAngel:	it's . . . u know, a long-sleeve shirt with a short-sleeve shirt on top of it, only the long-sleeve shirt is a fake-out, cuz except for the sleeves and collar it doesn't really exist. it's the layered look, so i can look slouchy-cool w/o half-trying.
mad maddie:	**oh, angela, no.**
SnowAngel:	but it's really really cute! the long-sleeve part is white and the short-sleeve part is baby blue to match my eyes.
mad maddie:	**next thing u know, ur gonna be buying fake vintage t-shirts from old navy. ppl will say, "ooo, where'd u get that great shirt? have u really been to bob's hawaiian luau?" and u'll blush and stammer and say, "uh, no, i found it at a thrift**

store," which will be such a lie! UR LIVING A LIE, ANGELA SILVER!!!

SnowAngel: well, it's my aunt sadie's fault. she's the one who whisked me off to the mall. she said i needed some good old-fashioned girl time.

mad maddie: that's nice, altho it's a little unnerving that your aunt sadie considers herself a "girl."

SnowAngel: as opposed to what, a man?

mad maddie: as opposed to a WOMAN. as in, a grown-up adult-acting person our parents' age. not that u'd know it to look at her.

SnowAngel: i know—isn't she adorable? she shops in Gap Kids cuz the jeans there r cheaper, and she's tiny enough that she can get away with it. i wanna be just like her when i grow up.

mad maddie: or when u fail to grow up, as the case may be. lemme guess: your aunt played hooky from work to take u shopping.

mad maddie: did i nail it?

SnowAngel: maybe

mad maddie: and did she have all sorts of funky barrettes jammed in her hair? and was she wearing her hipster shoes with the mile-high platforms?

SnowAngel: so? what would u recommend—turning all matronly and wearing rubber-soled orthopedic loafers? *shudders*

mad maddie: i'm just giving u a hard time. u know i think your aunt sadie is cool.

SnowAngel: we had so much fun at Claire's, trying on all the tacky jewelry. i bought a sparkly dragonfly pin to go with my shirt-on-shirt.

mad maddie: well, aren't u clever

SnowAngel: why, yes i am

SnowAngel: hey, i'm gonna rewatch season one of "orange is

the new black" since it's about prison and since i'm
. . . well . . . you know. wanna come watch?

mad maddie: **oh, that reminds me. chive posted something**
funny on his blog. hold on and i'll copy it so u can
c . . .

SnowAngel: chive has a blog?

mad maddie: **a deadjournal, yeah**

SnowAngel: what's a deadjournal?

mad maddie: **it's like a livejournal, only better. instead of having**
"friends," u have "fiends," and your blog's called
your grave. the whole site is called the cemetery.

SnowAngel: sounds goth

mad maddie: **nah, just antiestablishment**

mad maddie: **here's his post. it's not about "orange is the new**
black." it's about reality shows. but it's still funny:

Hey, I know. Let's take a group of twenty-something
"actors" and let them pretend to live their lives as if
they don't know they're being filmed. Fake-boobed
Jersey girl gets punched in face? Check. Famous
"model" throws a tantrum in small room crammed
with a dozen other famous "models"? Check. "Hunky"
bachelor falls in love with not one but TWO lovely
ladies? Check.

But so what? It's all in the name of "fun"!

SnowAngel: why is he so obsessed with putting things in "quotes"?

SnowAngel: anyway, how does "chive" know so much about
reality shows if he doesn't watch them?

mad maddie: **i know, that's what's so funny. chive LOVES reality**
shows—he just rags on them for the hell of it. in
fact he thinks u should move to orange county
instead of el cerrito. then you cld be a "TV STAR"!

SnowAngel:	um. okay.
SnowAngel:	i'll run away and live in an alley on hollywood blvd.

⭐

mad maddie:	u, run away? and be separated from your straightening iron?
SnowAngel:	i could stash my straightening iron in my backpack. public bathrooms have electrical outlets, u know.
mad maddie:	no they don't
SnowAngel:	yes they do
mad maddie:	no, angela, they don't. trust me.
SnowAngel:	well . . . then i'd find a library and do my hair there. there are definitely outlets in libraries, cuz ppl use their laptops there.
mad maddie:	i can c it now. to the right are the studious computer folk, working hard on their papers, and to the left is angela, plunked down on the floor and straightening her hair.
SnowAngel:	and the problem is . . . ?
mad maddie:	sorry, darlin, u wouldn't last a minute as a runaway.
SnowAngel:	*sticks out tongue*
SnowAngel:	so r u gonna come watch with me or not?
mad maddie:	i can't—i told chive i'd hang with him. we're gonna watch "doctor who" and down a shot every time someone says "the doctor."
mad maddie:	but tell those prison hotties hi for me!

Fri, Dec 3, 4:15 PM E.S.T.

zoegirl:	hey mads. i'm at my mom's office, sitting in the most phenomenal swivel chair ever invented. can i have a swivel chair like this when i grow up?
mad maddie:	depends. r u gonna be a high-powered lawyer like your mom and make tons of money?
zoegirl:	uh . . .
mad maddie:	i, for one, plan to reject all worldly objects. u can

	come visit me in my trailer if you want. i will have christmas lights blinking all year long.
mad maddie:	so wazzup?
zoegirl:	have you ever heard of
zoegirl:	ok, this is embarrassing. i don't know how to say it. which is why i'm txting it.
zoegirl:	but have you ever heard of girls, like, pleasuring themselves by jiggling their legs?
mad maddie:	WHAT?!!
mad maddie:	omg, i am rolling on the floor, just so you know. just exactly how phenomenal IS that swivel chair?
zoegirl:	maddie! not *me*! god!
mad maddie:	and the term is "masturbating," zoe. u can say it. mas-tur-bat-ing.
zoegirl:	fyi, i don't do that. sometimes i wish i could, but i can't, so that's that.
mad maddie:	what do u mean, u can't?
zoegirl:	i can't, that's all
mad maddie:	r u serious?
zoegirl:	this is not actually what i texted to talk about. but yes, i'm serious.
zoegirl:	can u?
mad maddie:	can i MASTURBATE?
mad maddie:	uh, zoe, where is your mom? she's not in the room with u, is she?
zoegirl:	yes, she's standing right behind me and i'm reading our texts aloud.
zoegirl:	she's in a meeting, dummy! i've been stuck at her office *forever* because we're meeting my dad for dinner.
mad maddie:	well, in that case . . . yes, i can pleasure myself quite nicely, thank u very much. and i'm only telling u that cuz ur one of my dearest friends on the planet. but don't go asking for lessons.

zoegirl:	oh, gross!
mad maddie:	**what brought this up? what's this "jiggling their legs" business?**
zoegirl:	grrrrrrrrrrr
zoegirl:	chase dickinson, during french. he looked over at me and started cracking up, and i was like, "what? what are you laughing about?"
zoegirl:	he jerked his chin at my legs, which happened to be crossed, and he said, "i know why girls do that."
zoegirl:	"do *what*?" i said.
zoegirl:	and he goes, "jiggle your leg like that."
mad maddie:	**WERE u jiggling your leg?**
zoegirl:	maybe. i don't know. but so what if i was? i wasn't doing . . . what he said i was doing!
mad maddie:	**don't let it bother u. he's an immature freak.**
zoegirl:	i couldn't have been doing that even if i wanted to, not that i *ever* would have been doing it right there in french. i mean, god. but sometimes i think there's something wrong with me, maddie. why doesn't my body work the way other people's do?
mad maddie:	**hmm, cuz ur repressed?**
mad maddie:	**uh oh, ur not responding**
mad maddie:	**i was KIDDING, zoe!**
zoegirl:	that was not a nice thing to say
mad maddie:	**i'm sorry, i'm sorry. i was just teasing.**
zoegirl:	i don't want to be repressed. i just think . . . i don't know. that some girls are more naturally sexual than others. like you.
mad maddie:	**chive told me i'm sexy. he said i have great legs.**
zoegirl:	you do have great legs. you have great everything.
zoegirl:	are you *sure* the two of you aren't becoming an item? angela said you watched "Doctor Who" with him last night.

mad maddie:	yeah, and i totally made a fool of myself. not during the show, but after.
zoegirl:	uh oh. what happened?
mad maddie:	one of chive's friends from northside was there, a girl named whitney, and she was all over chive. it was disgusting. and i guess i was a little . . .
mad maddie:	i dunno. but somehow i ended up getting paired off with this guy named brannen, who also goes to n'side.
zoegirl:	what do u mean, paired off?
mad maddie:	the four of us were out by the pool, which was closed, but we climbed over the fence. whitney was like, "i'll kiss chive, and u kiss brannen, ok?"
zoegirl:	she calls him "chive" too?
mad maddie:	everybody does now. i love that.
zoegirl:	if you're the one who came up with his nickname, and you're the one who likes him, then *you* should get to kiss him.
mad maddie:	i know! but whitney already claimed him, so what was i supposed to do?
mad maddie:	anywayz, who cares? bodies r bodies r bodies.
zoegirl:	no, because bodies are connected to actual people, to hearts and brains and souls.
zoegirl:	was brannen cute at least?
mad maddie:	ehhh, too short for my taste. and u know what's bad?
zoegirl:	what?
mad maddie:	it turned into this totally horny go-for-it session, with my bra shoved up and his hands all over me, and now he won't quit txting. he's like, "do u wanna go to a movie? do u wanna go out for coffee?"
mad maddie:	i finally wrote back and said, "enough, all right? quit feeling sorry for me."

zoegirl:	i doubt he feels sorry for you, mads.
mad maddie:	that's what HE said. he's all, "what? no, i really like u!"
mad maddie:	whatevs
zoegirl:	i don't get it. you and chive have so much fun together, and it's obvious he thinks you're hot or he wouldn't have kissed you at donovan's wedding. so why would he kiss whitney instead of you?
mad maddie:	cuz she basically told him to. it's not like he was gonna tell her no.
zoegirl:	i don't see why not
mad maddie:	plus she's pretty, in a bouncy cheerleader-y way.
zoegirl:	did he even seem apologetic about it?
mad maddie:	it wasn't a big deal, zo. i refuse to be a ball and chain.
mad maddie:	anywayz, i'm gonna see him later tonight. he says he's got something planned, but he won't tell me what.
zoegirl:	is whitney going to be there?
zoegirl:	this is making me not like chive as much, that he would treat you like this.
mad maddie:	like what? i'm a big girl—i can make my own decisions.
mad maddie:	i can't even blame whitney for liking him. he's just got that kind of energy, where everyone wants to be around him. he makes everyone feel special.
zoegirl:	not special enough, apparently . . .
mad maddie:	i'm so glad u know everything about relationships, zo. i'm so glad ur such a pure and shining example of how to do things right.
zoegirl:	you're right. i'm sorry, i'm sorry.
zoegirl:	and if it makes u feel any better, i have boy problems of my own.

mad maddie:	plz elaborate.
zoegirl:	all right, but you *can't* tell angela. anyway, it'll probably come to nothing.
mad maddie:	what'll come to nothing?
mad maddie:	OMG—is it about u and doug?
zoegirl:	what?!! how did you know?
mad maddie:	it just came to me in a flash, cuz why else would u be all interested in this leg-jiggling business?
zoegirl:	maddie!
zoegirl:	never mind, i'm not dignifying that with a response.
mad maddie:	so you WERE flirting with him at dylan's. i knew it! zoe likes doug! zoe likes doug!
zoegirl:	shut up!
mad maddie:	omg, if angela finds out she's gonna FREAK.
zoegirl:	i know, but why? it's totally unfair for her to even care. yes, he had a crush on her last year, but now they're just friends.
mad maddie:	does angela know that?
zoegirl:	of course she knows that. she's the one who never reciprocated. how would she think they're anything BUT friends?
mad maddie:	cuz in angela's mind, doug is her safety date, the guy who'll long for her forever. and one day she cld have a change of heart, and they would live sappily ever after.
zoegirl:	that's not going to happen, maddie
mad maddie:	well, no, not with U in the picture
mad maddie:	but i'll tell u what: u can't give me a hard time about chive, not when ur sneaking around behind angela's back!

Sat, Dec 4, 11:09 AM E.S.T.

SnowAngel:	hi, mads. wake up wake up wake up!

mad maddie:	**ugh. too groggy. go away.**
SnowAngel:	then why'd ya respond to my text, huh? gotcha there, sucker.
mad maddie:	**can't talk. or text, whatever. downloading a song from a group chive told me about. go away.**
SnowAngel:	i'm not going away.
SnowAngel:	so how was your night? *folds hands and waits with a pleasant smile*
mad maddie:	**u really wanna know?**
SnowAngel:	yes, i really wanna know.
mad maddie:	**well, u can't flip out, but i'll tell u cuz ur my friend.**
SnowAngel:	hmm, intrigue. i luv it.
mad maddie:	**i smoked pot for the first time, ok?**
SnowAngel:	WHAT???
mad maddie:	**it was SO not a big deal. chive said he had a surprise for me, and that's what it was.**
SnowAngel:	chive's surprise was that the 2 of u were gonna smoke pot?!
mad maddie:	**and his friend brannen, which was a mistake. not the fact that i smoked pot, but the fact that brannen was there too.**
SnowAngel:	brannen from the kissy-kissy night?
mad maddie:	**if i'd known he was gonna be there, i might not have gone. cuz the pot, like, intensified everything, and partly that was cool, but partly it was uncool, especially in regards to brannen.**
SnowAngel:	why?
mad maddie:	**i dunno, cuz he kept staring at me with this "i'm interested in u" smile. it was gross.**
SnowAngel:	what about chive?
mad maddie:	**he was in his own world listening to music with earbuds in. i wish i could be more like that, just do whatever i feel like doing and be confident in**

	myself. but no. i had to deal with brannen making pop-eyes at me.
SnowAngel:	where were u guys this whole time?
mad maddie:	we sneaked into a housing development called cross creek condominiums. there's this big stretch of forest behind the condos, and that's where we went.
SnowAngel:	oh
mad maddie:	we called ourselves the cross creek crusaders. it was pretty funny.
SnowAngel:	i can't believe u smoked pot. i mean, i know ppl do, but i can't believe that U did.
SnowAngel:	what was it like?
mad maddie:	kinda a mixed bag
mad maddie:	ha, that's funny. a mixed BAG, get it?
SnowAngel:	no
mad maddie:	as in, a bag of pot. that's what u call it.
SnowAngel:	fascinating, now tell me what it was like
mad maddie:	well, it hurt sucking it in. and then ur supposed to hold it for as long as u can, but i kept coughing. and it made my eyes water.
SnowAngel:	sounds fun. NOT!
mad maddie:	chive says i'll get better with practice. he says the paranoid feelings will go away too.
SnowAngel:	huh
SnowAngel:	um, i know this'll sound kinda stupid, but what's the GOOD part about smoking pot? besides the fact that it was something u did with chive.
mad maddie:	well . . . i seriously had some wild sensations. it made everything blurry around the edges, like the boundaries of the world were melting away, and all these undercurrents of life were swirling around us. and i could SEE them. that's what made it so cool.

SnowAngel:	u could see what? the undercurrents of life?
mad maddie:	i know it sounds weird. i guess there's no way to explain it unless u've tried it yourself.
SnowAngel:	my life is blurry enough, thx
SnowAngel:	u gonna do it again?
mad maddie:	dunno. wish it didn't burn so much.
mad maddie:	but chive mentioned something about hooking up tonight, so maybe. wanna come?
SnowAngel:	er . . . doesn't really sound like my scene.
mad maddie:	yr always saying u want to get to know chive better, and zoe's working tonight so u have no excuse. u don't have to smoke if u don't want to.
SnowAngel:	i don't wanna sneak into that golf course, either
mad maddie:	it's not a golf course! it's just the woods behind some condos.
mad maddie:	how about this: why don't i call chive and see what's up, and then i'll give u more details. we'll do something legal if that's what u want.
SnowAngel:	uh . . . ok, i guess
mad maddie:	hey, that just gave me a good idea for a googlewhack.
SnowAngel:	qu'est-ce que c'est un googlewhack?
mad maddie:	i haven't told u about googlewhacks?
mad maddie:	oh yeah, that was zoe i told
SnowAngel:	*taps foot on floor*
mad maddie:	a googlewhack is an extremely delightful way to pass the time where u type in words on google and try to get only one hit. the "perfect 1," it's called.
SnowAngel:	sounds boring
SnowAngel:	or rather, sounds like something u should do ON YOUR OWN and not while your friend is twiddling away her toes.
mad maddie:	i'm gonna try "legal chive," whaddaya think? let me just do a little multitasking here . . .

mad maddie:	tarnation. 20,100 hits.
SnowAngel:	oh well 😕
mad maddie:	maybe "illegal chive" is the way to go, eh?
SnowAngel:	maddie, i do not wanna sit here while u googlewhack!
mad maddie:	716 hits. still shabby. wouldn't it be funny if all 716 were actually about chive and his illegal activities?
SnowAngel:	wouldn't it be even funnier if u actually talked to ME instead of googlewhacking off in the corner?
mad maddie:	ooo, u make me sound so perverted
SnowAngel:	good-bye, i'm leaving
mad maddie:	what? WHY?
SnowAngel:	cuz ur making my eyes glaze over. anyway, i've gotta clean up my room for an open house today. UGH.
mad maddie:	in that case maybe i'll go hunt down some breakfast—maybe some more of that pizza i had last night. u know, pizza hut pizza is truly amazing. it's been in our fridge for 2 weeks, but it tastes as good as ever.
SnowAngel:	did u say two weeks? *goes pale*
mad maddie:	i didn't even heat it up. mmm-mmm good! 🍕 🍕 🍕

Sat, Dec 4, 11:52 AM E.S.T.

SnowAngel:	omg, i just realized! chive IS a stoner!!!
mad maddie:	huh?
SnowAngel:	i said he was a stoner at dylan's party, and u were like, "nooooo." but he's TOTALLY a stoner boy.
SnowAngel:	u knew it all along, didn't u?
mad maddie:	well . . .
mad maddie:	he's more than that, tho. he's not JUST a stoner boy.

SnowAngel:	i'm just saying. *looks knowingly at friend*
SnowAngel:	u can't pull 1 over on me, madderoo!

Sun, Dec 5, 9:18 AM E.S.T.

SnowAngel:	mornin', sunshine. did u have fun at work last night?
SnowAngel:	zoe?
SnowAngel:	wow, it must have been REALLY good if you can't even take the time to text back yr dearest friend. either that or really bad . . .
zoegirl:	sorry, sorry, texting someone else
SnowAngel:	who?
zoegirl:	just someone
SnowAngel:	okay. WHO?
zoegirl:	it was doug, that's all. he texted me, i didn't text him.
SnowAngel:	doug texted u? why?
SnowAngel:	did he ask about me?
zoegirl:	you know, angela, it's not *always* about you.
zoegirl:	we were talking about work, that's all. about that little kid who cracks us up, graham cracker. last night graham kept presenting his cheek to me and saying, "you can kiss me if you want. little boys need lots of kisses."
SnowAngel:	aww, i love little kids. they're so pure. 😇
SnowAngel:	wanna know what i did last night? and just to give u a hint, "pure" would not be the way to describe it.
zoegirl:	that's right, you went out with maddie and chive! how'd it go?
SnowAngel:	AND meade AND brannen AND whitney.
SnowAngel:	i have to tell u, zoe, i'm feeling weird about it.
zoegirl:	how come?
SnowAngel:	i dunno. i've been trying to figure it out. i've been trying to figure out chive, mainly. maddie really likes him, u know.

zoegirl:	do you not?
SnowAngel:	no, i DO like him—at least when i'm around him. he's smart, even tho he talks so s-l-o-w-l-y. and he's funny. he was totally cracking me up last night, calling everyone "boogie." as in, "m-boogie, what's happening?" or "c'mon over here, a-boogie, and get yo-self some chips."
zoegirl:	he is pretty charming, isn't he? i remember that from dylan's party.
SnowAngel:	AND he's extremely hot
SnowAngel:	i can see why maddie's into him. i just think he holds too much power over her.
zoegirl:	like jana last year?
SnowAngel:	maybe . . . but different. chive isn't trying to use maddie, i don't think. and he DOES care about her, i can tell. he just doesn't care about her ENOUGH.
zoegirl:	maybe he doesn't care about anyone enough.
zoegirl:	you know he kissed whitney, right? but maddie was all, "it's no big deal, bodies are bodies, blah blah blah."
SnowAngel:	last night chive was giving maddie all kinds of attention—laughing at her jokes, looking at her in that lazy, bemused way of his—but he was sitting next to whitney and stroking her forearm the whole time.
zoegirl:	ick. *so* uncool. 😒
SnowAngel:	i'm sure maddie can't be too thrilled about that, but of course she won't admit it.
zoegirl:	i don't get it. there's no way i could watch the guy i like fool around with another girl.
SnowAngel:	"the guy u like"? who's the guy u like?
zoegirl:	what? nobody!
SnowAngel:	then why would u say that?
zoegirl:	why would i say what?

SnowAngel:	zoe, r u hiding something?
zoegirl:	angela, please. we're talking about chive, remember?
SnowAngel:	oh yeah
SnowAngel:	u know he's a stoner, right? well, guess what: now maddie's becoming one too.
zoegirl:	becoming a *stoner*?
zoegirl:	no way
SnowAngel:	she's tried it, tho. she really has.
zoegirl:	hold on. maddie tried *pot*?
SnowAngel:	yes, pot. 🍁 weed, ganja, doobage, gank.
zoegirl:	gank? gank is an extremely stupid word.
zoegirl:	and no, i didn't know she tried it, because of course she didn't tell me.
SnowAngel:	cuz she thinks ur a nun 👲
zoegirl:	that is so irritating. and she shouldn't be smoking pot. it kills brain cells. doesn't she know that?
SnowAngel:	i'm not even sure she liked it that much, from what she said.
zoegirl:	but i bet she pretends she does in front of chive. am i right? to protect her tough-girl image?
SnowAngel:	well . . . possibly. i was afraid they were gonna light up last night, but they didn't. brannen was like, "we're out of pot, dude. who's gonna go on a pot run?" but nobody ever did anything about it.
zoegirl:	lovely
SnowAngel:	crap, i g2g. my mom's yelling at me from downstairs—some family is here for a 2nd showing of the house.
zoegirl:	a 2nd showing? oh no!
SnowAngel:	don't worry, i have a plan. i heard the evil realtor say that the man wants to know about our neighbors, cuz his current neighbors r really loud. so as i leave, i'm gonna happen to mention the

thoroughly bitchin garage band that practices two
doors down. *snickers*

zoegirl:	what garage band?
SnowAngel:	exactly
SnowAngel:	ttfn!

Mon, Dec 6, 10:15 AM E.S.T.

mad maddie:	z-boogie! i saw u hanging out with doug at his locker, and unless i am mistaken (which i sincerely hope i am), i heard him saying something very disturbing.
zoegirl:	what are you talking about?
mad maddie:	ahem. and i quote, "u can kiss me if you want. little boys need lots of kisses." !!!
zoegirl:	oh gosh. you heard that?
mad maddie:	what kind of twisted games r u playing, zo? PLEASE tell me u don't pretend to be his mommy. PLEASE tell me u don't spank his iddle-widdle bottom.
zoegirl:	maddie, gross!!!
mad maddie:	WELL?
zoegirl:	it's an inside joke, from saturday night when we worked together. he wasn't being himself. he was just being . . . cute.
mad maddie:	"little boys need lots of kisses"?!!!
zoegirl:	please stop. you're making me blush.
mad maddie:	have u told angela yet? cuz i gotta say, if ur gonna be flirting with him in the hall, she's gonna find out.
zoegirl:	i know, i know . . . but there's so much going on with her right now. i don't want to make things more complicated. and i don't want to make her mad at me.
mad maddie:	ha—i would love it if she got mad at u. she NEVER gets mad at u.

zoegirl:	maddie, that's a terrible thing to say! why would you even say that?
mad maddie:	that's why u have to TELL her, u idiot. on every single sitcom in the world, this is how problems start. some idiot plays dumb and doesn't tell someone else what's really going on, and then there's mass confusion and mistaken assumptions and everything ends in chaos. u shld know this, zoe.
zoegirl:	i *do* know. i do. but when you're in the middle of it—in real life, not tv—it's completely different. it's harder than you think to tell the truth.
mad maddie:	not for me
zoegirl:	then you tell her!
mad maddie:	no ma'am, miss zoe. i'm having too much fun watching you squirm.
mad maddie:	but i do want u to swear to me that u'll straighten this whole mess out, mmmkay?
zoegirl:	fine. i will. i really will.
mad maddie:	when?
zoegirl:	tomorrow, i promise
mad maddie:	i'm doing this for your own good!

Tues, Dec 7, 9:09 AM E.S.T.

mad maddie:	dude! i know yr in class, but i'm bored!
zoegirl:	maddie, go away
mad maddie:	if you want me to go away, why'd you respond?
zoegirl:	because my phone's on vibrate. otherwise i wouldn't have.
mad maddie:	ooo, vibrate. is it as good as your special chair?
zoegirl:	😈
mad maddie:	have u told angela about doug?
zoegirl:	not yet
mad maddie:	u better!

Tues, Dec 7, 10:53 AM E.S.T.

mad maddie:	**how about now? have u told her by now?**
zoegirl:	stop texting me during class!
mad maddie:	**so u haven't?**
zoegirl:	ms. aiken is staring. i'm turning you off.

Tues, Dec 7, 1:48 PM E.S.T.

mad maddie:	**hi, zo. me again. do u feel like ur being spied on?**
zoegirl:	maddie, what are you doing here? this isn't your free.
mad maddie:	**peaches doesn't care. she loves me. anywayz, the media center isn't your own private idaho.**
mad maddie:	**have u told angela?**
zoegirl:	no, because i'm being stalked by a deranged lunatic who thinks it's more fun to text and make waggly eyebrows than to JUST COME OVER AND TALK TO ME.
mad maddie:	**okey-doke, i'll come over and talk to you. in a nice loud voice that everyone can hear.** 👁️👍👁️
zoegirl:	on second thought, don't. i'll tell angela as soon as i get home from school. are you satisfied? now go away. i have to finish this paper!

Tues, Dec 7, 3:45 PM E.S.T.

mad maddie:	***singsong voice* yr home from school! HAVE U TOLD HER?**
zoegirl:	you're a freak. i'm calling her right now. bye!

Tues, Dec 7, 4:12 PM E.S.T.

zoegirl:	hi, maddie. it's me.
mad maddie:	**oh really? u mean someone didn't steal yr phone? awesome!**
zoegirl:	shut up, smarty-pants.

zoegirl:	i just wanted to tell you that i called angela, just like i said i would, but i didn't tell her about doug.
mad maddie:	omg. what's your excuse this time?
zoegirl:	they sold the house, mads. her mom sold the house.
mad maddie:	WHAT?!!!
zoegirl:	they're moving as soon as finals are over!!!
mad maddie:	as soon as
mad maddie:	zoe, that's less than 2 weeks!
zoegirl:	i know
mad maddie:	i just
mad maddie:	i don't even
mad maddie:	they're seriously moving? this is real?
zoegirl:	angela could barely get the words out, she was crying so hard.
mad maddie:	holy fucking shit
mad maddie:	where r they gonna LIVE?
zoegirl:	the apartment mr. silver rented has three bedrooms, so they'll join him there. i guess that was the plan all along.
zoegirl:	what are we gonna do, maddie?
mad maddie:	i have no flipping idea
mad maddie:	but for now, we better get going.
zoegirl:	where, to angela's?
mad maddie:	where else?!

Thu, Dec 9, 9:14 PM E.S.T.

zoegirl:	hey, mads. did you read angela's FB status? it's so sad.
mad maddie:	i know. i was gonna txt her, but all those scowly faces made me think, "ooo, better back off."
zoegirl:	i had the same thought, but then i realized that right now is when she needs us the most. so i called her—and she sounded *very* depressed.

mad maddie: well, duh. she's moving 3,000 miles away.

zoegirl: it was like she wasn't even angela anymore. her voice was all pale and listless, and she kept saying, "this sucks. this just totally sucks."

mad maddie: that's how she was at lunch too

zoegirl: i tried in my nicest way to suggest that being depressed isn't gonna help anything, and she goes, "i think it's an appropriate response, zoe." like i was being stupid for trying to cheer her up.

mad maddie: we shld do something fun tomorrow night. maybe that would help.

zoegirl: yeah, sounds good. i feel bad that i can't do something with her tomorrow night *and* saturday night, but i've got to work.

mad maddie: where u'll c doug, nudge-nudge, wink-wink 😊

mad maddie: u still haven't told angela, have u?

zoegirl: it's so not the point right now. it would just make her feel worse.

mad maddie: ur playing with fire, zoe. mark my words, this is gonna come back and bite u on the ass!

Fri, Dec 10, 4:44 PM E.S.T.

mad maddie: hey, gal. since u never decided what u wanna do tonight, zoe and i decided for u. put your party hat on ... cuz we're going BOWLING!!!

SnowAngel: *lifts head from the depths of hell* bowling?

mad maddie: chop-chop! if we get there early, we can beat the rush.

SnowAngel: there's a rush to go bowling?

mad maddie: on a friday night? we're talking high drama, baby. ker-ash! she scores another strike!

SnowAngel: i haven't gone bowling since last year when i went with doug and steve and chrissy. doug and steve slipped notes into the holes in chrissy's ball and pretended they were from a mystery admirer, remember?

SnowAngel: that was so fun. but nothing will ever be fun again. 🙁

mad maddie: YES IT WILL. oh, and be sure to wear crappy shoes. don't ask—just do it.

SnowAngel: pardon me, but i don't own any crappy shoes

SnowAngel: hey, do u think doug would come with us if we called him? maybe that's what i need to perk me up, a dose of doug-love.

mad maddie: er . . . no doug. this is a girls' night, full of bonding and wacky hijinks.

SnowAngel: right, right

SnowAngel: but i have been thinking . . . maybe, before i leave, i'll give doug something to remember me by. *wink, wink* he's certainly waited for it long enough.

mad maddie: angela, no

SnowAngel: why? it would be the thrill of his life.

mad maddie: bad idea. trust me.

SnowAngel: yeah, i guess it wouldn't be fair. *sigh*

mad maddie: that's right. leave the poor guy alone.

SnowAngel: altho who said love was fair? and long-distance relationships CAN work, u know . . .

mad maddie: FORGET ABOUT DOUG

mad maddie: now go dig thru your closet and find your rattiest sneaks. i'm coming to pick u up!

Sat, Dec 11, 10:00 AM E.S.T.

SnowAngel: morning, zo

zoegirl: morning, angela. are you wearing your super-duper very own pair of official bowling shoes? 😀

SnowAngel: at ten in the morning? i'm in my bunny slippers, sweetheart. 🐰

SnowAngel: but yeah, i've got them right here beside me. *pats hideous bowling shoes lovingly* i didn't think we were gonna have fun . . . but we did, didn't we?

zoegirl: especially when you threw your ball into that truck driver's lane. (snicker, snicker)

SnowAngel: he could have been MUCH more understanding. it's not like i meant to.

zoegirl: and then you knocked over his beer when you went to reclaim it, ya big klutz.

zoegirl: poor guy!

SnowAngel: poor me! i'm under a lot of stress, zoe. i'm leaving in 6 days!!!

zoegirl: what i don't get is why you just didn't tell the truck driver guy that you spilled his beer, instead of leaving it glopped on the floor in a puddle. if you'd cleaned it up right then, nothing else would have happened.

SnowAngel: i didn't tell him cuz i didn't want him yelling at me again. duh!

zoegirl: and that strategy sure worked

SnowAngel: it's not MY fault. who knew beer was so sticky?

zoegirl: and who knew our truck driver friend would attempt his patented foot-slide approach right after stepping smack into it?

SnowAngel: i think he needs to alter his diet. a slimmer man wouldn't have fallen so hard.

zoegirl: too many cheese fries

SnowAngel: at least it caused a distraction as we stole our shoes. frankly, zo, i'm still surprised you went along with it.

zoegirl: the operative word is "trade," angela. we gave them a more than fair trade.

SnowAngel: in your case, maybe. i gave them a pair of chrissy's old tap shoes from when she used to take lessons.

zoegirl:	um, angela? why did u just insert a pirate smiley?
SnowAngel:	i dunno. cuz it's cute?
zoegirl:	you're such a goof
zoegirl:	so what are you doing for the rest of the day?
SnowAngel:	i'm PACKING. how's that for a mood kill?
zoegirl:	oh, angela
SnowAngel:	come keep me company, please-please-pleasy-please?
zoegirl:	sure, only i have to go to work at 5:00. and at some point, i should probably study for finals.
SnowAngel:	finals. *vomit*
SnowAngel:	there is no way i can be expected to study when my whole life is being ripped apart.
zoegirl:	maybe we can study together after i help u pack.
SnowAngel:	just come over. i don't care what we do, as long as i'm not alone!

Sun, Dec 12, 3:30 PM E.S.T.

mad maddie:	hey, a-boogie
SnowAngel:	hey, m-boogie
SnowAngel:	how long r u gonna stay on this "boogie" kick?
mad maddie:	for-boogie-ever. got a problem wid dat?
SnowAngel:	ur a freak
SnowAngel:	so wazzup?
mad maddie:	nothing, just procrastinating. i SHLD be studying, but let's just say i'm not.
mad maddie:	wanna go get krispy kremes?
SnowAngel:	heck yeah!
mad maddie:	boogie-licious!

Mon, Dec 13, 5:23 PM E.S.T.

zoegirl:	hey, angela. guess what happened in biology today?
SnowAngel:	what?
zoegirl:	mr. mack tripped on the smart-board cable, and

	he went down hard. he hit his head on his desk and ended up with a gash from his eyebrow to his hairline. blood. everywhere. it was crazy.
SnowAngel:	poor mr. mack!
zoegirl:	he's okay. head wounds bleed a lot even when they're pretty minor, he said. but for the rest of the period (after taping a paper towel bandage to his head with masking tape), he pretended to have amnesia. every time someone asked a question about our exam, he'd be like, "what's your name again?"
SnowAngel:	that's gonna be me at my stupid new school. i won't know a single person's name except stupid glendy.
SnowAngel:	i wish I'D get clonked on my head—at least then i'd be put out of my misery.
zoegirl:	angela!
zoegirl:	i told you about mr. mack to cheer you up, not make you more depressed!
SnowAngel:	oh
SnowAngel:	well . . . ha
zoegirl:	that wasn't very convincing
SnowAngel:	HAHAHAHAHA
SnowAngel:	was that better?
zoegirl:	er, thanks for trying
SnowAngel:	yeah, u too

Tues, Dec 14, 4:09 PM E.S.T.

zoegirl:	i can't believe finals start tomorrow—help!
SnowAngel:	which means only 3 more days until . . . never mind.
zoegirl:	i know
zoegirl:	that's all i can think about, even though i've *got* to focus on studying.

SnowAngel:	there's no way i'm getting any studying done. i've just accepted it.
SnowAngel:	sorry i'm typing so slow, btw. i cut my thumb on the packing tape dispenser, and the band-aid's making things tricky.
zoegirl:	that's okay
SnowAngel:	ms. higgins gave us the question for our take-home essay. wanna hear it?
zoegirl:	sure
SnowAngel:	it's awful. it's like she WANTS to torture me, as if that was her evil plan. "using any three works of literature from this semester, discuss the following quote: 'home is where the heart is.' support your position with examples."
zoegirl:	oh man
SnowAngel:	i know
SnowAngel:	hey zo . . . do u ever just feel sad for no reason?
zoegirl:	i do, yeah.
SnowAngel:	me too
SnowAngel:	*sigh*
SnowAngel:	guess my bracelet didn't work, huh?
zoegirl:	what bracelet?
zoegirl:	oh, your "believe" bracelet
SnowAngel:	i kept thinking that maybe this was all a joke, that maybe it would all go away. i've been closing my eyes and rubbing the "believe" part, as if my wish might actually come true. isn't that stupid?
zoegirl:	not stupid at all. i wish it *would* come true.
SnowAngel:	oh well
zoegirl:	i don't want u to move, angela.
SnowAngel:	me neither 😔

Wed, Dec 15, 6:59 PM E.S.T.

| zoegirl: | three finals down, two to go! |

SnowAngel:

zoegirl: i hear you. it's like, yay that we're over half done, but the pressure's still on.

zoegirl: i've been mowing my way through my mongo bag of snack-size snickers, which i convinced my mom i have to have in order to study. i don't know how it started, but now every year at exam time she stocks up on snickers and coke.

SnowAngel: while my mom, on the other hand, asks questions like, "have u cleaned out your closet yet? the moving truck will be here tomorrow afternoon, u know."

zoegirl: do you have to be there for that? because maddie and i want to take you out, since it's your . . . you know.

SnowAngel: since it's my last night in atlanta?

zoegirl: yeah. we want to spend every minute we can with you.

SnowAngel: at least someone does.

SnowAngel: other than you two, do you know that hardly ANYONE has acted the slightest bit devastated that i'm moving? they act sad for like a second, and then they're all, "omg, have u finished your take-home yet? have u memorized the formulas for chemistry?"

zoegirl: people just don't know how to handle it, angela. everyone hates it that you're leaving.

SnowAngel: it's like when u get a haircut and u go to school all self-conscious and waiting for ppl to comment on it, and then no one notices at all. that's what it's gonna be like when i'm gone.

zoegirl: not for us, angela

zoegirl: you will leave a hole the size of france.

SnowAngel: me again. my mom says it's fine if i go out with u guys tomorrow night. she said she already assumed that's what i'd be doing.

zoegirl: good!

SnowAngel: i can stay out as late as i want, which i guess is nice of her.

SnowAngel: but it's not enough.

zoegirl: no, it's not.

SnowAngel: ☹

mad maddie: we're done!

zoegirl: yay!!!

mad maddie: do u have the candles & food & quilt?

zoegirl: i do. do you have the pictures?

mad maddie: yes ma'am, in my backpack.

zoegirl: she's going to cry, you know. we all are.

mad maddie: NO WE'RE NOT. c ya at collier park!

mad maddie: woot! woot!

SnowAngel: oh god, i JUST turned my paper in. i'm the last person left in the room.

mad maddie: meet me at back parking lot!

SnowAngel: YEAH!!!

zoegirl: omigosh, maddie. ☹

mad maddie: i know

zoegirl: she's *gone*. she's really gone.

mad maddie: do u have to say it like that?

zoegirl: but it's the truth. as of exactly one hour ago, angela doesn't live here anymore.

mad maddie:	i don't know how to
mad maddie:	i feel so
zoegirl:	wrong?
mad maddie:	yeah
mad maddie:	w/o her, everything feels wrong

Sat, Dec 18, 10:21 PM P.S.T.

SnowAngel:	well, here i am in crudballs california. i cldn't txt before now cuz stupid me cldn't find stupid charger and . . . yeah.
SnowAngel:	r u there, zo?
SnowAngel:	ohhhhh. it's, what, after midnight there? so yr probably in bed, while here i am, not even in the same TIME ZONE as u anymore!
SnowAngel:	i hate this so much, zo.
SnowAngel:	and guess what? my bracelet broke. i snagged it on the corner of the ticket counter at the airport, and the leather snapped and the silver part flew off and i couldn't find it anywhere and now it's ruined, just like my whole entire life.
SnowAngel:	so just in case u were wondering, let me enlighten u:
SnowAngel:	i
SnowAngel:	don't
SnowAngel:	b
SnowAngel:	lieve

Sat, Dec 18, 10:33 PM P.S.T.

SnowAngel:	maddie?
SnowAngel:	oh, ma-a-a-a-ddie!
SnowAngel:	great, even UR asleep.
SnowAngel:	i lost my "believe" bracelet. ask zoe, she'll tell u what happened.
SnowAngel:	i want it back, mads.
SnowAngel:	i want my life back.

Sun, Dec 19, 2:11 PM E.S.T.

zoegirl: hey, mads. i talked to angela this morning. she's incredibly sad, big surprise.

mad maddie: fill me in

zoegirl: she hates her apartment, for one thing. and she hates el cerrito.

zoegirl: it's so weird imagining her in a brand-new place. i keep telling myself it's true, but it doesn't *feel* true.

mad maddie: i know what u mean. i drove by her house yesterday, even tho i know i shouldn't have. it looked so . . . empty.

zoegirl: i bet

zoegirl: she told me again how much she loved our moonlight picnic, though. and the photo album. she said looking at it is the only thing keeping her sane.

mad maddie: that was a good time 👍

zoegirl: i don't know if i'd say it was a "good" time, but i know what you mean.

zoegirl: i told you we'd be sobbing, though. even u, miss i'm-so-tough-maddie. sometimes i think you're the biggest softie of us all.

mad maddie: oh please

zoegirl: in a good way!

mad maddie: ok, well, enough of this drama, cuz i'm off to meet chive. wanna come?

zoegirl: no thanks. i guess i feel more like being alone.

mad maddie: u deal with things your way, i'll deal with them mine.

mad maddie: laters!

SnowAngel: maddie maddie maddie! hey, maddie!

mad maddie: **a-boogie! wassup?**

SnowAngel: FINALLY! omg, i've been trying to reach u forever!

SnowAngel: u haven't been avoiding me, have u?

mad maddie: **WHAT?**

SnowAngel: u haven't texted me, and u haven't returned my calls. i thought maybe u were sick of me cuz i'm such a downer all the time

mad maddie: **don't be crazy—i've just been busy.**

mad maddie: **so what's new in el cerrito?**

SnowAngel: my pillow got lost in the move. isn't that just dandy? the movers arrived this morning, and my pillow wasn't in the truck!

mad maddie: **that high-tech squishy pillow from the sleep store?**

SnowAngel: it's the only good pillow i've ever had in my life. now i have to use this crap pillow that mom ran out and bought me at some crap store, and it's one more thing in my life that utterly sucks. it's thoroughly and wrongly fluffy, and i'm never gonna be able to sleep again, i just know it. i tried it out on my bed, and i can hear my pulse thru it!

mad maddie: **wtf?**

SnowAngel: it presses on my neck wrong. it jams up against my carotid artery or whatever the hell it's called, and it makes my pulse ring in my brain. thump! thump! thump! that's all i can hear!

mad maddie: **ur losing it, lady**

mad maddie: **repeat after me, "it is good to have a heartbeat."**

SnowAngel: not if u have to HEAR it all the time. i HATE hearing my pulse!

mad maddie: **so sleep on your back!**

SnowAngel: i can't sleep on my back. i can only sleep on my side.

SnowAngel:	r u purposefully trying to upset me?
mad maddie:	er, i don't wanna name names, but someone is freaking . . .
SnowAngel:	*folds arms over chest* zoe would understand.
mad maddie:	one sec, something just came on tv that i wanna watch
SnowAngel:	ur watching tv while i pour my heart out? tv's more important than ME?
SnowAngel:	maddie?
SnowAngel:	maddie!!!
mad maddie:	good god, i just saw THE most horrifying newsclip. u can catch on fire at the gas station if u touch the gas pump with too much static electricity—did u know that? they showed this girl putting the nozzle in her gas tank thingie, and then she got back in her car while it was pumping. she was wearing a sweater, and apparently it rubbed against the seat and got her all staticky. she went back to grab the pump . . . and KAPOW! she burst into flames!
SnowAngel:	is this supposed to cheer me up? "sorry u lost your pillow, but at least u avoided self-immolation"?
mad maddie:	sweater girl survived, but the news guy said that other people have actually died.
mad maddie:	damn. 🔥 🔥 🔥
mad maddie:	u be careful, u hear?
SnowAngel:	why do i need to be careful? i don't even have a car. i wanted a car, but instead i got to move to california, remember?
mad maddie:	well, when and if u DO get a car, don't get back in it while ur in the middle of pumping gas. and touch the side of the car before u grab the gas pump again. that way the static electricity will flow out of u.

SnowAngel: thanks for the tip *regards friend sourly*

SnowAngel: do u have anything else to say?

mad maddie: umm . . . don't wear fluffy sweaters when u go to the gas station?

SnowAngel: gbye, maddie!!!

Tues, Dec 21, 10:30 AM E.S.T.

zoegirl: hey, angela. is it too early for me to be texting? i can never remember the time difference.

zoegirl: angela?

zoegirl: okay, guess that's a yes. but i just wanted to tell u that i mailed you a present today—snail mail! old-school!—so you should get it soon, hopefully by christmas eve.

zoegirl: i love you, angela! text me!!! 🩶

Wed, Dec 22, 4:43 PM P.S.T.

SnowAngel: hey, zo. sorry i missed u yesterday—i was sleeping in. it's like all i do is sleep these days, and i'm STILL tired.

zoegirl: that's okay. i would have called u back last night, but i picked up a shift at Kidding Around.

SnowAngel: was doug there?

zoegirl: he was, yeah

SnowAngel: i had a dream about him, isn't that weird? it was actually about BOTH of u. u had dyed your hair blond to impress him.

SnowAngel: which leads me to ask: u haven't started liking him, have u?

zoegirl: *angela*

SnowAngel: i'm sorry, i'm sorry *grimaces*

SnowAngel: why am i so needy? is it just cuz i'm stuck 3,000 miles away from u guys, and i feel like everything's being torn apart?

zoegirl: you're being silly. nothing's being torn apart.

SnowAngel:	i hope not
SnowAngel:	so have i mentioned that life sucks? i told mom AGAIN that i wanna move back to atlanta and live with my aunt sadie, but she was like, "u haven't given california a chance. ur gonna love it, u'll see."
zoegirl:	maybe you will. i can see you as a california girl, all tan and beautiful. hey—maybe you'll learn to surf!
SnowAngel:	???
SnowAngel:	seriously?
zoegirl:	sorry. just trying to be optimistic.
SnowAngel:	u know what i miss that i didn't even realize i was gonna miss? magnolia trees. i never knew how much i loved them until i moved here.
SnowAngel:	it is a barren wasteland of sadness. that is where i live now. *single tear*
zoegirl:	i love magnolia trees too
SnowAngel:	plus i HATE our apartment. i still have boxes all over my room. isn't that depressing? it's like i can't bear to make myself unpack.
zoegirl:	sorry you hate it, but describe it anyway so i can see you in my mind.
SnowAngel:	it's tiny. it's beige. there's wallpaper in my room with stupid rosebuds on it, and i can hear traffic thru my window. mom says rentals here r super-expensive and we're lucky dad found a three-bedroom place, but i disagree.
zoegirl:	have you met anybody else in the apartment complex?
SnowAngel:	no, and i don't want to. the family below us has a kid, but she's five. she speaks korean.
zoegirl:	she's five years old and she speaks korean? impressive.

SnowAngel:	no, i meant she speaks korean cuz she IS korean.
zoegirl:	oh
zoegirl:	well . . .
SnowAngel:	yes, zoe? if u can put a positive spin on my sucky life, then believe me, i wanna hear it.
zoegirl:	um . . . at least it's almost christmas? 🎄
SnowAngel:	at least it's almost christmas. *sigh*

Thu, Dec 23, 6:02 PM E.S.T.

mad maddie:	dude! chive gave me a nickel bag of pot to celebrate the birth of christ. isn't that righteous?
SnowAngel:	what a guy
SnowAngel:	but don't u think that's sacrilegious?
mad maddie:	i gave him a cool marble pipe i bought at the head store in little five points. oh, and i made him a fantastic playlist that for the record was way more complicated to make than it shld have been. why does iTunes make it so hard to gift playlists instead of individual songs???
mad maddie:	we're gonna make use of it all tomorrow night— if i can escape the fam.
SnowAngel:	maddie, tomorrow's christmas eve. u can't smoke pot on christmas eve!
mad maddie:	why not? the three wise men followed a frickin STAR all the way to Bethlehem. ur telling me they weren't under the influence of a certain illegal substance?
SnowAngel:	tsk, tsk
SnowAngel:	i think u need to start going to church with zoe, young lady!
mad maddie:	yeah, that'll happen
SnowAngel:	does this mean u've learned how to smoke it in a way that doesn't hurt?

mad maddie: i wouldn't say that, exactly. that's why i bought the pipe—it's supposed to make it a smoother ride. but anything'll get better the more u do it, right?

SnowAngel: uh, i guess

mad maddie: it's bound to

mad maddie: btw, chive says u can score some really good pot in california, so keep your eye out for me. ͡° ͡°

SnowAngel: yeah, that's what i need, to get busted for drugs on top of everything else.

mad maddie: whine, whine, whine. nobody actually gets busted for buying pot. you only get hassled if ur a big-time cocaine dealer or something.

SnowAngel: omg, u haven't tried COCAINE, have u?

mad maddie: angela, chill. pot is my drug of choice, thank u very much.

mad maddie: so check it out: i bought your christmas present, and you are going to LOVE it. wanna know what it is?

SnowAngel: a totally rockin marble pipe?

mad maddie: haha. no, microwavable slippers.

SnowAngel: aw, maddie, thanks! 😊

SnowAngel: and what, exactly, will i do with these microwavable slippers?

mad maddie: microwave them, of course! the bottoms have these pouches of rice or beans or something in them, and when u microwave them, they get roasty-toasty. they're for cold feet, u goof.

SnowAngel: ooo, they sound wonderful. it gets really chilly here at night, like unbelievably so. and our apartment is always freezing.

mad maddie: i'll put them in the mail tomorrow—that is, unless i don't. but i'll mail them soon, i promise.

SnowAngel: no rush. i haven't even picked out anything for u or zoe.

mad maddie:	so what's up with zoe these days? i haven't seen her all vacation.
SnowAngel:	why not?
mad maddie:	dunno, just haven't. it's not for any BAD reason.
SnowAngel:	well, she's fine as far as i know. she's working a lot, it sounds like.
SnowAngel:	with doug
mad maddie:	why do u say it like that, "with doug"?
SnowAngel:	i dunno. i can't get him out of my mind.
SnowAngel:	u don't think there's anything going on between him and zoe, do u?
mad maddie:	did zoe say there was?
SnowAngel:	no, of course not. i'm just being silly.
mad maddie:	listen, i've g2g. i've gotta stash my pot somewhere so the moms won't find it. i'm thinking the box from the set of "thank u" notes u gave me when we were thirteen. perfect, yeah?
SnowAngel:	gee, i'm touched
mad maddie:	why did u give those to me, anyway? i mean, c'mon. thank u notes?
SnowAngel:	i don't know, cuz they were cute. they were decorated with strawberries.
SnowAngel:	do you have any left?
mad maddie:	i have every single one of them left, and u know why? cuz they're cute and they're decorated with strawberries, fool. 😊
mad maddie:	but the box makes a PERFECT hiding spot for my pot.
SnowAngel:	cute little strawberries, cute little baggie of pot . . .
mad maddie:	organic! yeah!

Fri, Dec 24, 3:33 PM P.S.T.

SnowAngel:	zoe, the pressie u sent me came today! thank u sooooo much!!!

zoegirl:	oh, angela, you are sooooo welcome!
zoegirl:	u like?
SnowAngel:	it's beautiful. SHE'S beautiful, i shld say. i put her on my bedside table so i can see her first thing when i wake up. she's the only decoration in my entire room.
zoegirl:	she's the angel of hope, which you probably already know if you looked at the sticker on the bottom. i know it's dorky, but i thought it could be kind of like your "believe" bracelet, although it's not something to wear.
SnowAngel:	aww, zoe, ur so sweet
zoegirl:	i looked for another "believe" bracelet, by the way. i went to the store where u got it, but i couldn't find anything like it.
SnowAngel:	cuz it was the only 1. ever.
SnowAngel:	but THANK U for my angel. 😇 i love her, love her, love her. *sends big smoochie kisses to dear friend zoe*
zoegirl:	plus, the whole "angel" thing, with you being our SnowAngel and all.
SnowAngel:	she's great, and god knows i need all the angels i can get.
zoegirl:	i almost got one for myself, but then i thought, "no, it should just be something special for angela."
SnowAngel:	we can share her, how bout that?
zoegirl:	yay!
SnowAngel:	so whenever u think of doing something bad, u can remember that she's watching over u from california, and u can change your erring ways? 😇
zoegirl:	haha
zoegirl:	can u believe it's christmas eve?
SnowAngel:	no, i thoroughly cannot. i haven't done ANY shopping, which for my family is just too damn bad. but for u and maddie, i feel terrible.

zoegirl:	please don't, you've got enough to worry about. seriously, we don't care in the slightest.
SnowAngel:	but i do
SnowAngel:	hey, i know! i'll mail ME back to atlanta for your present!
zoegirl:	yeah!!!
SnowAngel:	how much does a plane ticket cost, u think? i've got $250 in savings. is that enough?
zoegirl:	i don't know. i bet it's a little more than that. but maybe?
zoegirl:	are you really thinking about coming?
SnowAngel:	i doubt my parents would let me. 😈
SnowAngel:	but if it's my money, then i can do what i want, right?
zoegirl:	er . . .
SnowAngel:	i'm gonna go check plane fares.
SnowAngel:	don't worry, i'm not REALLY gonna take off w/o my parents' permission, but it would be good info to have in the back of my brain—just in case.
zoegirl:	just in case what?
SnowAngel:	what's that one website called? canoe-something-or-other?
SnowAngel:	i'll figure it out. bye!

Sat, Dec 25, 1:01 PM P.S.T.

SnowAngel:	merry christmas, zoe!!! 😄 🎄 😄
zoegirl:	merry christmas! you seem happy. are you happy?
SnowAngel:	i am—or at least this is the happiest i've been since we moved. my mom made cinnamon rolls for breakfast, and our tree looks so beautiful, even tho it's not nearly as big as the one we had last year. and tomorrow we're gonna drive into the city for the after-christmas sales.

zoegirl:	cool
zoegirl:	when you say "the city," do you mean san francisco?
SnowAngel:	yeah, ppl here just call it the city. anyway, we're gonna get a hotel room and stay for a couple of nights, do some of the touristy stuff. so i might be less text-y for a while since my parents hate it when i use my phone when we're supposed to be having QUALITY FAMILY TIME.
zoegirl:	same here, actually. we're going to my grandmom's house tomorrow. we won't be back till wednesday.
SnowAngel:	and maddie's already left for her aunt and uncle's. she was planning on taking her stash with her, did she tell u?
zoegirl:	her "stash"?
zoegirl:	of what?
SnowAngel:	of pot. that's what chive gave her for christmas.
zoegirl:	is she actually gonna *smoke* it?
zoegirl:	oh man, angela. i am not liking this "maddie + pot" combo. i think it's a bad idea. and i think it's a really bad idea that she'd even consider getting high with her family around.
SnowAngel:	she said it's a coping mechanism based on years of family tradition, just that her relatives use alcohol instead of pot. and then she was like, "not that i have anything against alcohol, don't get me wrong . . ."
zoegirl:	you should tell her how dumb she's being
SnowAngel:	what do u mean, "i" should? ur the one who's still in town with her!
zoegirl:	yeah, but *you're* the one she talks to about this stuff. she never brings it up with me.
SnowAngel:	cuz she knows u'd scold her

zoegirl: i bet she's doing it to impress chive, so that when she gets back in town, she can be like, "hey, i smoked the stash u gave me."

SnowAngel: no, here's what she'd say: "duuuuude. good times, buddy. good times."

zoegirl: i don't like it. it worries me.

SnowAngel: it worries me too

SnowAngel: so . . .

zoegirl: so . . . ?

SnowAngel: so we'll tell her, ok?

SnowAngel: for real, w/o holding back

zoegirl: yeah, okay

Thu, Dec 30, 11:33 AM P.S.T.

SnowAngel: madigan, long time no talk! how was your trip?

mad maddie: hey, a. one sec while i finish this email . . .

mad maddie: ok, i'm back. i was responding to a delta airlines customer service dude. alas, still no word on your bracelet.

SnowAngel: u emailed delta about my bracelet? aw, mads!!!!

mad maddie: he checked their claim area, but no "believe" thingie.

SnowAngel: damn

SnowAngel: but that was incredibly sweet of u to try

mad maddie: yeah, i know

SnowAngel: so did u have a good time with your relatives?

mad maddie: the usual. the cousins breathed garlic in my face, the dads got ripped and made fart jokes.

mad maddie: but i wanna hear about U! how was the city?!!

SnowAngel: oh, maddie, it was AWESOME. the only un-awesome thing was that u and zoe weren't there, cuz u guys would have loved it. there's so much going on— omg, it's so different from atlanta. OR el cerrito, which doesn't even compare.

SnowAngel: there was this street musician on the sidewalk who totally made me think of u. he played the guitar, and he had a harmonica on a frame by his mouth, and he had cymbals strapped to his knees. i was like, "maddie would love this guy."

mad maddie: sounds cool. atlanta is pretty boring when it comes to street life.

SnowAngel: san francisco is definitely not boring. there are ppl EVERYWHERE. vendors selling jewelry, hot dog stands, guys with knockoff watches. oh, and we went to chinatown, which was sooooo fun. u go thru this archway thing, and it's like stepping into a different world. everyone was chinese—der—and they had these cute little shops with satin slippers and sparkly barrettes. touristy stuff too, like miniature trolley cars and I ♥ SAN FRANCISCO shirts.

mad maddie: did ya get me 1? did ya, did ya?

SnowAngel: sorry, no tacky souvenir shirt

mad maddie: damn. chive loves that campy stuff.

SnowAngel: i got u something better. i got u lots of stuff, actually—u and zoe both. from chinatown i got u guys candy, like Hello Kitty suckers and gum in weird flavors like cantaloupe and blueberry. and from the ferry building, which is this place down on the waterfront, i got u both boxes of the most awesome chocolates in the world, called Scharffen Berger chocolates. i got u a mix-and-match assortment with infusions of lavender and chile—which sounds gross, but it's not—and i got zoe a box of these super-thin pear slices dipped in dark chocolate. i hope u guys like them.

mad maddie: we will, i'm sure. thanks, a.

SnowAngel: and b-t-dubs, i LOVE my slippers. i've got them on right now.

mad maddie: angela. u do realize that it takes longer to spell out "b-t-dubs" than to just type "by the way," don't you?

SnowAngel: *blinks like a lizard* *like an expressionless lizard*

mad maddie: back to yr slippers. did u microwave them?

SnowAngel: i did. chrissy was like, "ew, what's that smell? it smells like burnt straw!"

mad maddie: hey now—the guy said they were supposed to smell good!

SnowAngel: i like the smell, it's just chrissy who doesn't. anyway it doesn't matter, cuz they feel so lovely and warm. 😍

mad maddie: i'm glad u like them. and i'm glad ur doing better in the land of california.

mad maddie: u are doing better, right?

SnowAngel: i dunno. a LITTLE, i guess.

mad maddie: take it and run with it, girl. u deserve it.

SnowAngel: except school starts on tuesday. that's five days away!

mad maddie: nyah, nyah! u have to start a day earlier than we do!

SnowAngel: i just hope all the girls aren't like glendy. i have to spend tomorrow night with her, cuz mr. boss invited our whole family over for new year's eve, and of course my dad said yes.

SnowAngel: can u imagine a worse way to ring in the new year? i begged my dad to let me stay home, but he refused.

mad maddie: bastard

SnowAngel: what about u? what r u gonna do for new year's?

mad maddie: i'm hanging with my man chive, and probably meade and brannen and whitney. we're going to a concert at the omni. it's a battle of the bands.

SnowAngel: huh. r whitney and chive still an item?

mad maddie: do u know how much he would hate it if he heard u call them that? an "item"?

SnowAngel: so r they?

mad maddie: i guess, altho they can't be THAT serious, cuz sometimes chive and i still fool around. like yesterday we were on a beer run, and at a stoplight he just leaned over and kissed me out of the blue. a LONG kiss.

SnowAngel: and u let him?

mad maddie: what do u mean "let" him?

mad maddie: whitney may be his girlfriend, but that's just cuz . . . i dunno. cuz she's pretty. cuz she does the girl thing and pouts when he doesn't call her. but i'm the one he talks to about music and life and shit. we've got, like, a connection.

SnowAngel: hmmm

SnowAngel: but then—don't be mad—why does he make u hide it?

mad maddie: give me a break. we're not into rules, angela. the world is bigger than that.

SnowAngel: oh

mad maddie: what does that mean?

SnowAngel: nothing!

mad maddie: yes it does. u said it like u don't believe it, i can tell.

SnowAngel: did u smoke the bag of pot he gave u?

mad maddie: as a matter of fact i did. do u have a problem with that too?

mad maddie: it's just POT, angela. nobody's gonna get hurt from a little pot.

SnowAngel: if u say so

SnowAngel: just . . . be careful, all right?

mad maddie: i'm having fun, angela. be happy for me.

SnowAngel: ok, ok

mad maddie: good luck tomorrow night with glendy. call and tell me how it goes!

Fri, Dec 31, 5:30 PM E.S.T.

zoegirl: helloooo! i can't chat for long—i've got to get ready for tonight—but i wanted to talk to u one last time before the new year. is that dorky or what? i'm turning into my grandmom. every year, on the night before my bday, she calls and says, "i just wanted to talk to u one last time while you're __, honey."

SnowAngel: awww

SnowAngel: what r u getting ready for? do u have big new year's eve plans?

zoegirl: oh

zoegirl: um, not really, just a party

SnowAngel: a party? with who?

zoegirl: actually, it's not a party, it's more like people are just going to hang out from work.

zoegirl: it's no big deal

SnowAngel: will doug be there?

zoegirl: huh, i don't know

zoegirl: but i wish i was doing something with *you* instead. you and maddie, that is. like last year when we made chocolate fondue and maddie fondued a tomato. remember?

SnowAngel: u could still do something with her even tho i'm not there.

SnowAngel: why aren't u?

zoegirl: cuz we both have plans already, i guess

SnowAngel: that's lame. have u seen her at all this whole vacation?

zoegirl: well, we've both been out of town

SnowAngel: i talked to her about chive.

zoegirl:	you did? what did she say?
SnowAngel:	she got defensive, and then i felt bad for bringing it up. and then . . . i dunno. i decided to let it go.
zoegirl:	angela!
SnowAngel:	i don't wanna spend my time with her arguing— i get so little time with her as it is.
SnowAngel:	anyway, it's her life. she knows what she's doing.
zoegirl:	does she?
SnowAngel:	as much as any of us, i guess

Sat, Jan 1, 11:34 AM E.S.T.

zoegirl:	mads! happy new year!
mad maddie:	oof, if u say so
mad maddie:	can u txt me later? i'm kinda hurting here.
zoegirl:	hurting how? are you hungover?
mad maddie:	maybe just a tad
zoegirl:	just give me a second. it's important.
mad maddie:	*groans* wassup?
zoegirl:	i have something to tell you, that's all. it's about . . .
mad maddie:	yessss?
zoegirl:	hold on, first let me ask you something. things aren't weird between us, are they?
mad maddie:	huh?
zoegirl:	angela thinks it's strange that we haven't seen each other much over vacation. but that's just because we've been busy, right?
mad maddie:	duh. why else?
zoegirl:	no other reason at all. i just wanted to make sure.
mad maddie:	so what's going on that u need to talk about?
zoegirl:	aaargh. it's about doug. we kind of . . . hung out together last night.
mad maddie:	oh yeah? did u go to a new year's eve party?

zoegirl:	no, it was just the two of us.
mad maddie:	**as in a DATE?**
mad maddie:	**does angela know???**
zoegirl:	er . . . that's part of the problem.
mad maddie:	**yeah, i'll say. angela's gonna think u purposely waited till she was gone, and then BAM! u stole her man.**
zoegirl:	he's not "her man." sheesh!
mad maddie:	**well, is he YOUR man?**
zoegirl:	that's the other part of the problem. because i don't know, maddie. i just don't know!
mad maddie:	**explain**
zoegirl:	we went to dinner at La Fonda, and that was great. i love their guacamole. and then neither of us wanted to go home, so we went and hung out in the basement of trinity church. doug's an acolyte, so he's got the key to the youth group lounge.
mad maddie:	**oh god, zoe. again?**
zoegirl:	what do u mean, again?
mad maddie:	**this doesn't ring any bells for u? any CHURCH bells, per chance?**
zoegirl:	what are you talking about?
mad maddie:	**oh, nothing. definitely not a certain holy-roller teacher of yore . . .**
zoegirl:	do u wanna hear my story or not?
mad maddie:	**by all means, pray continue**
zoegirl:	we were sitting there talking, and it was chilly, so doug told me to come sit on the couch with him because it would be warmer. so i did, and . . . we kissed.
mad maddie:	**holy cow** 🐮
zoegirl:	that's not all. we *kept* kissing . . . and kissing and kissing and kissing. and it's not like i was swept away or anything, but at the same time i

didn't stop him, you know? i didn't want to hurt
his feelings.

mad maddie: u didn't wanna hurt his feelings? u did NOT just
say that, zoe.

zoegirl: anyway, we somehow ended up with both our
shirts practically off, but not completely. they
were just pushed up really high.

zoegirl: actually, i was wearing a sweatshirt—and i wasn't
wearing a bra underneath. it was thick enough
that i didn't need to! i didn't *expect* anyone to
find out!

mad maddie: whoa, zoe! u hussy!

zoegirl: i know! i'm sure he was pretty startled. but i
didn't *plan* it that way—it just happened!

mad maddie: and in the church basement, no less. what is it
with u and jesus? does he, like, turn u on?

zoegirl: can we let go of that, please? i knew you would
have to say that, and now you have, so that's over.

mad maddie: first mr. h, now doug . . . u give religion a whole
new meaning. "hussies for christ"!

zoegirl: what if doug *does* think i'm a hussy? what if
he woke up this morning and was like, "there's
something wrong with her"?

zoegirl: we did more last night than i've ever done with
anyone. what if he looks down on me now?

mad maddie: zoe, u r so insane i can hardly stand it. i'm sure
he went home with a stiffie, while visions of zoe
danced in his head.

zoegirl: i just wish i didn't feel guilty. why do i feel
guilty?!

mad maddie: i have nooooo idea. all u did is fool around.

mad maddie: ooo, do u think u made his scrotum tighten?

zoegirl: *what*?

mad maddie: chive's been reading james joyce, and apparently

	there's something in one of the books about some guy's scrotum tightening. it cracked me up.
zoegirl:	okay, please do not talk about that particular part of the body in reference to doug ever again, all right?
mad maddie:	doug has a scrotum, doug has a scrotum!
zoegirl:	i mean it, maddie
mad maddie:	cuz u think it's DIRTY? cuz u think it's NASTY?
mad maddie:	zoe, u need to learn how to relax if ur gonna have a boyfriend.
zoegirl:	i don't think any of those things. i just think that not everything is a joke, and that fooling around should count for something. it shouldn't be a free-for-all.
zoegirl:	maybe that's something *you* need to learn if *you're* ever going to have a boyfriend.
zoegirl:	maddie? you still there?
mad maddie:	nothing like a cold dose of reality from one of your best friends, eh, zo?
zoegirl:	maddie . . .
mad maddie:	no need to hold back, u know. just tell me how u really feel.
zoegirl:	look, u started it.
zoegirl:	but i didn't tell u about doug so that you and i could get into a fight. i told you because of *angela*. what am i supposed to do about angela?
mad maddie:	two words, zoe, and i've said 'em before: TELL HER, U IDIOT.
zoegirl:	that's four words
mad maddie:	i'm giving u the bird, just so u know
zoegirl:	ack—she's calling me right now!! i'm not ready to talk to her, so i'm going to turn my phone off and hide it. bye!

SnowAngel: hola, maddie. happy new year!

mad maddie: same to u, a-boogie

SnowAngel: do u know where zo is, by any chance? just called her but went to voicemail.

mad maddie: huh, fancy that

SnowAngel: oh well. i'll try her again later.

SnowAngel: how was your new year's eve??? any smoochy-smoochy action with chive???

mad maddie: ixnay on the oochie-smoochy-say . . . at least b/w me and chive. altho SOMEONE was smoochy-smoochy-ing last night, i can tell u that.

SnowAngel: oh yeah? who?

mad maddie: er . . . no one in particular. i just mean that surely someone was getting it on, cuz after all it was new year's eve, right?

SnowAngel: r u just being random? cuz sometimes i don't know what ur talking about.

mad maddie: forget it. yeah, i was being random.

SnowAngel: so how was the concert?

mad maddie: the bands sucked, but we had a blast. this one band played a cover of "stairway to heaven" and we turned on the flashlights on our phones and waved them over our heads like lighters.

SnowAngel: aw, fun

mad maddie: by the end of the song u could see glowing lights from one end of the amphitheater to the other. it was pretty cool.

mad maddie: also, chive bought us all beers with his fake, so we were verrrrry happy. at least until chive spilled his on the guy in front of us, who happened to be bald. the guy whipped around all mad and fuming, and i was like, "oh shit! sorry, man!"

SnowAngel: what did chive do?

mad maddie: he just sat there cracking up. i was elbowing him and going, "dude, U spilled it!" but he fully let me take the blame. it was hilarious.

SnowAngel: oh yeah. it sounds hilarious. *deadpans to show hilarity*

mad maddie: but i'm hurting today, i'll tell u.

SnowAngel: well, that's too bad

SnowAngel: but i don't feel sorry for u, wanna know why? cuz while u were out whupping it up with chive, i was trapped in glendy's room watching "The Sisterhood of the Traveling Pants" on netflix.

mad maddie: wowzers. dipping into the oldies, huh?

mad maddie: but i thought u liked that movie

SnowAngel: i do!

SnowAngel: but only with u and zoe. i mean, c'mon. four girls, friends forever? that's US, except with three instead of four.

mad maddie: and we're cooler. and we say words like "fuck."

SnowAngel: u, maybe. zoe and i r more refined. *adopts snooty expression and sips from teacup*

mad maddie: fuck, fuck, fuck

SnowAngel: but it wasn't just the choice of movie, altho that WAS the most horrible awful irony imaginable. it was the fact that glendy was such a baby the whole night. they didn't have any popcorn, so she asked her mom if she'd go to the store and buy some. her mom said no, so she worked up these fake tears and tried again with her dad. she was all, "oh, daddy, please? i REALLY need popcorn when i watch a movie. and my friend's here, and she needs popcorn too. please, daddy, please?"

mad maddie: and her dad gave in? bad move, buster.

SnowAngel: i know. she is such an only child.

mad maddie: ha. like zoe?

SnowAngel:	no, cuz zoe's parents r strict.
SnowAngel:	i guess it's possible that glendy's mom is too, but it makes no difference since mr. boss gives in whenever she pretends to cry.
mad maddie:	**and yr sure she's 16 and not 6?**
SnowAngel:	omg, exactly!
SnowAngel:	she kept talking through the whole movie—of course she's a movie-talker—and she was like, "i'm lena, the beautiful one. she's so me."
SnowAngel:	and i was like, "uh, no, ur bailey, the annoying kid who leeched onto tibby. only bailey turned out to be cool, and u r the epitome of uncool."
mad maddie:	**maybe glendy'll get a terminal disease like bailey did**
SnowAngel:	maddie!
mad maddie:	**those sisterhood chicks wouldn't say that either, i know. but it made u laugh, didn't it?**
SnowAngel:	anyway, i couldn't get away from glendy fast enough. and yet, this is who i get to go to school with on tuesday, cuz maddie, we're CARPOOLING!!! mr. boss is gonna drop us off each morning so my mom can drive chrissy to junior high.
mad maddie:	**yuck**
mad maddie:	**u better just move back here. hop on that plane like u said.**
SnowAngel:	plane fares cost more than i thought. 😢 the cheapest was $454, which is $200 too much. *grrr*
mad maddie:	**that sucks**
SnowAngel:	maybe i should ask glendy for a loan, or rather, get her to ask her daddy for 1. what do u think?
mad maddie:	**i think u need to give the glendinizer the boot. just quit talking to her. she'll get the message.**
SnowAngel:	like i can do that when we're squished together in the same car every freakin morning.

mad maddie: oh—i have to tell u one more funny thing that happened at the concert. whitney and i had to pee, but the line in the ladies' room was ridiculously long as usual. so whitney starts whining about how she REALLY has to go, and i'm like, "what do u want me to do about it?" she goes, "i dunno. something!" so i clapped my hands super loud and said, "listen up, ladies. ten seconds apiece! that's your limit!"

SnowAngel: oh god

SnowAngel: and how did u enforce this limit?

mad maddie: i started counting down from 10 to 1 each time someone stepped into a stall. at first ppl just stared at me, but then this big ol' trucker gal with a beer belly started chanting with me, and then other ppl in the line joined in too.

SnowAngel: did it work?

mad maddie: that was the best part! girls started charging out of the stalls with their pants unzipped, trying to beat the clock. one woman yelled, "i need 20! i had dinner at Max's Burritos!"

SnowAngel: good lord

mad maddie: heh heh heh

SnowAngel: i hope whitney appreciated your gesture of goodwill.

mad maddie: r u kidding? she was mortified. AND she took longer than her allotted 10 seconds. she got booed by trucker gal.

SnowAngel: ha!

SnowAngel: i can so see that whole scene. it makes me miss u, mads.

mad maddie: i miss u 2, a

SnowAngel: it's not fair that i have to spend new year's day alone

mad maddie: well, do something nice for yourself.

SnowAngel: like what?

mad maddie: i dunno, whatever u feel like doing. and now i've g2g, cuz it's time for a little nappie. byeas!

Sat, Jan 1, 4:42 PM P.S.T.

SnowAngel: zoe, where r u? and why is yr phone turned off??? i can't get hold of u no matter how hard i try!

SnowAngel: it's the beginning of a new year, and i want to TALK to u.

SnowAngel: *pouts*

SnowAngel: fine. i am gonna take maddie's advice and do something fun for a change. i've snagged a bottle of the champagne mom and dad bought for last night—don't worry, it's mini-size, just right for me!—and i'm going to hide out in my room and watch "pitch perfect" and laugh and cry.

SnowAngel: i just wish u and mads were here to watch it with me!

Sat, Jan 1, 6:01 PM P.S.T.

SnowAngel: zooo-eeee! oh, zoooo-eeee! where r u, girl?

SnowAngel: seriously? yr seriously still gon?

SnowAngel: *gone, sorry. new thumbs, tee hee. i think i'm a little tipsy.

SnowAngel: AND ALSO I NEED SOMEONE TO KISS!!! BECAUSE THE KISS AT THE END OF PITCH PERFECT IS SO PERFECT!

SnowAngel: wait! so *pitch* perfect, hahahaha!

SnowAngel: so, hypothetically, do u think doug would kiss me, if he were here? i think he would. i even thought about kissing him before i left. did u know that?

SnowAngel: hmm, i think i'll give him a ring-a-ling. *wink, wink*

zoegirl:	oh crap. oh crap crap crap!
zoegirl:	have you talked to angela today?
mad maddie:	**yesterday, but not today. why?**
zoegirl:	did you tell her about me and doug? and don't lie!
mad maddie:	**chill! i didn't tell her, i swear.**
zoegirl:	then how did she know? why did she pick last night, of all the nights in the world, to suddenly ring doug up and offer herself to him? huh???
mad maddie:	**what r u talking about?**
zoegirl:	she drank some champagne and got all sappy watching "Pitch Perfect," from what i can tell. and then she called up doug, out of the blue, and said things like, "hey, doug. do you miss me? because i miss you!" and "if you were here, i would kiss you. i should have a long time ago!"
mad maddie:	**how do u know all this?**
mad maddie:	**oh. cuz doug told u.**
mad maddie:	**this is NOT good**
zoegirl:	you think?
zoegirl:	and now doug's all weirded out because it was obvious to him that angela didn't know about us, because if she did then why would she be hitting on him, and he doesn't understand why i haven't told her.
zoegirl:	and angela . . . well, who knows how she's doing.
zoegirl:	crap, crap, crap!
mad maddie:	**i warned u that this was gonna happen. u know i did.**
zoegirl:	could u possibly say something the least bit supportive? i didn't plan this. it just happened!
mad maddie:	**sure, that's what U say, cuz ur the one who screwed up. can i just tell u how happy i am that it's u for once and not me?**

zoegirl: you know what? you're not helping. it's like . . . it's like you're *enjoying* this!

mad maddie: i'm not "enjoying" it, zoe. get real.

zoegirl: i've got to go. this is so messed up.

mad maddie: wait! what did doug say to angela after she threw herself at him? u never told me!

zoegirl: and i'm not going to. you'd just find some way to make fun of me.

mad maddie: zoe!!!!!!

Sun, Jan 2, 11:13 AM E.S.T.

zoegirl: hi, angela. it's me, your friend, who is so so sorry about . . . u know.

zoegirl: i saw your tweet about how california sucks, but at least it isn't full of big fat liars. i assume i'm the big fat liar you're talking about?

zoegirl: but angela . . .

zoegirl: aaargh

zoegirl: i should have told you about me and doug. i know that. but i just . . . i don't know.

zoegirl: anyway, nothing *had* happened between doug and me when you and i talked about it, so i wasn't actually lying. and the only reason i didn't mention it later is because i didn't wanna hurt you.

zoegirl: and come on, if you hadn't been so jealous in the first place . . .

zoegirl: never mind

zoegirl: i'm sorry, angela. i really am.

Sun, Jan 2, 8:20 AM P.S.T.

SnowAngel: i just got the lamest series of texts from zoe, which of course i didn't bother to reply to. did she tell u what happened? with doug?

mad maddie: yes, she told me that u've been a very naughty girl. did u drink and dial, young lady????

SnowAngel: WHAT?

SnowAngel: this is NOT about me. it's about ZOE! i'm never gonna forgive her as long as i live.

mad maddie: well, we both know that's not true. but we can pretend if you like.

SnowAngel: i'm serious, maddie. she's all, "i didn't wanna hurt u, blah, blah, blah," but come on. am i so needy and pathetic that i can't even handle the truth?

mad maddie: hmm. do u really want me to answer that?

SnowAngel: she even had the nerve to blame it on me! cuz i was "jealous," and that's why she didn't tell me about her and doug. is that not the most ridiculous thing u've ever heard?

mad maddie: yes, it's the most ridiculous thing i've ever heard, and yes, she should have told u. i told her that a thousand times. and now she's completely freaked that ur mad, but i told her, "sorry, zo, u brought it on yourself."

SnowAngel: thank u. i needed to hear that. i mean, it would have been different if

SnowAngel: wait a minute—U knew too?

mad maddie: about zoe and doug? uh . . .

SnowAngel: u knew they were a couple and u didn't tell me?!!!!

SnowAngel: omg, how long has this been going on???

mad maddie: now listen. IT WASN'T MY PLACE TO TELL. i told zoe she was screwing up, but that was her decision. i'm not her mommy, angela. i'm not either of your mommies.

SnowAngel: nice, maddie. try and shift the responsibility. do u not have any conscience at all?

SnowAngel: obviously not, or u wld have told your best friend that yr other best friend was dating a certain person who someone else still happened to like!

mad maddie: **that's crap, angela. u didn't like doug. u just liked him liking u.**

SnowAngel: that's so not true! why is everybody ganging up on me?

SnowAngel: i told zoe i was glad i moved to california, and guess what? i thoroughly and completely mean it!

Sun, Jan 2, 11:45 AM E.S.T.

mad maddie: **well, i talked to angela.**

zoegirl: and?!!

mad maddie: **she's mad as hell. ur at the top of her shit list, my friend.**

zoegirl: ah, crap.

zoegirl: i'm so stupid! stupid, stupid, stupid!

mad maddie: **no comment**

mad maddie: **r u ever gonna tell me what doug said to her, after she said all that about kissing him?**

zoegirl: he got really nervous, that's all. he blurted out something like, "angela, i'm dating zoe. didn't she tell u?"

mad maddie: **he said that out loud? that u 2 r dating?**

zoegirl: well, yeah. and that part was totally sweet. but i doubt it made angela feel any better, since even he assumed i'd told her.

mad maddie: **u r so screwed**

zoegirl: i know

mad maddie: **well, nothing i can do about it. i'm off to meet chive. laters!**

Mon, Jan 3, 3:30 PM E.S.T.

zoegirl: angela, are you ready to talk to me yet?

zoegirl: angela, come on. i know you're there. and don't

you remember when maddie stonewalled us like this last year, after everything fell apart with jana? i can't believe you're doing the same thing.

zoegirl: *please* don't be this way.

zoegirl: call me!!!

Mon, Jan 3, 6:01 PM P.S.T.

SnowAngel: hi, mads. i am SO not psyched to be me right now.

mad maddie: why? cuz yr still feuding with zoe?

SnowAngel: god, who even cares

SnowAngel: but yeah, i guess so, if by that u mean am i still mad at her. altho what makes me even madder is that i don't WANT to be mad at her. how pathetic is that?

mad maddie: why don't u wanna be mad anymore?

SnowAngel: cuz even tho i hate her right now, i miss her too. *scowls and kicks over trash can*

mad maddie: so get over yourself, freak. u BOTH need to get over yourselves.

SnowAngel: whatever

SnowAngel: anyway, tomorrow's my 1st day at El Cerrito High. i'm nervous.

mad maddie: don't be. u'll be fine.

SnowAngel: what if no one likes me? what if no one talks to me?

mad maddie: well, there's always glendy. maybe u'll have adjoining lockers.

SnowAngel: oh thx

SnowAngel: it's so unfair that i have to be starting over in my junior year.

mad maddie: i agree. u belong back here with us.

SnowAngel: IS there still an "us"?

mad maddie: wtf?

SnowAngel: u and me and zoe. are we still an "us"?

SnowAngel: nvm

SnowAngel:	so what shld i wear tomorrow??? shld i be cool and casual or sleek and sophisticated?
mad maddie:	**christ, angela, i don't know. wear whatever u want.**
SnowAngel:	when we were in the city, my mom bought me this off-the-shoulder sweater that i wear with a tank top underneath. i call it my slutwear, cuz it's pretty tight. and cuz of the shoulder thing. do u think i have good shoulders?
mad maddie:	**uh . . .**
SnowAngel:	she also bought me this fuzzy white sweater with three-quarter-length sleeves. i call that one my kate upton sweater cuz it makes my boobs look ginormous. (well, ginormous for a 34B)
mad maddie:	**good god**
SnowAngel:	so which should i wear??? cuz even tho my life sucks, i do wanna make a good impression.
mad maddie:	**a slutty impression?**
SnowAngel:	NO. *narrows eyes* hot, but classy. not like a woman of the night.
mad maddie:	**zoe's worried that doug thinks she's a woman of the night. isn't that hysterical? apparently the two of them got down and dirty in doug's church's basement, and things went further than zoe intended.**
SnowAngel:	maddie!
SnowAngel:	stop and think for one single second. do u really think i wanna hear this?
mad maddie:	**ur telling me u don't?**
SnowAngel:	just how down and dirty did they get? and why were they in the church basement?
mad maddie:	**i thought u didn't wanna hear!**
SnowAngel:	i don't. *puts hands over ears*
SnowAngel:	it's just, why is he getting down and dirty with zoe instead of me?

mad maddie: why do u think? cuz u never acted the slightest
bit interested in him until after zoe got interested.
that's why this whole fight is so ridiculous.

SnowAngel: okay. awesome. thx for nothing!!!

Mon, Jan 3, 9:55 PM E.S.T.

mad maddie: ok, angela, here's something to cheer u up. it's
Professor Poopypants' Name Change-O-Chart
2000. u type in your name and it spits back your
new "silly" name. wanna hear yours?

SnowAngel: is this your peace offering?

mad maddie: your silly name is "stinky pizzabuns," and i'm
"pinky pottybutt." i love it.

SnowAngel: not that i care . . . but what's zoe's?

mad maddie: she's got the best of all. "zsa zsa toiletsniffer."

SnowAngel: hmmph

SnowAngel: should i introduce myself tomorrow as "stinky
pizzabuns," do u think?

mad maddie: angela, that would be so awesome. u should, u
totally should!

SnowAngel: uh . . . no

mad maddie: why not? it's a chance to be a whole new u!

SnowAngel: i don't wanna be a whole new me! i just wanna be
the normal old me, but how can i do that if no one
even knows who i am?!!

Mon, Jan 3, 10:00 PM E.S.T.

mad maddie: zsa zsa, hey. i just talked to angela, and she is
seriously un-stoked about her new school.

zoegirl: maddie! i'm so glad u texted. i've been feeling
lonely. but why did u call me zsa zsa?

mad maddie: no reason. so when r u guys gonna get over this
stupid fight?

zoegirl: *i'm* not fighting. *she* is. and you're right,

it's stupid. i left her a message on her voicemail earlier today, and i was like, "angela, come on. in the grand scheme of things, this is not that big a deal."

mad maddie: **i bet that made her feel validated**

zoegirl: i just meant that our friendship is stronger than this. and i've sent her tons of emails, since she won't respond to my texts or my calls.

mad maddie: **she's weakening. i can tell.**

zoegirl: i dunno, but i hope so. guess i'll try her again tomorrow.

Tues, Jan 4, 4:37 PM P.S.T.

SnowAngel: I HATE EL CERRITO HIGH SO MUCH!!!

mad maddie: **ah, shit. what happened, a?**

SnowAngel: they have METAL DETECTORS, maddie. everyone has to line up and walk thru this security gate, with an armed guard standing right there. it is so so so different from atlanta. it's terrible. 😫

mad maddie: **ick, that would freak me out.**

SnowAngel: and they've got all these stupid rules, like "4 Bs and a U"

mad maddie: **wtf?**

SnowAngel: it's their dress code. no breasts, bellies, backs, or butts, and no underwear. meaning, u can't have any of those things exposed. this guy in my homeroom goes, "it's like we're under control of Al-Qaeda, man." and my homeroom teacher, whom i hate, goes, "yes, only we won't skin u alive. the word for that is 'flay,' by the way."

SnowAngel: what a wanker

mad maddie: **what about the kids? u meet anyone cool?**

SnowAngel: no. not a single person talked to me except glendy (who was wearing high-rise jeans, fyi) (ALSO, fyi, while I know that some ppl claim that high-rise is back in . . . NO. not on glendy.) she glommed onto me like we were best buds, and i could see everyone looking at me and going, "L-O-S-E-R." *puts L on forehead*

mad maddie: **u've gotta ditch the glendinizer, angela**

SnowAngel: yeah, but how???

SnowAngel: she gave me a little plastic Care Bear to clip onto my backpack! i tried to stuff it in the bottom compartment, and she pulled it right back out again and clipped it onto the zipper!

mad maddie: **egad**

mad maddie: **which care bear is it?**

SnowAngel: Friend Bear!

SnowAngel: SHE IS NOT MY FRIEND!!!

mad maddie: **lose the glendinizer, that's all i can say**

SnowAngel: gee, thanks, ur a big help

mad maddie: **chin up, angela. this was only your first day— things'll get better.**

SnowAngel: if they don't, i don't know what i'll do

mad maddie: **well, were there any cute guys?**

SnowAngel: no

mad maddie: **any fun teachers?**

SnowAngel: no

mad maddie: **any good snack machines, for god's sake?**

SnowAngel: they sell apples and raisins and granola bars, maddie. *bares teeth in horrid semblance of a smile*

mad maddie: **no licorice whips? no devilishly good ding dongs?**

SnowAngel: it's meant to stimulate better brain growth. freakin california!

mad maddie: **ok, now ur depressing ME**

SnowAngel: as if my life wasn't bad enough, i have to read three
               chapters of biology and write a response to the first
               20 pages of "The Heart of Darkness." *glowers*
               I'LL show 'em a heart of darkness.

mad maddie: the horror! the horror!

                    Wed, Jan 5, 7:45 PM E.S.T.
zoegirl: hi, angela. everyone missed you at school today,
               just so you know. especially me.

                    Wed, Jan 5, 4:45 PM P.S.T.
SnowAngel: ok, i've decided to talk to u. but i'm still extremely
               mad.
zoegirl: angela!
zoegirl: hurray, hurray, hurray!
SnowAngel: i TOLD u, i'm still mad at u.
zoegirl: i know, and i totally deserve it. and if it makes you
               feel any better, doug was mad at me too. we, like,
               had our first fight.
SnowAngel: how tragic—by which i mean "yay."
SnowAngel: u fought over me?
zoegirl: well, we didn't exactly fight, and it wasn't exactly
               over you. i mean, not in *that* way. but he
               thought i'd put you in a really bad position by not
               telling you about the two of us, and that by doing
               that, i put him in a really bad position.
zoegirl: neither of us meant to hurt your feelings, angela
SnowAngel: *glares silently*
zoegirl: please don't be mad anymore. i just got caught in
               my own stupidness, that's all. i really did think
               you didn't like him, because that's what you've
               always said.
zoegirl: do you forgive me?
SnowAngel: no

SnowAngel:	but one day if u text me again, maybe i'll text back. and if u call my cell, i MIGHT pick up.
zoegirl:	well . . . that's a start, i guess
SnowAngel:	only i've had enough for right now, cuz u shouldn't get off scot-free after being such a jerk. so, good-bye.
zoegirl:	angela . . .
zoegirl:	are you serious?
zoegirl:	ok, fine. but come back soon!!!

Thu, Jan 6, 6:04 PM P.S.T.

SnowAngel:	hi, zoe
zoegirl:	angela, hi! you DID text me back, you did! what's up?
SnowAngel:	nothing, except i guess i wanna say that i forgive u for real.
zoegirl:	you do? thank god!
SnowAngel:	my mom says it was a coping strategy to be so angry at u, that it gave me something to focus all my anger at. i can't control being stuck in california, but i CLD control being mad at u.
zoegirl:	huh
zoegirl:	i did kind of wonder if u were taking things out on me . . . but i also know that i really did screw up.
SnowAngel:	u got that right
zoegirl:	and like i said, i'm sorry
SnowAngel:	*deep, cleansing breath* and i forgive u
SnowAngel:	so now u have to tell me about him, since u didn't for all this time.
zoegirl:	who, doug?
SnowAngel:	no, benedict cumberbatch. of course doug!!!
zoegirl:	well . . . he's wonderful. he's funny and he's sweet and he's got a poster of kermit the frog in his room.
zoegirl:	are you sure u want to hear this?

SnowAngel: no, turns out i don't

SnowAngel: just tell me 1 thing. do u honestly like him? like, a lot?

zoegirl: yeah . . . i do.

SnowAngel: why? i'm not being a brat, i really wanna know.

zoegirl: oh, angela

zoegirl: i like him because when we talk, it feels real.
               like, last night we sat on the floor of the den and
               watched this candle burn down, and we talked
               about all kinds of things—our families, what we
               want to do when we're older, what we believe in
               terms of God.

zoegirl: it's just so rare to find someone—a guy!—who gets
               me, you know? who doesn't make me feel fake
               when i say what i'm honestly thinking.

SnowAngel: yeah, i can see that

zoegirl: although then it was weird when we finally
               stopped talking and it was time for him to go.
               he kept jingling his keys, but he wouldn't get up
               from the sofa and walk out the door. because i
               guess he was . . . thinking we should fool around.

SnowAngel: what???

zoegirl: never mind, that just slipped out. i didn't mean
               to bring up a touchy subject.

SnowAngel: too late now. tell me!

zoegirl: you sure?

SnowAngel: if u don't, it will just make things worse.

zoegirl: well, on our 1st date we fooled around kind of
               more than we should have, maybe. only why do i
               feel like that? like we *shouldn't* have? tons of
               people fool around. maddie fools around all the
               time. so if doug and i want to fool around,
               we should, right?

SnowAngel: is this my little zoe, all grown up? should i be putting
               on my mom's "Fiddler on the Roof" cd? *strikes

	melancholy pose* "Is this the little girl I carried? Is this the little boy at play? I don't remember growing older. When did they?"
zoegirl:	are you making fun of me?
SnowAngel:	"Sunrise, sunset. Sunrise, sunset. Swiftly flow the days!"
zoegirl:	stop singing!!!!!!!
SnowAngel:	ok, let's recap. u got down and dirty on your first date, and last night doug wanted an instant replay. did u give him one or not?
zoegirl:	*not*
zoegirl:	we kissed, but i didn't let it go further than that. finally i said, "doug, we have to get some sleep. you have to go." he didn't take the hint, so i pulled him up and propelled him to the door and very unsubtly pushed him toward his car.
zoegirl:	now i'm worried he thought i was being a jerk.
SnowAngel:	yeah, he probably did
SnowAngel:	jk
zoegirl:	i didn't know it would be this complicated. the physical stuff, i mean.
SnowAngel:	just remember that as much as it pains me to say this, it really is ok to fool around or kiss or whatever. as long as you like each other, then that's a GOOD thing.
zoegirl:	i know
SnowAngel:	and there's a difference b/w fooling around and hooking up.
SnowAngel:	ur not maddie, zoe. don't worry.
zoegirl:	ouch
zoegirl:	but thanks. i know this can't be the easiest thing for you to talk about.
SnowAngel:	get real. what kind of twisted friend would freak out over a guy she'd never even gone out with???

SnowAngel:	anyway, that's what i'm here for, even if i AM 3,000 miles away.
zoegirl:	wait! we forgot to talk about YOU! do you want to tell me about your new school?
SnowAngel:	nah, i'm pretty wiped. i'm just glad things r good b/w us.
zoegirl:	me too. night!

Fri, Jan 7, 6:50 PM E.S.T.

mad maddie:	u know what i hate? ppl who hate everyone. ppl who walk around so wrapped up in their own bullshit that they can't possibly imagine that everyone else might NOT be as fake as they wanna think they r.
SnowAngel:	and hello to u 2. what r u going on about?
mad maddie:	just cuz i don't wear all black, that makes me a sellout? that automatically implies that i worship taylor swift?
SnowAngel:	i like taylor swift. she's amazing.
mad maddie:	don't tell katie thompson and her minions that. they were trolling the halls today in their black eyeliner and their "wacky" clothes, and all i cld think was, "god, i'm sick of school already, and i've only been back three days." the katies think they're so DIFFERENT, but they can only be different in a group. have u noticed?
SnowAngel:	i did back in the good old days, yes. but in case u've forgotten, katie and i no longer live in the same state.
mad maddie:	i know that. DER.
mad maddie:	i just mean that if ur gonna be different, u should be different for real, not cuz of some bullshit desire to be different. like—well, hold on, chive says it better than me. here, this is from his deadjournal:

Chet Baker is the man. Never learned to read music, because he heard the music in his soul. Lived hard and fast, because that's what living is for. He lost his teeth in a street fight, but still he was the best jazz trumpet player this world has ever seen. The prince of cool.

Check it out, from "Chet Baker's Unsung Swan Song" by David Wilcox:

My old addiction
Makes me crave only what is best
Like these just this morning song birds
Craving upward from the nest.

mad maddie:	**doesn't that say it all?**
SnowAngel:	i don't get it. who's chet baker?
mad maddie:	**just the best trumpet player ever. it says it right there.**
SnowAngel:	what's the bit about the birds craving upward from the nest? is it poetry?
mad maddie:	**it's a SONG by david wilcox. don't u know who david wilcox is?**
SnowAngel:	no
SnowAngel:	did U, pre-chive?
mad maddie:	**it's about how chet b. died by falling out of a hotel window. he was wasted, apparently. hence, like a bird leaning out of its nest.**
SnowAngel:	a bird that was wasted?
mad maddie:	**the point is that chet baker lived his life on his own terms, unlike katie thompson. he took risks. he was unpredictable.**
SnowAngel:	u don't have to be wasted to be unpredictable. i'm not goth or emo or anything, and I'M unpredictable.

mad maddie:	U? hahahahahaha
mad maddie:	i love u, angela, but ur as predictable as they come. type in "16-year-old girl" and out pops "angela silver."
SnowAngel:	excuse me? name ONE thing about me that's predictable!
mad maddie:	uh, let's c. your ryan gosling obsession? your need to shop? and let's not forget the fight ur having with zoe, which is over the most predictable thing in the world—a guy.
SnowAngel:	what fight? we worked things out.
mad maddie:	come again?
SnowAngel:	i still think she handled everything completely wrong . . . but MAYBE i shouldn't have made such a case out of her hanging out with doug. maybe i sorta knew that she liked him all along.
mad maddie:	oh
mad maddie:	that doesn't make it ok, tho. she LIED to u.
SnowAngel:	i know she did
mad maddie:	more than once, i might add.
SnowAngel:	what's your point? do u not want me to forgive her?
mad maddie:	no, i do. of course i do.
SnowAngel:	good, cuz i did
SnowAngel:	and u wanna know what's weird? it was a total power trip to let her off the hook. i didn't know it was gonna be, but it was. it was such a role reversal— the great zoe messing up!
SnowAngel:	does that make any sense?
mad maddie:	you got to be the magnanimous one. you got to choose whether to let her live or die.
SnowAngel:	yeah. i'm not saying i'm glad it happened . . . but part of me liked having her grovel.
mad maddie:	i can totally understand
SnowAngel:	plus, what else was i supposed to do?

SnowAngel: she's my zoe, just like ur my maddie. i can't live w/o either of u.

mad maddie: lucky for u, u don't have to.

SnowAngel: which is good, cuz now i won't have to get wasted and fall out a hotel window.

mad maddie: haha, very funny!

Sat, Jan 8, 11:45 AM E.S.T.

zoegirl: wake up, angela! wake up, wake up!

SnowAngel: *rubs sleep from eyes* it's not noon here, zoe. we're three hours earlier, remember?

zoegirl: oh yeah, i forgot

zoegirl: so that makes it . . . 8:45? wow, ur up early.

SnowAngel: *smiles wanly*

zoegirl: so what's going on? you have any big plans for tonight?

SnowAngel: no, cuz i have no friends, cuz apparently i suck.

zoegirl: what about glendy?

SnowAngel: haha. glendy is WORSE than no friends.

SnowAngel: yesterday she cornered me at lunch and made me go to the bathroom with her. she needed me to run the water in the sink while she . . . did her business. what a baby!

zoegirl: why run water?

zoegirl: ohhhhh. to cover the sounds?

SnowAngel: she doesn't want anyone to hear her peeing. isn't that something ur supposed to be over by the time ur 16? i was like, "we ALL do it, glendy. every single 1 of us pees, even mother teresa."

zoegirl: i have a hard time peeing around other people too, though. in my head i'm like, "just pee, just pee!" but sometimes my body refuses to cooperate.

zoegirl: oh gosh. does that mean i'm repressed?

SnowAngel: huh?

zoegirl:	maddie thinks i am. she says i'm a prude.
SnowAngel:	no offense, but compared to maddie, anyone would be a prude
SnowAngel:	oops *claps hand over mouth*
zoegirl:	sometimes i worry she's right, though. like with doug, i still get nervous about all the body stuff. i can never just let go and enjoy it, not all the way.
zoegirl:	am i allowed to talk to you about this? i don't wanna make you feel bad.
SnowAngel:	the only time u make me feel bad is when u say things like "i don't wanna make u feel bad."
SnowAngel:	so when u say u can't just let go and enjoy it . . . does that mean things have been progressing?
zoegirl:	well, doug wants them to. i keep kind of redirecting him.
SnowAngel:	ahhh, redirecting him. that's a good way to put it.
zoegirl:	why do i have to be this way? it's like i'm stuck in my stupid head, thinking, "crap, did i shave? do i smell? are my breasts too small? is my butt too big?"
SnowAngel:	zoe, your butt is NOT too big. if your butt is too big, then the rest of us should jump over a cliff and be done with it.
zoegirl:	and even worse . . .
zoegirl:	never mind. i don't want to say.
SnowAngel:	SAY IT
zoegirl:	no, cuz then you'll *really* think i'm a prude!
SnowAngel:	u don't like to pee around him?
zoegirl:	angela! as if.
SnowAngel:	then what?
zoegirl:	it doesn't have to do with peeing noises, it has to do with . . . other noises.
SnowAngel:	other noises? like body noises, u mean? like slurps and squelches?

zoegirl: okay, please let's not put names on them. i'm totally turning bright red.

zoegirl: but yeah, *those noises*

zoegirl: i want to get over it, i really do. i want to let go and let whatever happens happen. but i can't!

SnowAngel: wait a minute. if ur worried about noises, then u guys must have gone pretty far . . .

zoegirl: below the shirt, below the underwear. *but just barely*

SnowAngel: his or yours?

zoegirl: uh, both?

SnowAngel: holy cats!

SnowAngel: zoe, u r not a prude, ok? in fact i'd say ur turning into a sex guru. shit, girl, ur gonna outpace us all!

Sat, Jan 8, 3:33 PM E.S.T.

mad maddie: it is a mistake to wear low-riders if u have an ass the size of texas. i am not saying this to be mean, but because it is the truth.

zoegirl: oh great! i just asked angela straight out if i have a big butt, and she said no!

mad maddie: U? ur a size two, zoe.

mad maddie: the ass in question is margo pedersen's. she was working at java joe's when i went by for a latte, and she had to lean over to get the milk. nuff said.

zoegirl: oh

mad maddie: u gonna c doug tonight?

zoegirl: yeah, at work. and we'll probably do something afterward.

mad maddie: ooh-la-la. give him a kissy for me!

Sun, Jan 9, 12:50 PM E.S.T.

zoegirl: hey, angela. i have something i want to tell u, but i'm not sure i should, only i really want to because it's making me all smiley inside.

zoegirl: can i tell you, or will it secretly make you sad?

SnowAngel: what r u blithering about? does this have to do with doug?

zoegirl: yeah, and i can't tell maddie because she'd make fun of me. so can i tell you, or would you rather i not?

SnowAngel: OMG, DID U HAVE SEX??????

zoegirl: angela, shhhhh!

SnowAngel: what, u think everyone in cyberland can hear?

SnowAngel: SO DID U????

zoegirl: no! of course not!

SnowAngel: darn

SnowAngel: altho not really cuz i don't think i'm ready for that

zoegirl: *you're* not ready? what about *me*?

SnowAngel: not everything is about U, zoe

SnowAngel: do u remember saying that to me, back when u first started lying? now u know what it feels like!

zoegirl: why are you snapping at me? are you in a bad mood?

zoegirl: talking to you isn't as fun as i thought it was going to be.

SnowAngel: i'm sorry, i'm sorry *drops to knees and hugs friend's legs*

SnowAngel: PLEASE tell me. i'll stop being obnoxious, i promise.

zoegirl: well . . . now it doesn't even seem like a big deal anymore. only, it is.

zoegirl: doug wrote a poem for me—isn't that sweet?

SnowAngel: awww! can i read it?

zoegirl: yes, because he posted it on poetry.com, which means anyone can read it. i think that's so cool, because it means he's not hiding it or anything. he wants the whole world to know.

SnowAngel: shld i go to the site right now?

zoegirl: i can just paste it in. but later you should visit the site and see for yourself how official it looks.

zoegirl: here it is. it's called "Miraculous Thing."

Miraculous Thing

Today all of the news is good news.
This morning a robin
lands on my porch
and beeps her hip hop
until dark.
I can't help tapping my foot.
I take her by the wing
and we dance into flight.
It is you, Zoe,
lifting me higher and higher
into the starry night
that reminds me
of your eyes and the sparkling
touch of your skin.
I may never sleep again.

zoegirl: isn't it beautiful and wonderful and perfect??? or do i just think so because it's about me?

SnowAngel: it's different from the poem he read at the poetry slam last year, that's for sure. that 1 was about dirty underwear.

zoegirl: no one's ever written me a poem before.

SnowAngel: no one's written me one either.

SnowAngel: ur lucky, zo

zoegirl: i know. thanks for being so cool about it.

zoegirl: but when it comes to maddie, mum's the word!

mad maddie: hey, a-boogie. chumley the psycho kitty scratched the hell out of my leg, and now i have three long gashes on my thigh. they look really cool.

mad maddie: is that sick, that i like the look of pain?

SnowAngel: yes

mad maddie: tell me ur not the same, tho. like when u get a bruise, don't u feel tough?

SnowAngel: i've always secretly wanted a black eye, to tell the truth

mad maddie: YES! that's exactly what i mean!

SnowAngel: we r sick little freaks, aren't we?

mad maddie: never said we weren't

mad maddie: so wassup?

SnowAngel: nothing much. i txted zoe earlier—she's doing well.

mad maddie: oh yeah?

SnowAngel: in fact i shouldn't tell u this, but i'm going to anyway.

SnowAngel: doug wrote her a poem.

mad maddie: oh good lord

SnowAngel: it's called "miraculous thing."

mad maddie: "miraculous thing"? what, now zoe's a bona fide miracle?

SnowAngel: it's sweet. it really is. it's posted under his name on poetry.com if u wanna check it out.

mad maddie: heck yeah, i'm gonna pull it up right now.

SnowAngel: did u find it? is it there?

mad maddie: "i take her by the wing and we dance into flight"??? we're not the freaks—he is!

SnowAngel: *chortle chortle*

SnowAngel: i take it that chive hasn't written U any love poems . . .

mad maddie: NO, thank god

SnowAngel: doug must really like her a lot. *deflates a little, like a balloon* i'm embarrassed to say it, but it makes me the TINIEST bit jealous.

mad maddie: why??? cuz u wanna be compared to a robin?

SnowAngel: ha, i knew u'd make me feel better. 😊

SnowAngel: seriously, tho, u can't tell zoe i told u.

mad maddie: excuse me, but it's on the world wide web. it's fair game.

SnowAngel: i know, but don't mention it anyway.

mad maddie: she should have told me. i hate it when she keeps secrets.

mad maddie: but don't worry, i know how to keep my mouth shut!

Mon, Jan 10, 8:35 PM E.S.T.

mad maddie: hey, zo. have u noticed mary kate's new way of talking? it's driving me up the wall.

zoegirl: what's she doing?

mad maddie: she, like, makes all her vowels long, like "agane" instead of "again." and she calls her mom "mum." i wanna vomit every time she opens her mouth.

zoegirl: i don't get it. is she trying to be British?

mad maddie: god only knows. it is nauseatingly pretentious.

mad maddie: anywayz, that's all i've got. i'm off to meet chive at the awful waffle.

zoegirl: wait! that's it?

mad maddie: yeah, so?

zoegirl: nothing, it's just that we haven't talked in forever.

mad maddie: cuz u've been busy with doug

zoegirl: and *u've* been busy with chive, only you've told me hardly any details

mad maddie: whereas u, on the other hand, make it a point to tell me everything?

zoegirl: huh? what's that supposed to mean?

mad maddie: i've gtg, i'm supposed to be at the waffle house in 15 minutes.

zoegirl: then call me when u get back. or txt.

mad maddie: it'll probably be late, but fine. but you'll probably be asleep!

Mon, Jan 10, 11:39 PM E.S.T.

mad maddie: zo-ster! here i am txting u, just like i promised. u awake?

zoegirl: maddie, hi!

mad maddie: oh yeah? how high r u?

zoegirl: ???

zoegirl: so how'd the night go? did you have fun?

mad maddie: mmmm, waffles. i could eat five more right now. and chive played the jukebox and the jukebox played him. hehehehe.

zoegirl: what do u mean, the jukebox played him?

mad maddie: i mean what i say and i say what i mean.

mad maddie: aren't jukeboxes COOL, tho? i mean, it's like back in the good ol' days. a blast from the last.

zoegirl: i think you mean a blast from the *past*

mad maddie: oh man, do u ever feel like your teeth r too sharp? my teeth r really, really sharp.

zoegirl: what are you talking about? are you ok, maddie?

mad maddie: special lady! waitin on me at the waffle house. she's amazin! calling all those orders out. special lady!

zoegirl: omg, are you stoned?!

mad maddie: hey, i resemble that remark! hehehehehe

zoegirl: i'm serious. are you????

mad maddie: it's a song from the waffle house jukebox. am i chive's special lady? i wanna be chive's special lady.

mad maddie: and no, i'm not stoned. the word i could easily write to show u that i'm not would be trilogy. or in stone in frye in capsula. or i could go to bed even tho i know i'll be in big trouble.

zoegirl: why r u gonna be in trouble?

mad maddie: cuz the moms thought that too, ya know. about being stoned.

mad maddie: oh man, i just realized something! u and the moms, ur like twins! u were separated at birth!

zoegirl: maddie, i don't see the point in talking to you right now unless you're going to start acting normal.

mad maddie: define normal. what's normal, zoe? r U normal?

zoegirl: bye, mads. you're making me feel really sad.

mad maddie: sad mad glad. how weird that they all rhyme.

mad maddie: u should go eat a waffle! u can't be sad if u eat a waffle!!!

Tues, Jan 11, 10:34 AM E.S.T.

zoegirl: angela, you awake? what time is it there, like 7:30 in the morning?

SnowAngel: awake, yeah, but glendy's dad is gonna be here to pick me up any minute. what's up?

zoegirl: angela, maddie texted me last night when she was stoned. it was *awful*

SnowAngel: she was stoned? how could u tell?

zoegirl: it was impossible not to. she kept going on about these random things and none of her sentences made sense and it was just scary. it's like she wasn't even herself.

SnowAngel: yikes 🙀

zoegirl: i know. it's one thing to suspect that she's playing around with being a pothead, but it's another to see it in action. i didn't like it, angela.

SnowAngel: did u tell her that?

zoegirl: no, because there was no point. she was *stoned*

SnowAngel:	well, r u gonna tell her today?
zoegirl:	i saw her before homeroom, and i just played it cool. but she had to have known that something was up.
SnowAngel:	not necessarily. ppl see what they wanna see.
SnowAngel:	crap, mr. boss just pulled up in front of our apartment. TELL HER, ZOE! SHARING MEANS CARING!

♥

Wed, Jan 12, 8:44 PM E.S.T.

zoegirl:	hi, maddie. i have to tell you something.
mad maddie:	yeah, wazzup? did u catch mary kate's brit-speak today?
zoegirl:	it's not about mary kate. it's about u.
mad maddie:	meaning?
zoegirl:	meaning that i'm worried about you. it's been like this unspoken thing between us—even though i've noticed you feel quite comfortable telling *angela* about it—but i don't want to shove it under the rug anymore.
mad maddie:	shove what under the rug?
zoegirl:	think about it: with the whole doug thing, i didn't tell angela because i didn't want to upset her, and of course that just made everything worse.
zoegirl:	maybe friends *have* to upset each other once in a while. maybe that's what being a real friend means.
mad maddie:	is this about the other night? i was just messing with u, u know that.
zoegirl:	no, you weren't. u were . . . freaky, maddie.
zoegirl:	it scared me.
mad maddie:	oh please. ur such an old woman.
zoegirl:	i'm an old woman because i don't want you smoking pot?

zoegirl: you weren't YOU, maddie. you could hardly string three words together.

mad maddie: zoe, chill. THIS is why i never bring it up with u.

zoegirl: no, you never bring it up with me because you don't want anyone pointing out that it's wrong!

mad maddie: it's "wrong"? smoking pot is "wrong"? when did U get to be the morality police?

zoegirl: it's wrong because it's bad for you—and you know it

mad maddie: says who?

mad maddie: u may not like the choices i make, but at least i'm LIVING. at least i won't look back at my life when i'm 100 years old and say, "i was too afraid to try that and i was too afraid to try that."

zoegirl: because you won't have any brain cells left, that's why

mad maddie: omg. maybe ur happy leading your boring safe life, but i'm not taking that route. i refuse to numb out.

zoegirl: which is why you get stoned and drunk? because you don't want to numb yourself out?

mad maddie: pot AMPLIFIES the experience, zoe

mad maddie: forget it. u've never tried it, so how can u even talk?

zoegirl: because i'm not stupid. because i like my brain in full working order, thank you very much. and because i'm not about to get high just to impress a guy who thinks life is one big party.

mad maddie: god, ur self-righteous

zoegirl: you don't have to get drunk or smoke pot in order to live life to the fullest, maddie.

mad maddie: oh yeah? what DO u have to do? study really hard? be a good little girl and do everything everyone tells u to do?

zoegirl:	you're trying to make this about me, but it's not
mad maddie:	**name one thing u've done recently that pushed u out of your comfort zone, that made your heart pound. and u can't say fooling around with doug, cuz that doesn't count.**
mad maddie:	**anywayz, u can't even give yourself fully over to that, can u? tell me that's not incredibly pathetic.**
zoegirl:	i can't believe you said that
mad maddie:	**are u saying it's not pathetic?**
zoegirl:	well, it's not as pathetic as fooling around with someone else's boyfriend! it's not as pathetic as pretending that's the way you want it when really you wish he was yours!
mad maddie:	**exsqueeze me?**
zoegirl:	"i want to be chive's special lady." that's what you said when you were high.
mad maddie:	**i did NOT**
zoegirl:	those were your very words—go back and look! and i know that's why you're smoking so much, to make yourself stand out from whitney. but whitney's the one he's with, isn't she?
mad maddie:	**so?**
zoegirl:	so you're lying to yourself, maddie!
mad maddie:	**whoa—i am so over this convo. u should hear yourself, man. u r majorly worked up.**
zoegirl:	don't tell me i'm not living my life fully. don't tell me that i'm the one with the problem.
mad maddie:	**"most men lead lives of quiet desperation." that's u in a nutshell.**
zoegirl:	omg. show off for chive, not me.
zoegirl:	why are we even friends, maddie?
mad maddie:	**WHAT?**
zoegirl:	i'm serious. why are we even friends? i'm not trying to be mean—i'm honestly wondering. we

both get along great with angela, and when we're all three together, everything's fine. but we're not all three together. when it's just the two of us, everything seems to fall apart.

mad maddie: don't say that. that's not true.

zoegirl: i don't *not* want to be friends.

zoegirl: but it's like everything gets blown up between us. everything gets rubbed the wrong way.

mad maddie: not always. not even usually.

zoegirl: lots, though

mad maddie: i just think that if ur gonna point all this blame at me, then u have to look at yourself too. ur not perfect, zoe.

zoegirl: i never said i was

mad maddie: u sure act like it sometimes

Thu, Jan 13, 10:35 PM E.S.T.

mad maddie: hey, a. did u hear about zoe's and my big blowout? i'm sure u did.

SnowAngel: yeah, zoe called this afternoon. i'm so sorry!

mad maddie: she drives me up the wall. u should have heard how self-righteous she was being.

SnowAngel: well, like i said, i'm sorry.

SnowAngel: but . . . i kinda need to tell u that i don't entirely disagree with her. i mean, i've been worried about u too. *shies back to avoid wrath*

mad maddie: u don't need to be. god.

mad maddie: anywayz, the moms had already been riding me before zoe txted. i didn't tell zoe, but that's part of why i jumped all over her.

SnowAngel: riding u about what?

mad maddie: the same thing zoe was, my "alleged" poor decision-making skills. she was all, "ur not smoking marijuana, r u maddie?"

mad maddie: only she pronounced it mare-uh-joo-wah-nah. so lame.

SnowAngel: shit, maddie, does she KNOW?

mad maddie: she has her suspicions, which i neither confirmed nor denied.

mad maddie: actually, i denied the hell out of them. but where does the moms get the right to come down on me? she and dad are the worst role models ever. and has SHE smoked pot? yes, she has. last night she told me that she and the dads smoked "mare-uh-joo-wah-nah" at some party when i was a kid, and it almost cost her her marriage.

SnowAngel: whoa, your MOM smoked pot? your parents are so cool. why did it almost cost her her marriage?

mad maddie: she got all flirty with some other guy or something. it was like her little cautionary tale to scare me straight.

mad maddie: but the point is that the moms had laid all that on me—very serious and "this is your life, maddie"—and then zoe texted me and gave me the exact same lecture, only worse. can u see why i got upset?

SnowAngel: i guess

mad maddie: AND i somehow managed to lose my wallet at the waffle house, which is a major drag. i didn't have much cash in it, but it means i don't have my license. aaargh.

mad maddie: anywayz, i just wanted to explain the whole story. i don't want everyone hating me.

SnowAngel: nobody hates u, maddie. we could NEVER hate u.

mad maddie: u wanna know what's weird? and i could never ever tell zoe, so u better not either.

SnowAngel: what?

mad maddie: contrary to popular opinion, i don't actually LOVE getting stoned.

SnowAngel: i know, cuz it burns

mad maddie: yeah, there's that. but it also just kinda ... makes things icky.

SnowAngel: like how?

mad maddie: it changes things. it's like everyone gets all distorted, and i can see what they're really thinking, and i don't like it. i can see how desperate we all are, cuz the layers get peeled off, and we're just these naked bundles of need.

SnowAngel: er, i'm not exactly following

mad maddie: like, ok, monday night at the waffle house? we're all crammed into this booth, and whenever brannen says something, he looks at me in this overly eager way. only i'm too busy looking at chive, who's too busy looking at whitney ...

mad maddie: ugh. i guess i can't explain it.

SnowAngel: why do u do it, then? get stoned?

mad maddie: i dunno. cuz sometimes it's bad, but it can also be hilarious. like mad-laughing hilarity, where u just go on and on and on and u don't even know what set u off. that part's awesome.

SnowAngel: but we do that without pot, like when zoe was trying to learn how to drive stick shift and she kept rolling down the hill. remember? 😃

mad maddie: yeah, i know

SnowAngel: we USED to have mad-laughing hilarity, that is. we haven't for a long time.

mad maddie: i hear u

SnowAngel: tell me something funny. tell me something to make me laugh.

mad maddie: um ... i can't think of anything

mad maddie:	wait, i know. today in english, mariah rath goes, "mr. phelps, it is SO cold in here. aren't u cold?" and mr. phelps goes, "noooo, i'm a little teacup."
SnowAngel:	???
mad maddie:	u know, from that song. "i'm a little teacup, short and stout. here is my handle, here is my spout."
SnowAngel:	it's teapot, not teacup
SnowAngel:	and that's not very funny
mad maddie:	it was at the time. mr. phelps is such a dork, u can't help but love him.
SnowAngel:	*blinks noncommitally*

Fri, Jan 14, 7:02 PM P.S.T.

SnowAngel:	zoe, why do ppl wear nude-colored hose? i am asking this as a serious question.
zoegirl:	um, because they think they look good?
SnowAngel:	but they don't. they never do.
SnowAngel:	glendy wore nude-colored hose today, with open-toed white leather sandals, no less. in january!!!
zoegirl:	ooo, that's bad
SnowAngel:	this morning she was all worked up about a bit of blueberry in her teeth that a guy she likes may or may not have seen, and i was like, "girl, u have bigger things to worry about."
zoegirl:	like nude-colored hose?
SnowAngel:	exactly
zoegirl:	poor thing
SnowAngel:	poor thing my foot!
SnowAngel:	she invited me to spend the night tomorrow night, can u believe it? i politely declined, and she goes, "oh, would tonight be better? cuz we can do it tonight, no problem." i told her i couldn't do that either, cuz mom wants me to get my room put together so that it doesn't look like i'm living in

a refugee camp. so glendy goes, "well, i'll come
help u. i know! i know! we can get matching
comforters!"

zoegirl: she did not

SnowAngel: she DID, zoe. and i've seen her comforter—it's this
crappy polyester deal with dolphins all over it.

zoegirl: so is she going to come help you decorate?

SnowAngel: r u kidding? glendy may have this illusion that we're
friends, but we're not. i already have my friends,
thank u very much.

SnowAngel: *droops* they're just not with me.

zoegirl: oh, angela. i wish i were there to help you
decorate.

SnowAngel: i don't wanna decorate. i don't even care about
decorating.

zoegirl: what did you say to glendy?

SnowAngel: i said, "thanks so much for offering, but how boring
that would be for u." and she said, "no, i want to,
really!" and i said, "that is SO sweet, but i'm not
roping anyone in to do my work." i just kept smiling
and not backing down no matter what she said.

zoegirl: ack. it kind of makes me feel sorry for her.

SnowAngel: don't u DARE feel sorry for her. she's snively.

SnowAngel: after she finally got it thru her skull that i wasn't
gonna invite her over, she got all pouty and said, "i
thought southern girls were supposed to be nice."
i looked at her like, "what drug r u on?" and she
quickly said, "just kidding."

zoegirl: hey now, southern girls ARE nice

SnowAngel: the point was, she needed to frickin take the hint

SnowAngel: that pouty crap might work with mr. boss, but not
with me. *wipes her hands of the annoying glendy*

zoegirl: you crack me up

SnowAngel: so have u smoothed things out with maddie yet?

zoegirl:	i don't know. kind of? she's just acting like everything's normal, only everything *isn't* normal, so it feels depressing and wrong.
SnowAngel:	believe me, i know all about depressing and wrong.
SnowAngel:	in fact, i'm gonna go stick my head in the toaster oven. bye!

Mon, Jan 17, 12:23 PM E.S.T.

mad maddie:	oh, martin luther king junior, i thank u for this day of rest. for without u, i would be in SPANISH right now instead of the lovely java joe's, sipping my delicious chai.
SnowAngel:	jealous. me want chai!
mad maddie:	here, i'll pour some thru the computer. gurgle, slurple, gack.
SnowAngel:	mmm, thanx. only now my keyboard's all sticky.
SnowAngel:	so zoe says ur being all fakey around her. r u?
mad maddie:	what?
mad maddie:	no, i'm not being fakey. how annoying that she would say that.
SnowAngel:	she says ur acting normal, but that things AREN'T normal.
mad maddie:	if things aren't normal, it's cuz of her. she thinks i'm too wild, but the reality is, she's too much of a wimp. she's like a timid little mouse. she's afraid to live in the real world.
SnowAngel:	ohhhh, i see
SnowAngel:	and it's your job to make her realize this?
mad maddie:	i never said that
mad maddie:	only . . . yeah! ur brilliant, angela. maybe it is!
SnowAngel:	maybe it is what? now i'm confused.
SnowAngel:	maddie?
SnowAngel:	come back! explain!!!

Tues, Jan 18, 6:40 PM E.S.T.

mad maddie: hey, zo. wazzup?

zoegirl: nothing much. you?

mad maddie: nothin. i thought of u today in english, tho.

zoegirl: why?

mad maddie: cuz of something the little baptist girl said.

zoegirl: what little baptist girl?

mad maddie: she was talking really loudly to her friend with the mole, and out of her mouth came, "no way! shut the hell up!" it was very unexpected.

zoegirl: are you talking about alicia arnold? you shouldn't call her the "little baptist girl."

mad maddie: true, she's more of a big baptist girl, isn't she? anyway, the whole class heard and she turned bright red. and then she said, "it's your fault, mr. phelps. i picked it up from u, and now it's stuck in my brain!"

zoegirl: mr. phelps says "shut the hell up"?

mad maddie: in a jokey way. like, he'll look at us at the beginning of class and say, "all right, all right, shut the hell up. who's finished chapter 12 of 'Things Fall Apart'?" but now he says he'll quit on account of corrupting the big baptist girl.

zoegirl: huh. weird.

zoegirl: but why in the world did that make u think of me?

mad maddie: cuz i started wondering, have U ever said "shut the hell up"? if alicia arnold can, then surely u can too. i give u permission.

zoegirl: haha

mad maddie: no, seriously. i think it would be good for you. ur so afraid of screwing up, but it IS ok to break a rule or two every once in a while. maybe if u did, u wouldn't be such a chickenshit.

zoegirl: i'm a chickensh*t?

(137)

mad maddie: um, yeah. just think about the whole angela/doug mess: if u weren't so wimpy, u would have told her in the first place. u said it yourself.

zoegirl: u can't use that as an example. it's over and done with.

mad maddie: but ur still a chickenshit—that's my point.

zoegirl: i am not. stop saying that.

mad maddie: then prove me wrong. pick anyone—anyone u want, as long as it's not me or angela—and tell them to shut the hell up. i dare u.

zoegirl: that's the stupidest thing i've ever heard.

mad maddie: why, cuz ur scared?

zoegirl: no, because it's *stupid*

mad maddie: that proves it—ur a chickenshit!

Tues, Jan 18, 6:55 PM E.S.T.

mad maddie: hey, a. i totally called zoe on her bullshit! it was hilarious.

SnowAngel: it was? what'd u do?

mad maddie: i dared her to tell someone to shut the hell up. can u imagine those words ever coming out of zoe's mouth?

mad maddie: i was like, "see! u criticize me for being willing to take risks, but isn't that better than being the perpetual good girl, locked in your land of repression?"

SnowAngel: whatever, mads. u sound a little wacko to me.

mad maddie: nah, i'm just gloating. u should have heard how defensive she got—hahahahaha!

SnowAngel: u shouldn't gloat about your friends. u should love them. and when they're feeling defensive, or left out, or just lonely, then u should do whatever u can to make them feel better. u should only want what's best for them!

mad maddie: huh?

mad maddie: well, this IS what's best for her—to realize she's flawed just like the rest of us.

mad maddie: and now, off for a celebratory glass of nestle quik. l8rs!

Wed, Jan 19, 5:05 PM E.S.T.

zoegirl: ok, mads, i did it. are you happy?

mad maddie: u did what?

mad maddie: no u didn't. ur lying.

zoegirl: i'm not. i told chase dickinson to shut the hell up!

mad maddie: bullshit!

zoegirl: he was talking to kurt manheim in french about all kinds of disgusting stuff, that's what started it. he was all, "my rep's getting pathetic because i haven't had sex in over a month," and "that's why i need a girlfriend, someone older who can teach me stuff. someone who'll give me head."

mad maddie: he said all this in french?

zoegirl: not *in* french, as in parlez-vous francais. but right there in the middle of class, yeah. he sits behind me.

mad maddie: he's such a scuz. no way ANY girl would have sex with him.

zoegirl: so kurt said, "dude, you're crazy," as in, "people can hear you," but chase was all, "chill, nobody's listening." kurt said, "what about her?" meaning me. chase laughed and said, "zoe? she doesn't even know what 'giving head' means." then he poked me in the back and goes, "do you, zoe? do you know what 'giving head' means?"

mad maddie: what a dick

zoegirl: so i turned around and looked him dead in the eye and said, "shut the hell up, chase."

zoegirl: i really really did it!!!!!

mad maddie: whoa! nice work, zo!

zoegirl: i know!!! 😊

mad maddie: altho it's kinda pathetic that u see this as a big deal. any other girl would say that to him as a matter of course.

zoegirl: i took your dare, simple as that. don't go downplaying it now.

mad maddie: no, it's great. really.

zoegirl: doug said so too. he was very proud of me.

mad maddie: how r things going with ol' dougie?

zoegirl: just fine, thanks very much. we went out for coffee after school, although actually we had mexican hot chocolate. have u ever tried?

mad maddie: too cinnamony for me. in a bad way.

zoegirl: i thought it was delicious. and doug and i had an awesome conversation, which was even better.

zoegirl: i *really* like him maddie.

mad maddie: didn't u already *really* like him?

zoegirl: but now i like him even more. the physical stuff is still . . . a little tricky, but everything else is perfect. plus it's such a relief to like someone normal again, someone i'm allowed to like.

mad maddie: as opposed to mr. h?

zoegirl: as opposed to mr. h.

zoegirl: i saw mr. h with cameron bryant today. it freaked me out. he was leaning close and smiling at her like he used to smile at me.

mad maddie: u know what i heard from some senior? that every year mr. h has a "special" female student that he pays a lot of attention to.

mad maddie: oops, i wasn't gonna tell you that—but now i did.

zoegirl: oh

mad maddie: sick, huh?

zoegirl:	yeah. sick.
mad maddie:	so u should be doubly glad u've got doug, that's all i'm saying.
zoegirl:	right, i am
mad maddie:	and that doug isn't pervy like mr. h
mad maddie:	or chase dickinson
zoegirl:	you know what else chase said? that he used to have this girl he "hung" with who gave him head for over an hour. is that possible?
mad maddie:	now that's just silly. blow jobs should not last over 30 minutes.
zoegirl:	ewww!
mad maddie:	ah, zoe, u still have a ways to go!

Thu, Jan 20, 4:04 PM P.S.T.

SnowAngel:	hey, zo. have u ever had wasabi cheese spread? it is sooooo good.
zoegirl:	isn't wasabi that super-spicy green stuff u get with sushi?
SnowAngel:	yeah, but this is a cheese spread with wasabi in it. it makes my mouth sting, but it's thoroughly addictive. *swipes last little bit up with cracker and smacks lips*
zoegirl:	mmm, you're making me hungry
zoegirl:	want to hear something sad? i saw mr. h hitting on cameron bryant—well, sitting really close to her in backwork—and maddie told me that cameron is his "special" student this year.
SnowAngel:	that's not sad. that's gross. he needs to go to a sex offenders' home.
zoegirl:	i know
zoegirl:	but the reason it's sad is because when maddie told me that, it made *me* feel sad.
SnowAngel:	WHY?

zoegirl:	i don't know
zoegirl:	because i wanted to be the only one?
SnowAngel:	zoe, no. u r soooooo much better off w/o him.
SnowAngel:	i take it u and maddie r talking again, tho?
zoegirl:	sort of, i guess
zoegirl:	huh. wonder how that happened?

Sat, Jan 22, 8:00 PM E.S.T.

mad maddie:	can't talk long—meeting chive for a night of wanton indulgence—but DUDE, am i brilliant. i have given zoe the best frickin dare ever.
SnowAngel:	dare? what do u mean, dare?
mad maddie:	it's just this thing we're doing. u gave me the idea, actually.
SnowAngel:	i did?
mad maddie:	i gave her the first one last week, and i just gave her the second. it's frickin genius.
SnowAngel:	what is it?
mad maddie:	can't tell. top secret. but it's going down tomorrow, on sunday, the day of our lord.
SnowAngel:	it's "going down"? what r u, a jewel thief?
mad maddie:	please. we're not stealing anything—in fact, the opposite.
mad maddie:	heh heh heh, it's so perfect to do it while he's at church.
SnowAngel:	do WHAT?
mad maddie:	g2g. byeas!

Sat, Jan 22, 5:07 PM P.S.T.

SnowAngel:	zoe, what r u and maddie up to? what's this "dare" business she's talking about?
SnowAngel:	zoe!
SnowAngel:	txt me!!!

zoegirl: oh man, angela. are you up?

SnowAngel: yes, but only cuz U NEVER TXTED ME LAST NIGHT and i'm dying to know what's going on!

zoegirl: omg, i haven't laughed like that in *forever*.
at first i was like, "no, maddie, we can't!" but we did, and it was totally . . . purging.

SnowAngel: will u please explain????

zoegirl: we plastered bumper stickers all over mr. h's car while he was at church! we were very sneaky. we were like spies. and we stuck them on with super-glue so they'll be really really hard to get off!

SnowAngel: no way! what did they say?

zoegirl: one said "sticks and stones will break my bones, but whips and chains excite me," and another said "i'd rather be spanked."

zoegirl: also included were "ass pirate," "i heart llamas," and, my personal fave, "jesus loves you, but i'm his favorite."

SnowAngel: holy cats. he's gonna die.

zoegirl: he already did. maddie and i hid at the other end of the parking lot until church let out, and we watched him walk to his car. he was with some friends—including a woman!—and when he saw the bumper stickers, he about had a heart attack. the woman got a pissy look on her face, but his other friends cracked up. it was *supremely* satisfying.

SnowAngel: i'll bet

zoegirl: it was also supremely satisfying to see him try to peel them off. hahaha.

SnowAngel: right, hahaha. when did u guys decide to do this?

zoegirl: we didn't really *decide* anything. maddie dared me to do it, and so i did.

SnowAngel:	how come u didn't tell me?
zoegirl:	oh. well . . . i guess it didn't occur to us.
SnowAngel:	it didn't OCCUR to u?
zoegirl:	it wasn't that big a deal.
zoegirl:	wait a second, are you upset?
SnowAngel:	no, of course not. why would i be upset?
zoegirl:	if anything, i thought you'd be glad that maddie and i are doing stuff again.
SnowAngel:	i am, i am
zoegirl:	you want us to be happy, don't you?
SnowAngel:	i suppose
SnowAngel:	but maybe i don't want u to be DELIRIOUSLY happy, that's all.
zoegirl:	oh, angela
SnowAngel:	it IS pretty funny, tho. what u did.
zoegirl:	it would have been even better if you'd been with us—and i'm not just saying that!

Mon, Jan 24, 5:22 PM E.S.T.

mad maddie:	hellooooo, zoe. prepare to face your darkest fears, for i am about to issue the best and most thrilling dare yet. r u ready?
zoegirl:	what? no!
mad maddie:	well, get ready, cuz this is not a dare to be denied. it is the Dare of the Century.
zoegirl:	i hate to break it to you, but i think we should be done with dares.
mad maddie:	done with dares? surely u josh!
zoegirl:	i think we're making angela feel bad.
mad maddie:	ohhhhh, the old "we're making angela feel bad" ploy. sorry, charlie, but i'm not letting u off the hook that easily.
mad maddie:	r u ready to hear the dare?
zoegirl:	no

mad maddie: good, cuz first i need to give u some background information. imagine if u will a brightly lit classroom. it is 6th-period english, and all the students are filing in. but—what's this? instead of taking a seat, theresa ketchum scowls and drags her desk to the other side of the room. "theresa," mr. phelps says with a look of confusion, "why r u moving your desk?"

zoegirl: maddie, i'm serious—no more dares.

zoegirl: plus, i just realized something: why are *you* the only one giving dares? why don't i get to give *you* a dare?

mad maddie: and theresa says, "i'm moving my desk cuz i don't wanna stare at wendy's butt. her crack's peeking out of her jeans."

mad maddie: btw, didn't i point out long ago that low-riders r not for those who r substantially endowed in the buttock area? why yes, i believe i did.

zoegirl: i don't know where you're going with this, but i am not taking any more dares. and i am most definitely not taking any dares that have to do with butt cracks.

mad maddie: plz. but watching this little slice of life got me thinking: what stresses zoe out more than anything? and my brain answered, "BODIES. bodies stress zoe out more than anything."

zoegirl: what? that is so not true!

mad maddie: so what does zoe need to do? zoe needs to loosen up. yes, that's right, she needs to overcome her fears of being a woman, with all that being a woman involves. she needs—drumroll, please— to embrace her sexuality!

zoegirl: no no no no no

mad maddie: the other dares have been warm-ups. rehearsals,

	if u will. for it is this ultimate dare that will bring u to the peak of self-awareness.
zoegirl:	good grief, maddie. could u be a little less full of yourself?
mad maddie:	here is your dare: you are to glue two marshmallows to yr shirt—the OUTSIDE of your shirt—at approximate nipple location. then you are to stroll from one end of the mall to the other.
zoegirl:	*maddie*!
zoegirl:	you have lost it. i'm leaving now.
mad maddie:	"the great marshmallow-nipple dare," i call it.
mad maddie:	is it illegal? nooooo. is it dangerous? nooooo. will ppl stare at u? hmm, they very well might. i would, if i saw some chick prancing along with marshmallows glued to her nipples.
zoegirl:	no way i'm doing that, so just forget it.
mad maddie:	then ur a wimp, and u finally have to admit it.
zoegirl:	wait.
zoegirl:	i told chase dickinson to shut the hell up. i pasted lewd bumper stickers on mr. h's car. u can *not* tell me i'm a wimp!
mad maddie:	but this one's the real dare, the dare that's about U. and if u don't take it, then u have to admit that ur afraid to live your life fully.
zoegirl:	prancing around with marshmallows on your nipples does *not* constitute living your life fully!
mad maddie:	wimp
zoegirl:	this is so unfair! *no one* would do this dare!
mad maddie:	i would, and u know it.
mad maddie:	it's very simple if u think about it. u just have to get over your inhibitions, which is something u've needed to do for a long time.
zoegirl:	you're doing me a favor, that's what you're saying?

mad maddie:	**tell ya what, they can be mini-marshmallows.**
zoegirl:	gee, thanks
mad maddie:	**so?**
zoegirl:	noooooooooooooo!

Mon, Jan 24, 5:36 PM E.S.T.

mad maddie:	**P.S. i googlewhacked "marshmallow nipple." four fucking million hits!!!**
zoegirl:	maddie, you need therapy
mad maddie:	**i'm just saying, that's A LOT of marshmallow nipples . . .**
zoegirl:	once and for all, *no*!!!

Mon, Jan 24, 6:30 PM E.S.T.

zoegirl:	angela! where are you???? you told me to include you in things, but how can i if you're never there? i've been calling you for over an hour!
SnowAngel:	hi, zo! i just this second got home from school, which, btw, sucked. can i tell u something depressing?
zoegirl:	uh, sure
SnowAngel:	i was watching this girl during lunch, one of the many girls who have no idea i exist. she was sitting in the courtyard, talking to someone on her cell, and she was so animated. yip yip yip, like a little dog. and then she said good-bye and snapped shut her phone, and all of a sudden there was just . . . nothing. her face was blank, her body was blank, it was like she'd snapped herself shut along with her phone.
zoegirl:	yikes
SnowAngel:	and i thought, "that's me, that's totally me."
zoegirl:	i feel that way sometimes. like when i'm around other people, i put on this show of being interested and eager, and then when i'm

alone, i don't always know who i am. and i think how if someone were watching, like my dead grandfather or God or someone, all they'd see is this incredibly boring person.

SnowAngel: for me it's u guys who make me feel alive, u and maddie. without u, i'm just this floating blob of nothingness.

zoegirl: angela, ur not a floating blob of nothingness.

SnowAngel: seriously, i am!

SnowAngel: someone had on a shirt today that said, "if i seem to be getting smaller, it's because i'm walking away." that's me, zo. i'm getting smaller and smaller, only i don't WANNA be walking away.

zoegirl: oh, angela

SnowAngel: *recedes into smaller and smaller dot* *POOF!* *disappears*

zoegirl: you are never never never going to disappear

SnowAngel: what do u think my aunt sadie would do if i just showed up on her doorstep? she couldn't turn me away, could she?

zoegirl: um . . .

SnowAngel: aaargh, i don't mean to be so boring *gives self firm shake*

SnowAngel: so why all the calls? u said u needed to talk.

zoegirl: oh, right

zoegirl: er, it was stupid, actually. i'll bug you about it another time.

SnowAngel: u sure? cuz if ur sure, i think i'm gonna go take a nap.

zoegirl: try to feel better, ok?

SnowAngel: ttfn!

Tues, Jan 25, 9:59 AM E.S.T.

mad maddie: u gonna do it?

zoegirl:	leave me alone, i'm supposed to be doing research.
mad maddie:	maybe we should ask peaches what she thinks. why look, there she is at her desk. should i call her over?
zoegirl:	leave peaches out of it!
mad maddie:	at least i didn't say you had to do the great marshmallow-nipple dare at school, zoe.
mad maddie:	think about it!!!

Tues, Jan 25, 2:07 PM E.S.T.

mad maddie:	u gonna do it?
zoegirl:	*no*!

Tues, Jan 25, 9:41 PM E.S.T.

mad maddie:	u gonna do it?
zoegirl:	go away!!!!!!!!!!!!!!!

Wed, Jan 26, 3:35 PM E.S.T.

mad maddie:	ur not gonna do it, r u? i mean, not that i care. i'm just saying.
zoegirl:	oh, right, you don't care. that's why you've been buzzing in my ear like a fly for the last 5,000 years. if i had a swatter, i'd swat you flat.
mad maddie:	i only care cuz i care about U. i don't want u going thru life like a scared little mealworm, that's all. isn't it better to be a fly than a mealworm?
zoegirl:	what?
mad maddie:	quiet desperation . . . quiet desperation . . . quiet desperation . . .
zoegirl:	fine. meet me at the mall in half an hour.
mad maddie:	seriously?
zoegirl:	but afterward, you belong to me. i'm going to give

you the worst possible dare, and you'll HAVE to do it!

mad maddie: **wh-hoo! i'll bring the marshmallows!!!**

SnowAngel: uh, maddie?

mad maddie: **hey, angela! man, what a day. wazzup?**

SnowAngel: i just got a really strange email from mary kate. she hasn't been in touch at all since i moved, and suddenly she emailed me this wacko message about zoe. u don't know anything about this, do u?

mad maddie: **u got an email from mk? omg, this is great. what did she say?**

SnowAngel: she said she saw zoe at the mall and that zoe had MARSHMALLOWS GLUED TO HER NIPPLES! *bores eyes into friend in extreme concern*

mad maddie: **it was awesome, angela. u should have been there.**

SnowAngel: it's TRUE? oh my freakin god. zoe won't answer my calls, and all i could think was, "maddie, maddie is behind this."

SnowAngel: u made her glue marshmallows to her nipples?!!

mad maddie: **well, to her shirt, not her bare skin. and i didn't MAKE her. it was a dare.**

SnowAngel: another one of your stupid dares? that's sick!

mad maddie: **don't think "sick," think . . . whimsical. playful. a breath of fresh air.**

SnowAngel: i can't believe she actually did it. i can't believe it.

mad maddie: **imagine if u will: the mall is packed with irritable shoppers, bored to tears with their predictable lives. but hark! from the distance comes a hazy apparition! it's . . . it's . . . it's zoe! she's charging thru the crowd, nipples a-blazin'!**

SnowAngel: omfg

mad maddie: her face was bright red and she kept her eyes straight ahead, playing the "if i can't see u, then u can't see me" game. she was walking so fast that ppl had to dive out of her way. if it wasn't for the security guard, she'd have been home free.

SnowAngel: the security guard?!!

mad maddie: but now zoe can add "run-in with the law" to her resume too. i'm so proud of her.

SnowAngel: but is she ok?? she must be mortified!

mad maddie: if only she'd made it to Macy's. there was a group of nuns out front collecting money for the poor.

mad maddie: damn that pesky security guard!

SnowAngel: *shakes head in disbelief*

SnowAngel: u don't understand, maddie. zoe isn't equipped to handle something like this. if i was there, i would have stopped u!

mad maddie: but u weren't, were u? heh heh heh!

SnowAngel: u should be ashamed of yourself, madigan kinnick!

Wed, Jan 26, 7:20 PM P.S.T.

SnowAngel: i keep calling zo, but still no answer. i'm really worried.

mad maddie: oh pshaw

SnowAngel: so does she get to dare U to do something, now that u've publicly humiliated her?

mad maddie: yeah, i have to do whatever she tells me to do. i'm sure she's gonna make me quit smoking pot, but i don't care. i was gonna quit anywayz.

SnowAngel: really?

SnowAngel: i mean, good! serves u right!

Thu, Jan 27, 3:46 PM P.S.T.

SnowAngel: zoe, why haven't you answered your phone? r u too embarrassed to talk to anyone? even ME?

zoegirl:	huh?
zoegirl:	i guess my ringer's on mute. oops.
SnowAngel:	well, i just want to say how SORRY i am that maddie did that to u. i don't know what she was thinking. and i'm so sorry u felt like u couldn't tell me that day when u txted and said u wanted to talk, only i was so depressed that all we did was talk about ME. i'm so sorry i let u down!
zoegirl:	angela, hold on. you didn't let me down, okay?
SnowAngel:	ur nice to say that, but i know i did.
SnowAngel:	i called u a zillion times yesterday and never got u. what were u doing—hiding out under your covers?
zoegirl:	well, actually . . .
zoegirl:	i *was* under the covers, but they weren't mine, and i wasn't exactly hiding . . .
SnowAngel:	i don't get it. what do u mean they weren't
SnowAngel:	OMG, what r u saying???
zoegirl:	oh man, angela. it was nuts. the security guard at the mall lectured me for half an hour about "proper behavior for young ladies"—while maddie stood there smirking!—and after that, i was so embarrassed that i fled to my car and zoomed off. i just wanted out of there. but then about halfway home, i was filled with this incredible rush.
SnowAngel:	cuz it was over, u mean?
zoegirl:	no, cuz i *did* it!!! i actually did maddie's ridiculous dare. and having that knowledge inside me was like, WOW.
zoegirl:	it made me feel so liberated!
SnowAngel:	yes, but the covers . . .
SnowAngel:	just how liberated were u?
zoegirl:	liberated enough to drive straight to doug's house instead of going home. his mom wasn't there,

and we had the whole house to ourselves. and it was really, really great.

SnowAngel: *gulps* r u saying what i think ur saying?

zoegirl: no, angela, we didn't have sex. geez.

zoegirl: but we went further than we've ever gone before, and the best part is, i just let myself enjoy it. i was, like, on this adrenaline high, and i felt like i could do anything. so i just let go of all my zoe stupidness and went for it.

SnowAngel: oh

SnowAngel: here i was imagining u in the depths of depression. i felt so bad that i wasn't there for u, while all the time . . .

SnowAngel: u really DIDN'T need me, huh?

zoegirl: oh, angela. i *always* need you. don't u know that?

SnowAngel: i can't believe things worked out so well for u. i mean . . . whoa.

zoegirl: it *was* whoa. i never knew my body could feel like that. i know that sounds ridiculous.

SnowAngel: it doesn't sounds ridiculous. it sounds . . . u know. like a good thing.

zoegirl: i've always felt so bad at that stuff. like how i told you i could never get out of my brain?

SnowAngel: i remember. u wanted to be less inhibited.

zoegirl: yeah, like maddie. i've never admitted this to anyone, but i've always been kind of jealous of her, of how easy it is for her to give herself over to the moment. secretly, i've always wished i was like that.

zoegirl: not in a fool-around-with-every-guy-that-shows-up kind of way, but i didn't want to be frigid, either. isn't that an awful word? i hate that word.

SnowAngel:	what, frigid? it doesn't sound like u need to worry about it anymore.
zoegirl:	that's what makes me so happy! because i *did* let go of my inhibitions and i *did* lose myself in the moment! and not to get too graphic, but i was like, "ohhhh, so *this* is what all the fuss is about!"
zoegirl:	i think doug enjoyed it too
SnowAngel:	nooooo, u think?
zoegirl:	all day long i've felt so strong inside, even when mary kate announced to our whole math class about the marshmallow-nipple thing. i just laughed like, "yeah? so?" and everyone looked at me like they couldn't believe it. like, "this is not the zoe we know."
SnowAngel:	so yr saying yr GLAD maddie made that dare
zoegirl:	no, i'm just saying . . . i'm not sure. that maybe it's not so bad to say "screw it" to the rules sometimes.
SnowAngel:	oh *blinks in amazement*
zoegirl:	wanna hear something awful, though? in my mad panic from the mall, i completely forgot about the marshmallows. so when i showed up at doug's, they were still there!
SnowAngel:	oh no! what did he do?
zoegirl:	let's just say that once i explained the whole crazy story, he took care of the problem. as in, the marshmallows are no more.
SnowAngel:	uh huh. what a gentleman.
zoegirl:	yeah, i love him
SnowAngel:	for real? u "love" him love him?
zoegirl:	omg, i didn't mean to say that. it just slipped out.
zoegirl:	but . . . crap, angela. i think i do.
SnowAngel:	*whistles* this is big
zoegirl:	it *feels* big

zoegirl: hey, thanks for listening. i'm sure it's boring to hear me go on and on.

SnowAngel: um, no. boring is sitting alone in my room while everyone in my life moves on without me.

SnowAngel: i'm happy for u, zoe, i truly am, but i swear i'm turning invisible.

zoegirl: invisible? what do u mean?

SnowAngel: last night at dinner i didn't say a single word. i didn't have anything to say, so i just sat there and ate my peas. no one even noticed.

zoegirl: i'm sure they noticed. that's so unlike you not to be chattering away.

SnowAngel: nope, cuz later i brought it up to my mom, and she was like, "oh, angie, u did so talk. of course u did."

zoegirl: hmm. not the most reassuring response.

SnowAngel: everybody else's lives r so exciting that they forget i even exist.

zoegirl: angela, i am so sorry, but i've got to go. the doorbell just rang downstairs, and it's doug.

SnowAngel: oh

zoegirl: i'll call soon, promise!!!

Fri, Jan 28, 10:03 AM E.S.T.

mad maddie: ah, we meet again in the lovely media center. so give me my stupid dare already, will ya? enough with the taunting looks, just get on with it.

zoegirl: do u ever actually do your work when ur here? ever?

mad maddie: i already know what it's gonna be, so don't think ur gonna pull one over on me.

zoegirl: you know what it is, do you? then why don't you tell me?

mad maddie: go on, just say it

zoegirl:	all right, then, here's your dare: tell chive how you really feel about him.
mad maddie:	**WHAT? that's not the dare ur supposed to give me!**
zoegirl:	that's the dare. are you a mealworm or are you a fly?
mad maddie:	**that's a stupid dare. that's the most stupid dare u could have possibly come up with.**
zoegirl:	oh yeah? then why is your face all red? i can see you, you know.
mad maddie:	**chive doesn't like me. he likes whitney.**
zoegirl:	then why does he kiss you? and why do you let him? and why are you packing up your books all of a sudden? has it gotten too hot in here for you?
zoegirl:	tell him how you feel. that's your dare!!!

Sat, Jan 29, 11:33 PM E.S.T.

zoegirl:	hey, angela. i know it's like two in the morning there, but . . . are you awake?
SnowAngel:	good god, zoe, i'm gonna have to strap a time-change clock to your forehead.
SnowAngel:	if it's 11:30 there, then it's 8:30 here, which means UR the one who's up late, at least for u. were u out with doug?
zoegirl:	yeah, we went out after work. but i'm not txting about doug for once. i'm txting to tell you what graham cracker said.
SnowAngel:	that 3-yr-old u think is so adorable?
zoegirl:	he fell and skinned his knee, and he got all worried when he saw that he was bleeding. it was just the tiniest bit, but he clamped his hand over it and said, "i am holding it in. i am holding it in." like if he didn't, it might all drain out.
SnowAngel:	poor little guy

zoegirl:	finally he let me put a band-aid on. he watched me really carefully, and then his eyes welled up and he said, "zoe, i miss my mommy." and i said, "i know. she'll be here soon." and he said, "i miss her because i love her. and when i love people, i want them with me always."
SnowAngel:	awww
zoegirl:	and it made my heart hurt, and i thought of you. ♥
zoegirl:	that's all.

Mon, Jan 31, 4:02 PM E.S.T.

mad maddie:	hey, zo. i'm at java joe's right now, and guess who i ran into?
zoegirl:	who?
mad maddie:	ian! with margo pedersen! AND THEY WERE HOLDING HANDS!
zoegirl:	ooo, maddie, ouch.
zoegirl:	you okay?
mad maddie:	am i ok? hell yeah i'm ok. it was a classic awkward moment, tho, the ex meeting the new flame. ian was like, "uh, maddie, this is, um, margo. she's, um . . . well, we were just . . ." and i was like, "dude, i know who margo is. we go to the same school. and ur allowed to date someone new, u know."
zoegirl:	weren't you upset?
mad maddie:	i did have the uncharitable thought of "she has a big ass, ha ha ha." but oddly enough i wasn't that upset. wanna know why?
zoegirl:	why?
mad maddie:	cuz i don't like ian anymore. i mean, as a human being, sure. but i'm not pining over him.
zoegirl:	ahhh
mad maddie:	he's not chive, that's the point.

zoegirl:	so you're admitting loud and clear in the light of day that YOU LIKE CHIVE. that's good, maddie. that's very good. now you just have to tell *him*.
mad maddie:	**wait for it, wait for it**
mad maddie:	**i'm gonna tell him this weekend. we're gonna hang on saturday—i'll tell him then.**
zoegirl:	for real?!
mad maddie:	**i haven't done it YET. but i figure if u can glue marshmallows to your nipples . . .**
zoegirl:	doug calls me "hot cocoa" now. warm and luscious with a delightful marshmallow topping.
mad maddie:	**good god, one little dare and out comes your inner deviant. 😈**
zoegirl:	ha ha ha. doug said the same thing, actually . . .
mad maddie:	**doug shld send me flowers. he owes me BIG time.**
mad maddie:	**but for now, i'm outta here. i finished my chai and i've got some errands to run.**
zoegirl:	like what?
mad maddie:	**never u mind. it has to do with angela (and MAYBE u if ur nice), and it's a surprise. i just hate it that she's so depressed. it kills me.**
zoegirl:	she left me a voicemail saying her mom's driving her into the city this afternoon. maybe that'll help.
mad maddie:	**that reminds me, the other thing i need to do is swing by the DMV and apply for a new driver's license. every time i drive somewhere, i think, "shit, what if i get pulled over."**
zoegirl:	why do u need a new license?
mad maddie:	**cuz i lost mine, didn't i tell u? byeas!**

Mon, Jan 31, 8:24 PM P.S.T.

SnowAngel:	maddie, my life has hit an all-time low. 😔
SnowAngel:	i know that hardly seems possible. how could i be lower than i already was? yet here i am.

mad maddie: but . . . i thought u went into the city today. i thought u loved the city!

SnowAngel: i do—it's the only good thing about being here. but guess who i saw while i was there? actually, don't bother, cuz u never will. i was buying a hot dog at the embarcadero, and the girl in front of me looked vaguely familiar. she turned around and it was JEANNIE STARR.

mad maddie: jeannie starr? she goes to northside, doesn't she? i think she's one grade above chive.

SnowAngel: yeah, she's a senior. that's why she was in san francisco, cuz she was visiting colleges. she says she wants to get as far away from home as possible.

SnowAngel: isn't that ironic? i was like, "here, u can have my life. wanna trade?"

mad maddie: that is so weird. i don't know that i'd even recognize her.

SnowAngel: it took us both a minute, cuz i barely know her and she barely knows me. but then she said, "wait a sec . . . aren't u angela silver? i thought u were dead!"

mad maddie: DEAD?

SnowAngel: she said, "i thought u died in a car wreck! that's what someone told me!"

SnowAngel: this is what my life has come to, maddie. i move away, and one month later everyone assumes i'm dead! 😲

mad maddie: that is so sad

SnowAngel: i said to jeannie, "what? no, i'm not dead." and she goes, "r u sure?"

mad maddie: good grief. she is 1 donut short of a dozen.

SnowAngel: i stuck out my arm and said, "u can pinch me if u want." and she did!!!

mad maddie: man. it's like that mark twain quote, "the reports of my death have been greatly exaggerated."

SnowAngel: but the reports of my pathetic-ness have not. i might
               as well be dead.

mad maddie: DON'T EVEN SAY THAT. EVER!!!

SnowAngel: and then—THEN—i came home to find glendy's
               name on our caller ID 13 times. what cld anybody
               have to say that's that important?

**mad maddie: how do u know it was the glendinizer? maybe it
               was mr. boss, calling for your dad.**

SnowAngel: nuh uh, cuz she didn't leave a message, which mr.
               boss would have done. anyway, dad was at work,
               so if mr. boss needed him, he'd have just gone to his
               office.

mad maddie: did u call glendy back?

SnowAngel: no, i hit delete, delete, delete. *jabs button 13 times*

mad maddie: lord, angela

SnowAngel: and now i am going to take a very long, very hot
               bath and use up all of my mom's aromatherapy
               beads. and even that will not wash away the stain
               of my pathetic-ness.

SnowAngel: i love u, maddie, but i hate my life!!!

                    Mon, Jan 31, 9:15 PM P.S.T.

SnowAngel: glendy called AGAIN, and i finally gave in and
               answered. wanna know what was so desperately
               important?

mad maddie: do i?

SnowAngel: apparently she felt unloved. apparently she'd saved
               me a seat at lunch today and i failed to notice.

mad maddie: so?

SnowAngel: exactly! i was like, "and this was so important that u
               had to call me 13 frickin times???"

mad maddie: technically, 14

SnowAngel: all i could think was, "great. everyone thinks i'm
               DEAD except for u, and ur the 1 person in the world

i don't wanna hang out with. LEAVE ME ALONE, U GROSS LEECHY PERSON!"

mad maddie: **ha**

mad maddie: **what'd u tell her for real?**

SnowAngel: seriously, maddie, i cldn't take it anymore, so i was kinda mean. i said, "i'm sorry i didn't see u flagging me down. clearly i am a worthless human being. next time just don't bother, ok?"

mad maddie: **ooo, way to tell it like it is**

mad maddie: **what did SHE say?**

SnowAngel: first there was dead silence, and then she said really coldly, "well, excuse me for trying to be nice. excuse me for thinking u actually wanted a friend. u pretend to be so sweet, but really ur just a bitch!"

mad maddie: **omg**

mad maddie: **angela, that was so uncalled-for. SHE'S the bitch—u know that, right?**

SnowAngel: it made me cry, maddie, isn't that ridiculous? after she hung up on me, i just sat on my bed and bawled.

mad maddie: **oh, sweetie**

mad maddie: **if i were there, i'd spray paint bad words on her locker for u. i'd take away all her Care Bears!**

SnowAngel: *sniffles*

mad maddie: **just think of it this way: maybe u've gotten rid of the glendinizer once and for all.**

SnowAngel: god, let's hope

SnowAngel: i'm going to call zoe and tell her about this stupidness, and then i'm going to bed.

SnowAngel: thanks for listening, mads. night!!!

Tues, Feb 1, 6:33 PM E.S.T.

zoegirl: hey, are you home from school???? because it's

3:30 in california, if i finally got the time change right.

SnowAngel: i'm home, yup. wassup?

zoegirl: i want to ask your advice about something—
but first you have to update me on the glendy situation. how was she when you saw her today???

SnowAngel: *makes guttural frankenstein noise*

zoegirl: not so good, huh?

SnowAngel: actually, it was fine. u know the drill: wounded cold shoulder and poisonous glares. but at least i have her off my back, right?

zoegirl: *absolutely*

zoegirl: i'm still sorry that happened, tho

SnowAngel: oh who cares. it's just like everything else in my life, a big pile of poo. 💩

SnowAngel: what's going on with u? what do u need my advice on?

zoegirl: well, my mom and dad are going to this big law firm shindig on saturday night. it's called the prom, isn't that dorky?

SnowAngel: your mom and dad r going to the prom?

zoegirl: it's really just a fancy party, with a seated dinner and a live band. but it's black-tie, so everyone gets all dressed up. one of the partners at mom's firm decided to call it the prom as a joke.

SnowAngel: oh those crazy grown-ups! 🌀

zoegirl: but what this means is that i'll have the house to myself.

zoegirl: eeek! i'm so excited!

SnowAngel: aha. r u gonna invite doug over?

zoegirl: i want to cook him a really nice dinner, wouldn't that be fun? and then . . . who knows where the evening will lead?

SnowAngel: hold on now. ur not thinking . . . i mean, are you finally planning to . . .?

zoegirl: no! you always ask that, and the answer is always no. the answer will *always* be no, okay?

zoegirl: but there's a lot you can do leading up to that . . .

SnowAngel: an empty house, a romantic dinner, a soft, inviting bed . . .

zoegirl: so my question is, where should i go to get some sexy lingerie?

SnowAngel: zoe! *jaw drops on floor*

zoegirl: what? that's allowed, isn't it?

SnowAngel: of course it's allowed! i'm just flabbergasted. who'd have thought that u, of all ppl, would be marching off to buy sexy lingerie? and for doug!!!

zoegirl: where should i go? victoria's secret?

SnowAngel: sure, that would work. what r u gonna get?

zoegirl: that's what you need to tell me. what *should* i get?

SnowAngel: hmmm *taps finger on chin*

SnowAngel: is this something u plan to model for him, or will it just be the delightful surprise beneath your clothes?

zoegirl: i'm not gonna model it for him! no, no, no. just something nice for when we . . . u know.

SnowAngel: then i'd say it's time to go for the thong, zoe. god knows ur the only girl on the planet who doesn't own one.

zoegirl: a thong? i am not a fan of thongs and you know it.

zoegirl: anyway, don't u have to have a really good butt to wear a thong?

SnowAngel: u DO have a really good butt. here's the criteria for a thong: firm butt (preferably tan), no dimples, no unruly hairs. do u meet the requirements?

zoegirl: ew, angela. does anyone really have hair on her butt?

SnowAngel:	well, not sprouting from the cheeks or anything. i'm talking about from within the crevice.
zoegirl:	angela! sick!
SnowAngel:	so, good. u don't have butt hair—u can cross that off the list. now, for the firmness element. *cups hands in air as if squeezing* i don't think u have any problem there.
zoegirl:	oh my gosh, i am getting so nervous just talking about this.
zoegirl:	but okay, a thong. *maybe*. what about on top?
SnowAngel:	just get a good push-up bra with a little lace or ribbon on it. u'll be able to find one to match the thong, and if u can't, just ask one of the sales ladies to help u.
zoegirl:	no way, too embarrassing
zoegirl:	aye-yai-yai—i wish u were here to go with me!
SnowAngel:	yeah, me too *crumples into sad sack of a person*
zoegirl:	oh no, have i made u sad?
SnowAngel:	no sadder than i already was
SnowAngel:	i'll be with u in spirit. now go shop, u love-crazed fool!

Tues, Feb 1, 8:11 PM P.S.T.

SnowAngel:	hi, maddie. i am feeling very worthless.
mad maddie:	**why?**
SnowAngel:	cuz zoe txted earlier to ask for fashion advice, and it made me so aware of how pointless my life has become. she has doug, u have chive—and more than that, u both have each other. but what do i have? a big fat nothing. i don't even have glendy now that she's stopped talking to me!
mad maddie:	**but glendy not talking to u—that's a good thing, remember?**
mad maddie:	**anyway, i don't "have" chive. not even close.**

SnowAngel:	except ur gonna confess your love to him on saturday, zoe told me. and then he's gonna throw himself in your arms and ur gonna waltz off in a spasm of happiness.
SnowAngel:	i, probably, will be at home staring at my toenails.
mad maddie:	**that's bullshit**
mad maddie:	**do u really think he's gonna throw himself in my arms?**
SnowAngel:	so to commemorate my sadness, i've shaved off all my hair. i just wanted to let u know.
mad maddie:	**WHAT? u've been trying so long to grow it out!**
SnowAngel:	yeah, but what's the point? i don't have anyone to look good for, so i shaved it all off. i can be daring too, u know.
mad maddie:	**skype me then. prove it.**
SnowAngel:	um, my skype machine is broken
mad maddie:	**yr "skype machine"? uh huh. is snapchat broken too?**
SnowAngel:	ok, let me clarify. i *cld* have shaved it all off. i THOUGHT about shaving it all off.
mad maddie:	**your hair is so pretty. don't shave it off.**
SnowAngel:	i'm just so depressed. i have to do something.
SnowAngel:	my mom says i can go to atlanta over spring break, but that's not good enough. that's so far away!
mad maddie:	**ur coming to atlanta over spring break? angela, that's awesome!**
SnowAngel:	yeah . . . but i wanna be there now!
mad maddie:	**when's your spring break?**
SnowAngel:	march 21–25
mad maddie:	**that seems like a long way off, but c'mon. this is very very very good news.**
SnowAngel:	then why doesn't it feel like it? 😦
mad maddie:	**hold on, girl. u'll be here before u know it!**

SnowAngel: still sad. so sad i've started cutting myself, just fyi.

mad maddie: **so sad what a bad liar u r.**

mad maddie: **u can't stand the sound of your pulse, but i'm supposed to believe u could slice your skin and watch your blood ooze out?**

SnowAngel: ugh 😖

SnowAngel: u should go into counseling, maddie

mad maddie: **what? i'm not the one with the problem here!**

SnowAngel: i don't mean as a patient. i mean as a counselor. i can just see u talking to some poor distraught girl—much like ME, i might add—and saying, "u cut yourself, do u? u slice your skin and watch the blood ooze out?" u'd cure her in no time.

mad maddie: **good. does that mean i cured u?**

SnowAngel: maybe i'll start slow and build up. this girl in my math class uses a pink eraser to rub raw spots on the inside of her arm. i could manage that, i bet.

mad maddie: **please don't hurt yourself, angela. even in jest. and i think we shld have a moment of silence to send good thoughts toward any real cutters out there, cuz i'm suddenly feeling bad for making a joke out of it.**

SnowAngel: *groans* *puts head in hands*

SnowAngel: yr right, of course. kk, moment of silence, then:

SnowAngel: 🙊 🙊 🙊 🙊 🙊

SnowAngel: r we done? r we good?

mad maddie: 👍

SnowAngel: subject change: did zoe ever make it to victoria's secret?

mad maddie: **ooo, baby. she just popped by to show me her purchases, and they're sexcellent. 👙**

mad maddie: **she didn't model them for me, for which i say a prayer of thanks, but she done made me proud.**

the bra is lacy and has a rosebud in the center,
and she bought a thong to go with it. i am
extremely impressed.

SnowAngel: she bought a thong? for reals? what's it look like?

mad maddie: er, like a thong? it's lacy too, and it's got the same
rosebud thing going on as the bra.

mad maddie: pelt-woman calls her jesus sandals "thongs," btw.

SnowAngel: can u imagine pelt-woman wearing a *thong*
thong? a real thong?

mad maddie: i will now slide a steel door over my eyes to
prevent that image from entering my brain.
there r few things i can think of that wld be more
horrifying.

SnowAngel: my mom says that the key to a successful marriage
is wearing pretty underwear. u might let pelt-woman
know.

mad maddie: your mom says strange things.

SnowAngel: if u think she's bad, u should try my aunt sadie. i
called her last night and said, "please can't i come
live with u? please please please please please?"
and she was like, "angie, i would love nothing more
than for u to come live with me. we'd be two hip
girls on our own. we'd have a blast! but hon, that's
between u and your parents."

SnowAngel: then she told me she had to go cuz she was getting
ready for a date, but before she hung up, she gave
me a handy tip which i shld prolly pass on to zoe.

mad maddie: which was?

SnowAngel: to lean over when u put your bra on and really jiggle
your boobs into place. "so many women have an
extra inch of cleavage that remains under-utilized,"
she told me. "it's over by your armpits. u just have to
shove it into place."

mad maddie: armpit cleavage. luverly!

SnowAngel: hi, mads! me again! 😃

mad maddie: **couldn't get enough of me, is that it?**

SnowAngel: i just wanted u to know how wrong u r about me, that's all. i may not be able to stand the sound of my pulse, but i'm quite fine with needles as it turns out.

mad maddie: **so ur saying . . . what? u've taken up cross-stitch?**

SnowAngel: i'm saying that i've pierced my nose. AND my nipple. i did it myself in my very own bathroom. just this second. *proudly thrusts out boob*

mad maddie: **angela. cupcake. ur picking the wrong girl for your charade. u need to be telling this to zoe, not me.**

mad maddie: **anywayz, if ur going for shock value, u should tell her u pierced your labia.**

SnowAngel: *eyes widen with appreciation* u r so right.

mad maddie: **but don't say u did it yrself. that's too much of a stretch, even for zo.**

SnowAngel: ah, yes. true true!

SnowAngel: zoe, i have something shocking to tell u, and i don't want u to get upset.

zoegirl: what happened? is something wrong?

SnowAngel: no, no, nothing wrong . . . other than everything, that is.

SnowAngel: it's just, well . . .

SnowAngel: i pierced my labia.

zoegirl: WHAT?

SnowAngel: i pierced my labia. i got this sudden urge, i don't even know why, so i walked into a body-art salon and just went for it.

zoegirl: omg. omg! did it hurt?

SnowAngel:	a little, yeah. well, ok, a lot. but i was very brave. in fact, the guy who did the piercing said i was the bravest of anyone he'd done.
zoegirl:	a *guy* did it? why, angela???
SnowAngel:	cuz he was the only person there. he does tattoos too. think i shld get a tattoo?
zoegirl:	angela, i don't know how to say this, but—and please don't be offended—is this a cry for help? sometimes people do really out-of-character things when they're unhappy. i mean, tattoos are fine, but do u honestly want to get one? you know how you are with needles.
zoegirl:	as for your . . . as for the other thing, if you took the ring or stud out right now, would the piercing close up?
SnowAngel:	oh, zoe. ur no fun.
SnowAngel:	no, i don't want a tattoo. and i don't want a pierced labia, either.
zoegirl:	you *were* just doing it for attention! poor angela!
zoegirl:	so go take the ring out RIGHT NOW! you've only had it for a day, right?
SnowAngel:	even less. i never got it done, zo.
zoegirl:	what do you mean, you never got it done? you just said
zoegirl:	oh. haha.
SnowAngel:	sorry
zoegirl:	did maddie put u up to this???
SnowAngel:	*blinks meekly*
zoegirl:	i should have known. what was i thinking? you can't even stand the sound of your own pulse.
SnowAngel:	must everyone go on and on about that? YES, i'm a blob. i admit it. you and maddie do these daring, exciting things, and what do i do? i plod thru school

with glendy trailing behind me like a cloud of doom. even when i go to the bathroom, there she is, glaring malevolently at me from over the top of the stall.

zoegirl: she does not stare at you from over the top of the stall.

zoegirl: does she?

zoegirl: anyway, what have i ever done that's daring and exciting?

SnowAngel: hmm, does parading thru the mall with marshmallow-nipples count? plus ur planning this fabulous night with doug, which requires its own kind of daring. and while ur cozying up with him, maddie's gonna be confessing her undying love to chive. that's braver than all the stupid-ass stunts she's pulled before.

zoegirl: well . . . ok, that's actually true. but you're brave too, angela.

SnowAngel: no, i'm not. if i was brave, i'd escape this stinking hellhole!

zoegirl: being in california isn't your fault, and being stalked by glendy isn't your fault either. just keep telling yourself, "spring break. spring break, spring break, spring break."

SnowAngel: u think it's that easy, but it's not. i can't talk about it anymore—it's only making things worse!

Thu, Feb 3, 6:02 PM E.S.T.

zoegirl: mads, you there?

mad maddie: i is, i is. wassup, girl?

zoegirl: well, i can't talk long because i'm heading out to dinner with my parents. i figure i should play the good-girl role while i can, so that they won't suspect anything about saturday night.

mad maddie: have u worked out the details with doug?

zoegirl: my mom and dad leave for the prom at 7:00, so i'll start cooking then. i'm making chicken parmesan, steamed broccoli, and crescent rolls.

mad maddie: i thought for a romantic evening u were supposed to eat oysters.

zoegirl: yeah, like i know how to cook oysters. if i even liked oysters, which i don't. anyway, i told doug to show up at 8:00. i don't want him coming over until the food is in the oven.

mad maddie: what about kidding around? don't u guys usually work on saturday nights?

zoegirl: we traded shirts.

mad maddie: u traded SHIRTS?

zoegirl: oops

zoegirl: *shifts. we traded shifts with other employees. this is our one opportunity to have the house to ourselves, and i intend to take advantage of every minute of it.

mad maddie: yeah, so that u can trade shirts, heh heh heh.

zoegirl: that was pretty freudian, huh?

zoegirl: i'm *nervous*, maddie. isn't that silly?

mad maddie: it's cuz ur having impure thoughts. just think, after saturday u'll be a soiled dove.

zoegirl: a soiled . . . ?

zoegirl: maddie, no. i told you already—we're not gonna have sex.

mad maddie: says who?

zoegirl: says me! *and* doug. we're not ready.

mad maddie: u say ur not ready, but what happens when the passion of the moment overtakes u? do u have a condom just in case?

zoegirl: oh, and where am i supposed to get a condom? you think i'm just going to march into the drugstore and

zoegirl:	*stop*! i am not having this conversation! doug and i are going to have a lovely romantic evening together, and maybe we'll fool around and maybe we won't.
mad maddie:	believe me, you will
zoegirl:	okay, we will. but we're *not* going to have sex.
zoegirl:	what about you? have you planned what you're going to say to chive?
mad maddie:	ur joking, right?
zoegirl:	if you're gonna confess your love to him, you need to know what you're gonna say. these things require thought.
mad maddie:	cuz ur the expert now?
mad maddie:	zo, u know i'm not a plan-it-out kind of girl.
zoegirl:	have you thought about it at all?
mad maddie:	dude, i have sweat stains the size of buffaloes blooming from under my pits.
zoegirl:	ick, maddie!
mad maddie:	just imagine how bad i'll be by saturday when i actually see him. THIS is why i don't wanna think about it. i'll just . . . say whatever i happen to say. don't stress me out, ok?
zoegirl:	fine, just as long as u don't wimp out. just remember: marshmallows!
mad maddie:	grrrr
zoegirl:	ack, my mom's yelling that it's time to go.
zoegirl:	but quickly, have u heard from angela today?
mad maddie:	no. u?
zoegirl:	she called from her cell a few hours ago. it was a little strange.
mad maddie:	strange how?
zoegirl:	because three minutes into our conversation, she said, "oh crap. here comes glendy."
mad maddie:	i thought glendy was giving her the cold shoulder.

zoegirl:	that's exactly what i said. and angela said, "i thought so too, but she's heading straight for me. and she's wearing a VEST."
mad maddie:	**i don't get it. what's the significance of a vest?**
zoegirl:	i don't know, that they're tacky?
zoegirl:	then in the background i heard this whiny voice, which i assume was glendy, saying, "angela? can we talk?"
zoegirl:	and then angela told me she had to go, but that she'd call me right back. and then she hung up.
mad maddie:	**huh. i wonder what happened.**
zoegirl:	and *i* wonder why she hasn't called me back.
zoegirl:	all right, bye for real!

Thu, Feb 3, 9:33 PM E.S.T.

zoegirl:	where in the world is angela? she still hasn't called or txted or anything!
mad maddie:	**give it a rest. she's FINE.**
zoegirl:	you don't think she's gone off and done something crazy, do you?
mad maddie:	**ANGELA? no, i don't think she's gone off and done something crazy.**
mad maddie:	**unless maybe it involves a daringly sparkly eyeshadow . . .**
zoegirl:	all right, all right. you don't have to make fun of me for worrying about my friend. sheesh!

Fri, Feb 4, 6:59 PM E.S.T.

zoegirl:	maddie, angela's phone is turned off, and i haven't seen her on FB or twitter or anywhere for two days. i called her parents' land line, and her mom says she's at *glendy's*!
mad maddie:	**at glendy's?**
mad maddie:	**that's unexpected**

zoegirl:	"unexpected"? that's all you can say?
mad maddie:	**what do u want me to say?**
zoegirl:	i want you to say that there's something very wrong with this picture, more than just "unexpected."
zoegirl:	she's disappeared off the face of the earth, and we're supposed to believe she's at *glendy's*?
mad maddie:	**she hasn't disappeared off the face of the earth. sure, her phone's turned off, but she probably just spaced it. as for not being online, she prolly just hasn't been online when U'VE been online. did u think of that?**
mad maddie:	**unless . . .**
zoegirl:	unless what?
mad maddie:	**unless the glendinizer locked angela into the basement and forced her into a vest!!! ahhhhhhhhhhhh!** 🤖
zoegirl:	shut up
mad maddie:	**maybe she and glendy had to do a school project or something. try to find glendy's number and call her there.**
zoegirl:	do u know her last name?
mad maddie:	**sorry, charlie, ur on your own.**

Fri, Feb 4, 11:59 PM M.S.T.

SnowAngel:	hi, zo. it's super-duper late, i know. so yr prolly not awake . . . huh?
SnowAngel:	yeah. (sigh.) figured.
SnowAngel:	i kinda need u, zo. like, i need to talk to u. can u tell i'm not so great at being all by myself at midnight with no one to talk to?
SnowAngel:	ok, well . . . i know i'm supposed to handle things on my own and all that, but i might not be that strong. i'll call u if i need u. mwah!

Sat, Feb 5, 12:04 AM M.S.T.

SnowAngel: maddie, are YOU awake?

SnowAngel: or are you snoring?

SnowAngel: *drums fingers on scratchy upholstery*

SnowAngel: yr snoring. fine. just don't call me unpredictable ever
               again!!!

Sat, Feb 5, 11:00 AM E.S.T.

zoegirl: maddie! i finally heard from angela, but it was
               weird. it was a late-night text, and it had to do
               with midnight and being alone and calling me if
               she needed me, only wanting to be strong enough
               not to have to. what was she talking about???

mad maddie: she txted me too. she made a cryptic comment
               about not being unpredictable, maybe cuz for
               once she was up past me??? does that count as
               unpredictable?

mad maddie: oh, and she said something about upholstery,
               which i didn't get.

zoegirl: well, i feel better knowing that at least she still
               exists. although her phone is still going straight
               to voicemail.

mad maddie: dude, she's fine. it's 8 in the morning california
               time. she's prolly sleeping, which is what i wanna
               do. power nap to rest up for my evening of sin
               and debauchery.

zoegirl: tell me you're kidding. you're taking a nap at 11 am?

mad maddie: nighty-night!

Sat, Feb 5, 7:29 PM E.S.T.

zoegirl: sooooooo . . . ? are you at chive's?

mad maddie: not yet. we're not heading to his house until after
               northside's basketball game, cuz whitney insisted
               they attend.

mad maddie: are u cooking your fancy dinner?

zoegirl: everything's in the oven, and all i've got left to do is decide what to wear. what do u think: jeans and my peasant blouse or my black j.crew skirt and my gray cashmere sweater?

mad maddie: i thought u were gonna wear your fancy underwear.

zoegirl: but on top, dummy? i'm not going to open the door in my bra and thong!

mad maddie: well, don't ask me. ask angela.

zoegirl: don't u think i would if i could reach her???

zoegirl: so what should i wear??? doug's gonna be here in 20 minutes!

mad maddie: hmm. your peasant blouse is one of those off-the-shoulder dealies, right? i say wear that, for easy access.

zoegirl: easy access to what?

zoegirl: never mind. god, maddie, you and your smutty mind. i'm wearing the sweater.

mad maddie: u ask for my fashion advice and then do the exact opposite? what kind of friend r u?

zoegirl: a smart one!

Sat, Feb 5, 7:43 PM E.S.T.

zoegirl: oh yeah, i forgot to say one thing.

mad maddie: what?

zoegirl: don't wimp out!!!

Sat, Feb 5, 8:12 PM C.S.T.

SnowAngel: zo?

SnowAngel: remember how i said i'd call if i needed u? well, i need u.

SnowAngel: so call me

SnowAngel: soon, ok?

SnowAngel: call me soon, plz!

Sat, Feb 5, 8:14 PM C.S.T.

SnowAngel: maddie? u there?

mad maddie: angela! hello, hello!

mad maddie: zoe's been worried sick cuz of not hearing from u,
btw. what's the dealio?

SnowAngel: i ran away. i'm txting from a greyhound bus.

mad maddie: hahaha. hence all the mystery? hence the veiled
reference to bad upholstery?

mad maddie: where r u really?

SnowAngel: ???

SnowAngel: i really am on a greyhound. i'll be in atlanta in 12
hours.

mad maddie: a-boogie, i already told u i'm the wrong girl for yr
games

mad maddie: and hey, sorry for bad timing, but text me later?
i luv u and can't wait to talk to u, but i'm kinda
in the middle of something. l8rs!

SnowAngel: maddie, wait!

SnowAngel: MADDIE!!!!

Sun, Feb 6, 10:00 AM E.S.T.

zoegirl: crap, maddie

mad maddie: u can say that again. 1 day—1 FRICKIN DAY—and
everything comes crashing down!

zoegirl: i *knew* something was up. i just knew it! and
now i feel terrible, like i should have done
something to fix it all!

mad maddie: what wld u have done? not even u cld have fixed
this one, zo.

mad maddie: wait a sec, how do u even know? oh god, my
mom didn't tell your parents, did she?

zoegirl: your *mom* knows? how?!

mad maddie: oh let's see . . . cuz she's the one who had to pick me up from the police station?

zoegirl: the police station?! maddie, what are you talking about?

mad maddie: i'm talking about everything that happened with chive, and . . . wait. what r U talking about???

zoegirl: i'm talking about *angela*! she ran away from home and she's at the bus station this very second! only i can't go pick her up because i'm grounded, so you have to go. you have to go now!

mad maddie: she's at the bus station? the ATLANTA bus station?

zoegirl: yes. alone and hungry and . . . alone. go get her!

mad maddie: omg, she was telling the truth!

zoegirl: she didn't give me the whole story because her phone died, but apparently she just couldn't take it anymore. so she hopped on a bus and traveled for two and a half days to get here!

mad maddie: holy shit

zoegirl: yea, shit. but backing up a sec—the police station?!

mad maddie: i got busted buying pot, zoe.

zoegirl: oh my god

mad maddie: um, yeah, so i'm grounded too.

mad maddie: hold on—there is way too much going on here. angela's at the bus station, i can't go get her cuz i'm grounded, and u just said u can't go get her cuz yr grounded too. what r U grounded for?

zoegirl: my parents came home early from the prom. they walked in on me and doug.

mad maddie: oh no.

zoegirl: oh yes. it was AWFUL.

zoegirl: it was completely mortifying, and my mother saw way more of doug than she ever wanted, and i'm forbidden to leave the house until i'm 43.

mad maddie:	fuck
zoegirl:	yeah
mad maddie:	and angela's waiting at the bus station.
zoegirl:	yeah again
zoegirl:	what r we gonna do?
mad maddie:	well, we have no choice, do we?
zoegirl:	but how? i seriously cannot leave the house, maddie. my mom is livid. she would physically block me from the door.
mad maddie:	lemme think
mad maddie:	ok, call the land line at my house got it? say you couldn't reach me on my cell. the moms will answer, and odds are she'll say i can't come to the phone cuz she'll want to punish me by keeping me from my friends. but that's good, cuz your job is to talk to her, not me.
zoegirl:	talk to her about what?
mad maddie:	about anything. use your good-girl charm and keep her chatting long enough for me to sneak out.
zoegirl:	how do you know she won't see you?
mad maddie:	cuz the phone's in the kitchen and my car's parked on the street out front. if all goes well, i'll be out and back without her even knowing.
zoegirl:	if not, you'll be even more dead than you already are.
mad maddie:	and so will you, cuz i guarantee that if all of this falls apart, my mom will call your mom pronto.
zoegirl:	crap
mad maddie:	yep
zoegirl:	well, are you ready?
mad maddie:	zoe, i was born ready.

Sun, Feb 6, 11:23 AM E.S.T.

SnowAngel:	hi, zoe

zoegirl:	angela. thank god. where are you???
SnowAngel:	i had maddie drop me off at my aunt sadie's. aunt sadie is flipping out, btw. first she made me take a shower while she called my mom. then she made ME call my mom to reassure her that i really was alive.
zoegirl:	what did your mom say? did she have any clue where u were this whole time?
SnowAngel:	of course! *huffs indignantly* what kind of daughter do u think i am?
zoegirl:	she *knew* you'd run off to atlanta?!
SnowAngel:	well, noooo, i didn't tell her THAT part.
SnowAngel:	what i told her was . . . well, it's confusing. lemme just walk u thru it.
SnowAngel:	thursday i cut school early and bought my bus ticket, and after i did that, i called my mom and said i was spending the night at glendy's. (as if!) i told her we had an english project to do.
zoegirl:	i *knew* you would have never gone to glendy's. that should have been my big warning sign. why didn't i listen?!
SnowAngel:	and then friday, i called and said i was gonna stay for the whole weekend since we were having such a blast.
SnowAngel:	that was a bit of irony in case u didn't notice.
zoegirl:	when u weren't answering yr phone, i called yr mom, and she just sounded happy that u were off having fun. in my head i was like, "with *glendy*? i don't think so." but i didn't say anything.
SnowAngel:	i'm glad—not that it would have mattered. by that point, there was nothing she could have done to stop me.
zoegirl:	man, angela. i can't believe u hopped on a bus and came all the way across the country. i just can't believe it.

zoegirl:	weren't you scared?
SnowAngel:	i wasn't scared, exactly. it was more like everything felt . . . unreal. like there i was, trapped in my sucky life, and there was absolutely nothing i could do about it, right? but then i DID do something—and it turned out to be so much easier than i would have thought.
zoegirl:	actually, i kind of know what u mean. like after the marshmallow incident, when i decided to just say "screw it" to being the uptight me that i'd always been.
zoegirl:	although it is true that the uptight me would never have been caught naked in bed with my boyfriend . . .
SnowAngel:	poor zoe! i need more details on that, u know. my phone died right when u were getting to the good part!
zoegirl:	there is no way we're gonna talk about me when you just crossed the entire country—by yourself!—on a greyhound. my god, angela, what was it like?
SnowAngel:	like a really bad, really long field trip. mainly it was boring, especially in states where everything looked the same same same. instead of "wyoming," i called it "i'm moaning." "kansas" was "can't stand us," and "missouri" was "misery." that's what i did to pass the time, i made up new names for the states i went thru. i guess it helped keep my mind off what i was doing.
zoegirl:	nobody bugged u? nobody was like, "young girl on her own—better call the cops"?
SnowAngel:	not a soul. i was still invisible, apparently.
SnowAngel:	altho there was this one horrible man who boarded in St. Louis. he didn't do anything gross like try to molest me, but he was big and smelly and of all the

	seats on the bus, he had to choose the one next to
	mine. his b.o. was REVOLTING, as in, i thought i was
	gonna barf. 😖
zoegirl:	ick
SnowAngel:	so i got up and moved, with no excuses and no
	apologies. i was like, i'm not escaping california and
	the horrible glendy just to end up next to this bozo.
zoegirl:	why *did* u escape the horrible glendy? i mean, i
	know why in general, but what happened that day
	when you and i were on the phone? i heard her in
	the background, and i heard her say that the two
	of you had to talk—did she say something specific
	that made you run away?
SnowAngel:	*does air-blowing-out thing so that lips make p-b-b-
	b-b sound*
SnowAngel:	i don't know if i can explain. mainly it's just that i was
	so unhappy already, with no end in sight. she just
	pushed me over the edge.
zoegirl:	what did she say???
SnowAngel:	she dragged me over to a private spot on the
	quad, looked at me very sternly, and said, "first of
	all, i'd like to apologize for all the things i've said to u
	in my head over the last few days."
zoegirl:	no!
zoegirl:	that's psycho, angela
SnowAngel:	then she said, "but i forgive u, cuz i know ur having a
	hard transition. your dad told my dad all about it."
zoegirl:	your dad discussed you with mr. boss?
SnowAngel:	she went on and on about how she wasn't gonna
	let me push her away no matter how hard i tried,
	cuz she knew i was just acting out of pain. and then
	she put her hand on my knee and leaned so close
	that i could smell her breath, which smelled like taco
	salad. she said, "i know u miss your old friends from

	atlanta, but they're not here. i am. and i will never leave u, i promise."
zoegirl:	ewww!
SnowAngel:	and then the reality of that hit home, how glendy was gonna be there forever and ever, and how u guys were still gonna be in atlanta. and i was like, "no. i just can't."
SnowAngel:	so . . . i left.
zoegirl:	oh, angela. i don't blame you!
SnowAngel:	*puts hands on hips defiantly* and i'm glad i did, even tho i know it's gonna cause all kinds of problems. and even tho my REAL friends can't even come see me cuz ur both grounded, u idiots!
zoegirl:	omigosh, that's right! what in the world happened to maddie last night? did she tell you?
SnowAngel:	yeah, and it's bad. but i'm too tired to explain—text her yourself.
zoegirl:	what? NO! tell me!
SnowAngel:	whoa. woozy. all of a sudden i can hardly keep sitting up straight. guess that's what happens after being on a bus for 3 days, huh? ttyl!

Sun, Feb 6, 12:01 PM E.S.T.

zoegirl:	hey, mads. can u talk? i mean text?
mad maddie:	well, no one's taken my phone yet, so yeah. u rocked with the moms, dude. she has no clue i was even gone.
zoegirl:	that's because i stayed on the phone with her for an entire hour!!! i was like her therapist. she was all, "i don't understand why maddie would do something like this. you would never make such bad decisions, would you, zoe?" later she asked who else of our friends "participates" in smoking marijuana, as if i was gonna give her a list.

mad maddie:	**what a freak**
zoegirl:	no, she just loves you. but the worst part was sitting there going, "uh huh, uh huh. no, i'm sure maddie doesn't have a drug problem," when i didn't even know the whole story.
zoegirl:	so while i'm very glad that you delivered angela to her aunt's, and i'm very very glad that angela herself is safe and sound, will you please tell me what happened to YOU last night?
mad maddie:	**u wanna hear the story of the Big Bust? fine, but it's not pretty.**
zoegirl:	spill
mad maddie:	**i met up with chive and whitney and brannen and meade after northside's basketball game, right? and brannen announced that he wanted some pot. so chive said, "ok, maddie and i will go buy it."**
mad maddie:	**now before u get all judgmental, I WASN'T PLANNING ON SMOKING ANY. but i figured it would be a good chance to get chive alone, so that we could talk.**
zoegirl:	oh no. it's my fault—because of my dare!
mad maddie:	**no, zoe, it's not your fault.**
mad maddie:	**actually, sure. let's make it your fault.**
mad maddie:	**anywayz, brannen goes, "i'll come too," which was extremely annoying cuz i knew HE was saying it to be with ME. so then chive goes, "look, u two just go on. i'll stay here."**
zoegirl:	aargh!
mad maddie:	**yeah, but what was i supposed to say? so brannen and i took off to downtown atlanta, and at echo street i took a wrong turn, which meant that brannen ended up on the side where the sellers were, which actually turned out to be very lucky**

	for me. so brannen bought a nickel bag, and off we drove.
zoegirl:	echo street? nickel bag? how do you know all this, maddie?
mad maddie:	do u wanna hear the story or not?
mad maddie:	five minutes later, i looked behind me and saw a police car. i didn't think anything of it, other than to remind myself AGAIN to get my damn license.
zoegirl:	i thought you already got your new license, that day you went on your secret errand.
mad maddie:	well . . . i kind of blew it off cuz the line was so long. nice move, huh?
zoegirl:	maddie. omg.
mad maddie:	uh huh, especially cuz it wasn't just a coincidence that the police were behind us. they turned on their lights and bleeped their siren, and i about crapped my pants.
mad maddie:	i pulled over, and the cops yanked me and brannen out of my car. they had us lean up against the door and they frisked us and put handcuffs on us. it was crazy. then one cop drove my car and the other cop drove me and brannen in the squad car, and we went to this big parking lot which was full of more cops and vans and other ppl who were obviously getting busted, just like we were.
zoegirl:	what are you saying, that it was a setup?
mad maddie:	the guy we bought the pot from turned out to be a cop named rudolph—no lie. rudolph took our names and asked which one of us had bought the "oatmeal," even tho they already knew it was brannen. then the other cop asked me for my license, which of course i didn't have.
zoegirl:	maddie! this is terrible!

mad maddie: they did a license check on a computer, and for some reason my license didn't come up—or maybe they just SAID it didn't. so the cop said to me, "why are you lying to us, girl? why are you lying?!" he was SO mean. and after a long hassle, they said that i could go, but that brannen was gonna get taken to jail. and then they told me that if i was caught out on the road again, then I'D be sent to jail.

zoegirl: can they really do that? send kids to jail?

mad maddie: guess so

zoegirl: but you didn't end up at jail. you ended up at the police station. i don't understand!

mad maddie: chill!

mad maddie: SO . . . i drove back to chive's and told everyone the story, and then chive and i took off to get brannen out of jail.

zoegirl: maddie, no!!!

mad maddie: but we had an unbelievably hard time trying to figure out where brannen was, and we drove around downtown atlanta for like two hours before finding the holding cell. turns out brannen's bail was $1,500, which meant that the bond would be $150. but we only had $98, cuz that's all we'd collected back at chive's. the bondsman we talked to told us that we needed to get the rest of the money and then come back with someone over 24 who had a responsible job. THEN he'd give us the bond.

zoegirl: good god, maddie. you know all this weird stuff that i would never in a million years dream of knowing.

mad maddie: believe me, i'd rather not. so we decided to drive to dunwoody and get my cousin donovan, only as

	we were walking back to my car we heard a man yell, "hey! you two! get over here!"
zoegirl:	oh no. what now?
mad maddie:	it was the exact same cops who had busted me and brannen after we bought the oatmeal from rudolph. i couldn't fucking believe it. they took us to the station and made us call our parents—and THAT'S why i'm grounded.
zoegirl:	ugh, what a mess. what an awful, awful mess.
mad maddie:	except there is one last thing. i did finish the dare.
zoegirl:	hold on. somehow in the middle of this, you found time to have your heart-to-heart with chive?
mad maddie:	we were sitting on this hard metal bench outside the police station, and i thought, "well, things sure as hell can't get any worse."
mad maddie:	actually, what i REALLY thought, cuz i'm an idiot, is that we were having, like, this big moment. we were going thru this really shitty thing, but at least we were going thru it together.
zoegirl:	so . . . what did u say?
mad maddie:	i told him that i liked him—more than just as a friend.
zoegirl:	and?
mad maddie:	it's not good.
mad maddie:	he put his head in his hands and said, "ahh, maddie." like he was in pain.
zoegirl:	uh oh
mad maddie:	he goes, "maddie . . . i'm with whitney." my heart was pounding really hard, but i made myself say, "why?" meaning, she doesn't get u. she can't keep up with u, she doesn't even get your jokes.
zoegirl:	but *you* do

mad maddie:	yeah, i do, and he KNOWS that, zoe. i could c it in his eyes. but he just shook his head really mournfully. he said, "i'm probably making a big mistake, huh?"
zoegirl:	like that's supposed to make it better? don't be man enough to actually *act* on it, just toss it out there like a consolation prize?
zoegirl:	he doesn't deserve you, maddie.
mad maddie:	then he took my hand and gave me one of his soulful looks and said, "we can still spend time together, tho. nothing has to change."
zoegirl:	is "spending time together" code for "fooling around"?
zoegirl:	i hope you told him to f*ck off!
mad maddie:	then my parents drove up, and that was that.
mad maddie:	the moms is totally bent out of shape. in fact i have to go, cuz she just knocked on my door and said in this pinched voice that she wants to talk to me. guess it's time for lecture #3 on The Evil of Drugs.
zoegirl:	maddie, i am so so so so sorry
mad maddie:	just another sucky day in suck land.
mad maddie:	u know what, tho?
zoegirl:	what?
mad maddie:	i am glad i told him, cuz now i know. 💔

Sun, Feb 6, 7:33 PM E.S.T.

zoegirl:	hey there, sleepyhead. you awake?
SnowAngel:	hey, zo. my aunt told me u called a couple of times, but she didn't wanna wake me. sorry.
zoegirl:	that's ok, i just wanted to check in and see how you're doing.
SnowAngel:	about like this, i'd say.
zoegirl:	what's that, you with tire tracks across your face?

SnowAngel:	i just got off the phone with my mom. she said she's really upset with me for running away, but that she's also really upset that she didn't know how unhappy i was living in el cerrito. i was like, "mom, u didn't know cuz u didn't WANT to know."
zoegirl:	is she going to make u go back?
SnowAngel:	NO, cuz i refuse to. i told her that flat-out, and she said, "angela, ur our daughter. u'll do what we say." *rolls eyes*
zoegirl:	so what does that mean?
SnowAngel:	we're in negotiation. let's put it that way.
zoegirl:	what about school?
SnowAngel:	if i stay here with aunt sadie, i'll go back to school with u guys. but not tomorrow. not till everything gets settled one way or another.
zoegirl:	wow. i am so impressed with u, angela. i really am.
SnowAngel:	what about u—how's life on the home front?
zoegirl:	ehh . . .
zoegirl:	on the bright side, i didn't run away, and i didn't get busted buying pot. on the un-bright side, my mother saw my boyfriend's naked butt.
SnowAngel:	the dark side of the moon, like that pink floyd song. hee hee.
zoegirl:	i'm glad you can laugh about it
zoegirl:	it's just so ridiculous, my mom coming home from the prom and catching me and doug all over each other. and poor doug! he sent me an email saying he's never stepping foot in my house again.
SnowAngel:	and ur never stepping foot out of your house again, if your mom has anything to say about it. which will make things tricky, huh?
zoegirl:	well, i'll see doug at school, of course.

zoegirl: you know what's weird? i'm not glad that mom walked in on us, obviously, but at the same time . . .

SnowAngel: at the same time what?

zoegirl: we stopped because my mom barged in on us. but if she hadn't . . . i don't know what would have happened. and that kind of scares me, because as you know, i wasn't planning on that.

SnowAngel: whoa

zoegirl: or maybe it wouldn't have happened anyway. it probably wouldn't have.

SnowAngel: this time u really r talking about sex, right? about u and doug going all the way?

zoegirl: we didn't even have condoms, angela. it would have been bad.

SnowAngel: r u gonna buy some for next time?

zoegirl: there's not going to *be* a next time for a very long time. i'm sure my mom's going to make it hard for me and doug to be alone together, even when i'm not grounded anymore. *if* i'm ever not grounded anymore.

SnowAngel: and how do u feel about this? *raises eyebrows inquiringly*

zoegirl: frustrated? relieved?

zoegirl: i don't know!

zoegirl: the whole night—until mom busted in—was amazing. and my body wanted more and more and more. but deep down i'm just not ready.

SnowAngel: how does doug feel about it?

zoegirl: he's like me—at least he says he is. although part of me thinks that if i said, "yes, let's go for it," he'd agree right away.

SnowAngel: nooooo, really?

zoegirl: i do love him, angela. it's just all so confusing.

SnowAngel: don't i know it. and not just boys, but EVERYTHING!

Sun, Feb 6, 10:01 PM E.S.T.

mad maddie: hey, u. u conked out?

SnowAngel: nah. i took a long nap. plus, my body's still on california time. it's only seven in el cerrito. isn't that weird?

mad maddie: do u wish u were back there?

SnowAngel: r u kidding??? not in the slightest.

SnowAngel: i'm sure i'll miss my mom and dad and chrissy eventually, but no, i don't wish i was there.

mad maddie: well, maybe i should take your place. think your parents would notice?

SnowAngel: madigan kinnick! *puts hands on hips* i came all this way to be with U. don't even tease me like that.

mad maddie: i just need a break from the moms, that's all. she can't get it into her head that my pot smoking days r over, that they were over even before the Big Bust.

mad maddie: the theme of tonight's lecture was that she thinks i have a "naive" philosophy toward life, which is that i have to try something out before i can make a decision about it. so she goes, "but u don't need to rob a bank to know that's bad, now do u? poison little children? put glass in halloween candy?"

SnowAngel: good grief

mad maddie: she also thinks that i was pressured into smoking, that chive made me do it. i told her, "why do u insist on believing that i can't possibly make a decision on my own? no one 'persuaded' me to do anything. it was not peer pressure!"

SnowAngel: huh. i'm not sure that's the angle i would have taken . . .

mad maddie:	the moms just shook her head and said, "i don't believe that, maddie. i simply don't believe that."
mad maddie:	aaargh
SnowAngel:	what about chive and brannen? have u heard from them?
mad maddie:	brannen's mom went down to the jail and got him. he's grounded, just like me, plus he has to do forty hours of community service. chive got off scot-free except for being yelled at by his mom. but i didn't talk to him long, cuz it made me feel too weird.
mad maddie:	i'm glad they go to n'side so i don't have to see either of them at school tomorrow.
SnowAngel:	as for me, i don't have to go to school at all. vacation day! vacation day!
mad maddie:	lucky dog
mad maddie:	will u do me a favor, then? i'd do it myself, but i can't, obviously.
SnowAngel:	what is it?
mad maddie:	i need u to go to 2620 moreland avenue. ask for a guy named willy.
SnowAngel:	excuse me? who's willy?
mad maddie:	tell him ur picking up the package for madigan kinnick. it's already paid for, so u don't have to worry.
SnowAngel:	maddie . . . what kind of errand r u sending me on? i thought u were done with your life of crime!
mad maddie:	oh plz. yeah, willy sells pot from behind the cash register, and i'm sending u to get it.
mad maddie:	give me a little credit, will ya?
SnowAngel:	what is it, then?
mad maddie:	don't open it until i tell u to. there's 1 for u, 1 for zoe, and 1 for me.
SnowAngel:	a surprise? 😊 i love surprises!

mad maddie: so u'll do it?

SnowAngel: of course. i have to go out anyway, cuz i need to buy a new charger for my phone. i kinda lost mine.

mad maddie: well, thx. text me tomorrow after school lets out!

Mon, Feb 7, 4:05 PM E.S.T.

SnowAngel: IMPORTANT MESSAGE TO YOU (MADDIE) AND ALSO TO YOU (ZOE) FROM ME (ANGELA)

mad maddie: yes?

zoegirl: hi!

SnowAngel: i have picked up the "surprises" per your instructions, maddie. i have delivered 1 to zoe and 1 to u, which your mom should have given to u now that ur home from school. did she?

mad maddie: i've got the box right here. u haven't opened yours yet, have u?

SnowAngel: no, but i am extremely tempted!

SnowAngel: i waited so that we can open them together. okey-dokey?

mad maddie: let's do it, then. does everyone have her box?

SnowAngel: 👍

zoegirl: yes!

mad maddie: 1, 2, 3 . . . open!

SnowAngel: omg!!! *squeals and jumps up and down in a frenzy*

zoegirl: maddie, it's beautiful!

mad maddie: yeah, yeah, yeah. i know.

SnowAngel: oh, mads, it's just like the one i lost!!!

SnowAngel: are y'all's the same? do they both say "believe" too?

zoegirl: mine does

mad maddie: mine too. aren't i corny, getting us matching bracelets? i am so corny i can hardly believe it. 🌱

SnowAngel: i love it sooo much!

zoegirl: me too, me too!

SnowAngel: but i'm confused. my original bracelet didn't come from that store on moreland ave. it came from curiosities. and zoe, didn't u go back to curiosities after i moved? and they didn't have any more!

zoegirl: that's true, they were all sold out.

mad maddie: when u want something bad enough, u MAKE it happen.

SnowAngel: but how???

mad maddie: dude, i went to every single store in little five points, and NOBODY had any "believe" bracelets. finally this lady told me to talk to willy at a store called moon daughter, cuz he's a silversmith and he makes stuff like that. so i told willy what i wanted, i even drew him a little picture, and he said, "sure, i can do that."

SnowAngel: aw, maddie, ur the best friend ever!

mad maddie: no, u r!

SnowAngel: no, U r!

zoegirl: hey—what about ME?

SnowAngel: *gives zoe a noogie* and u r 2, of course

SnowAngel: we're ALL the best friends ever! *melts into a mush pile of affection*

mad maddie: i put the order in for the bracelets a long time ago—back when u were still in california, angela. i wanted to cheer u up, and i hated that i couldn't do anything to make things better for u.

mad maddie: but then u made things better for yourself. ur a stud, girl.

SnowAngel: u know why, tho, right? cuz of u and zoe. if u guys were willing to take control of your lives, then i should be too.

mad maddie: fat lot of good it did us. we're both grounded!

SnowAngel: well, guess what? *giggles behind hand* i am too!

mad maddie: wtf?

SnowAngel: i told zoe already, when i dropped off her bracelet. zoe, tell maddie.

zoegirl: she's grounded at her aunt's house, supposedly until the end of time. but we think her sentence will eventually be lifted. it's mainly just angela's parents' way of proving they can be long-distance parents.

mad maddie: long-distance parents?

mad maddie: what r u saying?

zoegirl: she can stay!!!

SnowAngel: i can stay!!! 😄 😄 😄

mad maddie: r u serious?

SnowAngel: i am the epitome of all seriousness. i have grown a beard, that's how serious i am. i will only wear tweed, with leather elbow-patches.

mad maddie: u r punch drunk

SnowAngel: *twirls about giddily* it's true, i am. i'm drunk on magnolia trees and sweet tea and true-blue friends forever and ever. 😊

mad maddie: i'm still trying to soak this in. yr parents said, "sure, u can live in atlanta"? just like that?

zoegirl: just for spring semester, and then they'll re-evaluate. if things don't work out, or if angela's aunt says there's a problem, then angela gets shipped back pronto. but that's not going to happen.

SnowAngel: especially not since i'll have u two to keep me straight. after all, ur SUCH good influences.

zoegirl: haha

mad maddie: maybe it's good that we're all locked in our respective houses, huh? at least it'll keep us out of trouble.

mad maddie: in fact, i dare say . . . yes, yes . . . this calls for a googlewhack!

SnowAngel:	what r u gonna try? "grounded girlies"?
zoegirl:	"punished pals"?
SnowAngel:	"caged cuties"?
mad maddie:	ok, stop. ur starting to sound pornographic.
mad maddie:	i've got it, "virtuous rebels." cuz that's really what we r, right?
SnowAngel:	and what's the verdict?
mad maddie:	damn! 37,100 hits!
mad maddie:	will i ever find the one???
zoegirl:	i found the one, and it's doug.
mad maddie:	i meant "the one" googlewhack, fool. as in, the googlewhack that results in just one hit. must it all be about doug?
zoegirl:	i'm sorry, i'm sorry. it's just that it's only been two days of being grounded, and already i miss him so much!
SnowAngel:	oh, poo. stop being so dramatic.
zoegirl:	me, dramatic? you're calling *me* dramatic?
mad maddie:	quit yer whining. u'll see him saturday night at kidding around, won't u?
zoegirl:	yes, only my mom has informed me that she'll be dropping me off and picking me up so that there's no "unsupervised contact." joy.
mad maddie:	u want joy, try living at my house. the moms honestly and truly held up an egg this morning and said, "this is your brain." then she cracked it into the skillet. "this is your brain on drugs."
SnowAngel:	mmm, scrambled eggs!
SnowAngel:	now that the weight of the world is off my shoulders, i'm starting to get my appetite back.
zoegirl:	doug did something cute at school, though. he gave me a hug, and without telling me, he slipped a bendy heart into my jacket pocket. it has little

	rubber arms and little rubber legs and a glued-on picture of his face.
SnowAngel:	awwww!
mad maddie:	**retch, retch**
zoegirl:	he wrote me another poem too. it's about how he values our friendship just as much, if not more, than all this other stuff. it ends like this:

> But for now just let me hold you close
> As I hear your breath and feel your sighs,
> And let me take a healthy dose
> Of your essence, smile, soul, and eyes.

SnowAngel:	that's so sweet!
zoegirl:	isn't it?
SnowAngel:	*jabs maddie in the shoulder* don't u have anything to add, mads?
mad maddie:	**er . . . what angela said**
zoegirl:	maddie! i *know* you're rolling your eyes, so you can just stop.
zoegirl:	but i don't even care, because i know there's something between us. he really is the one.
SnowAngel:	i think that's great, zoe
mad maddie:	**it IS great. i thought i had that with chive, but obviously i don't.**
SnowAngel:	*puts arm around maddie sympathetically*
zoegirl:	anyway, i've been thinking a lot about it . . . and my honest prediction is that we will, you know, make love.
SnowAngel:	*lets out low whistle*
zoegirl:	just not anytime soon, obviously
mad maddie:	**unless u do it in the supply closet at Kidding Around . . .**

zoegirl:	maddie!
mad maddie:	**jk**
mad maddie:	**i, on the other hand, will NOT be getting any action in the near future, cuz i called chive and told him that we're done fooling around. now there's a twist, huh?**
SnowAngel:	maddie! i am SO proud of u!
mad maddie:	**well, it's like my dad says. why buy the cow if u can have the milk for free?**
zoegirl:	yes, absolutely. and you'll *know* when it's real, mads, you really will. just like i do with doug.
mad maddie:	**yeah, shut up. that sounds a little too much like rubbing it in.**
zoegirl:	maddie, no! i'm not trying to rub it in at all!
mad maddie:	**whatevs**
mad maddie:	**but we've discussed it enough, ok? it's not easy, even tho i know it's the right thing to do.**
mad maddie:	**i always learn my fucking life lessons the hard way.**
SnowAngel:	ah, mads. but at least u've got us. 😃
mad maddie:	**so . . . u guys really like your bracelets? really and truly?**
SnowAngel:	i love mine. i completely and fully love it.
zoegirl:	me too. i can't wait to see what it looks like on.
mad maddie:	**OH! that reminds me. the rule is that we have to put them on for each other. none of this "bracelet breakthrough, i-don't-need-anyone-but-myself-so-i'll-tie-it-to-a-necklace" business, got it?**
zoegirl:	huh?
SnowAngel:	she's talking about this great method i invented of putting bracelets on.
SnowAngel:	but she's right. her way is better.
zoegirl:	that means we can't wear them until we're all together, though.

mad maddie: no worries, we'll find a way around this foolish grounding business.

SnowAngel: surely your parents will let u come see ME, won't they? dear pitiful me who's been gone for so long?

SnowAngel: my aunt sadie could be our chaperone and make sure that no one smokes pot or does the nasty. 😊

zoegirl: haha, very funny

SnowAngel: ahhh, my friends. i think things r looking up.

mad maddie: yeah, life is good, even when it sucks.

zoegirl: we'll see each other soon, then?

SnowAngel: very soon. so altho i'm signing off—*draws hand to heart emotionally*—it is with the comfort of knowing that it is the most temporary of farewells.

zoegirl: you make me laugh, angela. but yeah, i should go too.

mad maddie: laters, dudes

SnowAngel: and btw, i DO believe! i do, i do!

mad maddie: u sound like tinkerbell, u nut

SnowAngel: *wiggles cute little bottom suggestively*

SnowAngel: ttfn!!!

OMG, IT'S SENIOR YEAR!
TURN THE PAGE
FOR A SNEAK PEEK OF

l8r, g8r

THE THIRD BOOK IN THE
BESTSELLING
INTERNET GIRLS SERIES.

zoegirl: maddie!!! i'm so excited, i can't sit still! i can't believe i'm going to see doug in 2 hrs!

mad maddie: i hear ya—even i'm kinda excited to c the guy. i wonder if he's changed?

zoegirl: do you *ever* check his instagram? he's gotten tanner. his hair is longer. he is even more handsome than he used to be, which seems impossible.

mad maddie: deeper changes. like, changes on the inside.

zoegirl: it's been SIX ENTIRE MONTHS. *6 months* of no doug!

zoegirl: aye-yai-yai—what if he doesn't like me anymore?

mad maddie: oh, please. doug is doug is doug, and no semester at sea is gonna change that.

mad maddie: anywayz, haven't you guys been skyping every single day?

zoegirl: that's true, but it's still different from being with someone in person.

zoegirl: what i liked even more than skyping—maybe— were the snail mail letters he sent. well, snail mail postcards, mainly, from all the different places they docked. sooo romantic.

mad maddie: speaking of romantic, what's doug gonna say when angela and i show up at the airport with you?

zoegirl: er . . . hi, maddie? hi, angela?

mad maddie: he's not gonna be pissed?

zoegirl: why would he be pissed?

mad maddie: that it's not just the 2 of you

zoegirl: course not. 1st of all, his parents are going to be there. and 2nd of all, i'm way too nervous to go by myself.

zoegirl: i have to have my maddie and my angela—he knows that!

mad maddie: how's he gonna feel, waltzing back to school in the middle of our senior yr? is that gonna be weird for him?

zoegirl: PAST the middle of the year. i was *supposed* to have him back at the beginning of the semester.

mad maddie: i'm still reeling from the unfairness of that, btw. let's pretend i was the lucky 1 who jaunted off to Sea the World. would the administrators let ME take an extra month off to travel with my parents? i don't think so.

zoegirl: but you don't have straight As like doug—no offense.

mad maddie: none taken. i'm proud of my Bs. 👍

zoegirl: doug's mom called it "cultural enrichment." that's the excuse she gave the school. but i say he's seen enough of the world. now he needs to see ME!

mad maddie: ah yes, now it's time for him to be enriched in OTHER ways, nudge-nudge, wink-wink.

zoegirl: maddie!!!

zoegirl: i'm just glad we're going to be together again. i mean, he had a great time, and i'm proud of him for doing it, but he's definitely ready to be home.

mad maddie: god, and i am definitely ready to NOT.

mad maddie: seriously, if i could graduate tomorrow, i would. i'd be like, hasta la vista, baby! g-bye, atlanta— hello, santa cruz!

zoegirl: *if* you get in. which you will. i hate that you want to go so far away, though.

mad maddie: blame angela. if we hadn't gone to california with her over the summer . . .

zoegirl: too ironic. she escapes california to move back

	to atlanta, and now all you wanna do is escape atlanta and move to california.
mad maddie:	U.C.S.C., here i come. go, banana slugs!
zoegirl:	is that honestly their mascot?
mad maddie:	it honestly is their mascot. it's 1 of the many cool things about them—their whole who-gives-a-damn attitude about typical college stuff like rah-rah football teams. that and the fact that they're 3,000 miles away, heh heh heh.
zoegirl:	oh, wow
zoegirl:	maddie . . . i just realized something
mad maddie:	what?
zoegirl:	things really are changing, aren't they? we're seniors, we're going to graduate in 3 months, we're all going to go our separate ways . . .
mad maddie:	and this comes as a surprise?
zoegirl:	no . . . i just don't know if i'm ready
mad maddie:	i sure as hell am
mad maddie:	repeat after me: change is good
zoegirl:	omg—no *way* did you just say that!
zoegirl:	if angela were here, she'd be rolling on the ground.
mad maddie:	pardon me, but all i said was that change is good. why is that funny?
zoegirl:	oh, mads. aren't you the one who was outraged when they switched brands of soap in the girls' bathroom?
mad maddie:	the old kind was better! it smelled like lavender!
zoegirl:	and you have a fit if you can't start the day with your pop-tart and dr pepper. i thought you were going to stage a riot that day the drink machine was out!
mad maddie:	i'm a growing girl. i need my caffeine.
zoegirl:	and every time facebook changes its layout,

	you swear you're going to shut down yr fb page forever
mad maddie:	**your point?**
zoegirl:	my point is that you *hate* change
mad maddie:	**no i don't**
zoegirl:	yeah, you do
zoegirl:	it's cute
mad maddie:	**i thought we were talking about marching off into the big bad world, not what kind of soap comes out when you squirt the thingie in the bathroom. and all i was saying is that we can't stay in high school forever, even if we wanted to.**
zoegirl:	i know that. but it still feels huge.
mad maddie:	**anywayz, no reason to get worked up about it now. there'll be plenty of time for weeping and gnashing of the teeth before it's over.**
zoegirl:	i already gnash my teeth—that's why i wear a mouth guard at night. my dentist says it's the curse of being an overachiever.
mad maddie:	**an overachiever? YOU?**
zoegirl:	haha
zoegirl:	hey, can i tell you something stupid that's totally not worth dealing with, but at the same time i'm kind of disturbed by?
mad maddie:	**shoot**
zoegirl:	it has to do with jana. still wanna hear?
mad maddie:	**oh god. not THE J-WORD.**
zoegirl:	you and jana have a past. i'm just trying to be sensitive.
mad maddie:	**you might have to excuse me while i retch, but other than that, go ahead.**
zoegirl:	well, right before i left school today, i ran into terri. now, normally we wouldn't have even exchanged hellos, because of the fact she's

jana's best friend. but terri had been crying—her eyes were red and her face was all puffy—and i would have been a complete jerk to not say anything.

mad maddie: **if i'd seen terri and she'd been crying, i wouldn't have said anything.**

zoegirl: yes you would've

mad maddie: **and if the situation were reversed, i wouldn't want HER to say anything, either.**

zoegirl: well, i am a good human, so i said, "um . . . terri? you ok?" which made her burst into tears all over again.

mad maddie: **c? that is why you should leave crying ppl alone.**

zoegirl: she was *horrified* to be falling apart like that in front of me, i could tell. she kept saying, "i'm fine, i'm fine," but she obviously wasn't. so i took her to the girls' room and gave her a wet paper towel to press against her eyes, and we ended up sitting down below the sinks and talking.

mad maddie: **so what was wrong? or rather, what terrible and awful thing had jana done to her?**

zoegirl: they'd gotten into a yelling match over terri's hair, if you can believe it. you know how it's now the same shade as jana's? jana had cussed terri out for being a clone, and i guess she took it too far and said some really nasty things.

mad maddie: **jana takes everything too far. she always has, but this year even more so.**

mad maddie: **she should go thru life armed with an apology and a complimentary bag of peanuts.**

zoegirl: well, i felt bad for terri, even tho she's not my favorite person. i hate it when i fight with you or angela.

mad maddie: **what r u talking about? we don't fight.**

zoegirl: so i said something like, "she shouldn't treat you that way," and terri said, "she treats *everybody* that way." i said she better stop or she won't have any friends left, and terri snorted. she was like, "poor little jana, alone in a corner. just her and her teddy bear."

mad maddie: HA

zoegirl: that's what *i* said. because it's such an oxymoron, the image of jana—mistress of death and destruction— clutching a teddy bear.

mad maddie: ooo, nice use of the word "oxymoron." i KNEW i should have taken that SAT prep course.

zoegirl: but terri goes, "for real, jana has this mangy old teddy bear that smells like spit. she takes it with her everywhere."

mad maddie: ???

mad maddie: i've never seen jana with a teddy bear

zoegirl: she leaves it in her car. that's what terri says. which is entirely possible. have you seen all the crap in the back of jana's station wagon?

mad maddie: it's a mobile junk heap. it's disgusting.

zoegirl: according to terri, jana's dad gave her the teddy bear when she was little, and she's unhealthily attached to it.

zoegirl: its name is Boo Boo Bear.

mad maddie: Boo Boo Bear???

mad maddie: omfg, i am loving this so much. Boo Boo Bear!

zoegirl: terri was like, "i can't believe i'm telling you— jana would *die*."

mad maddie: heh heh heh, jana whitaker is unhealthily attached to Boo Boo Bear. suddenly the world is a MUCH brighter place!!!

zoegirl: er . . . not necessarily. because 2 seconds later, jana herself stormed into the bathroom. "*there*

	you are," she says to terri, all fuming. "you're not even going to let me apologize?"
zoegirl:	then she noticed me, and her jaw dropped. she was like, "what are YOU doing here?"
mad maddie:	**plz, it's a public bathroom. does she think it's her private office?**
zoegirl:	my heart got all poundy, because—as you know— i'm a wimp, although jana had already switched to ignoring me. she said to terri, "get up, we're leaving."
mad maddie:	**ok, that is the perfect example of the evilness of jana. she's bossy and she's mean.**
zoegirl:	but amazingly, terri didn't obey. she said, "you can't treat me like dirt and then expect me to be your slave."
zoegirl:	"terri, get up," jana said, still very pointedly not looking at me. "we can talk about your 'issues' later."
mad maddie:	**oh god**
zoegirl:	so terri goes, "*my* issues? you're the one with issues! keep acting the way you're acting, and you won't have any friends left!"
mad maddie:	**which is exactly what YOU said!**
zoegirl:	i know! and for some reason that made me get all stupidly brave, and under my breath i said, "no one but Boo Boo Bear."
mad maddie:	**holy shit! u da BOMB!**
zoegirl:	i shouldn't have, though! it was totally unlike me!
mad maddie:	**that's what's so great!**
mad maddie:	**did jana hear?**
zoegirl:	she whipped her head toward me and was like, "WHAT did you say?" and terri goes, "she SAID, no one but Boo Boo Bear."
mad maddie:	**gee, thx, terri**

zoegirl:	jana was speechless. i've never in my life seen her speechless, but for that single moment she was. big splotches of color bloomed on her cheeks. it was freaky.
mad maddie:	cuz she IS a freak
zoegirl:	then she pulled herself together and said to me, "you've got nerve, sticking your nose up. not all of us live in a perfect plastic bubble, you know."
mad maddie:	exsqueeze me? what is that supposed to mean?!
zoegirl:	she was trying to make me feel like a spoiled little baby, in comparison to her, the jaded and worldly jana.
mad maddie:	who has a teddy bear.
zoegirl:	her tone said 1 thing—see how cool and detached i am? i couldn't care less that you know about my stupid bear—but her eyes said something else entirely. she looked like she wanted to kill me. i'm not kidding.
mad maddie:	well, duh. if anyone had to be there for that lovely moment, i'm sure you were the last person she'd pick. you or me or angela, that is.
zoegirl:	that thought crossed my mind, but i tried to tell myself, "no, you're being silly."
mad maddie:	except yr not. we have what jana doesn't have—actual true friends who lift each other up instead of tear each other down—and it's like a knife inside her heart.
mad maddie:	think of it like this: jana's a dragon (SO not a stretch) and terri exposed her secret piece of weakness. so now jana's screwed twice: 1st cuz u know about Boo Boo Bear, and 2nd cuz u know how easily terri would betray her.
zoegirl:	jana the dragon. i just hope she doesn't flame me.
mad maddie:	if she does, she'll have ME to deal with.

mad maddie: now isn't it time to pick up your long-lost boyfriend? it's 5:15.

zoegirl: it is? EEEEEK! IT IS!!!!!

zoegirl: go pick up angela from her aunt's house and then swing by here. i'll be the 1 gnawing my fingernails to the quick!

mad maddie: i'm heading out the door. l8r, g8r!

Why were your books banned and do you personally believe that they should have been?

Lots of my books have teen girls in them. Teen girls sometimes talk about sex. Teen girls sometimes have sex. Lots of grown-ups would like to believe that this is not true. I am not one of those grown-ups, and I think it's important and meaningful to give readers stories that reflect reality—in a respectful way. Like, not salaciously, but with the intent of saying, "Let's look at how this story played out. How'd it seem to work out for so-and-so?" And then the readers—who are SMART, damn it—can grapple with those issues themselves. And no, I do not believe my books should have been banned. I do not believe that any author should be banned, ever. Freedom of speech, dude. :)

What's your response when you are censored? Are you ever frustrated, or do you take pride in it?

At first I cried. And called my editor and apologized, because I felt so terrible about it. Now I take pride . . . but it requires a bit of emotional effort, because it still hurts to have people say, out loud and with venom, "Your books suck. YOU suck."

What was your favorite part of writing the Internet Girls series?

My fave part of writing this series was NOT HAVING TO WRITE SETTING. I hate setting. In other books that aren't purely written in text/IMs, my annoying (awesome) editor makes me include setting, and it is hard.

Which of your characters is most like you, and which character do you wish you were more like?

I'm most like Winnie from the Winnie Years series. She's a good girl, funny, tries to do the right thing. Often gets into embarrassing situations. I once ran over a squirrel on my bike.

Whom do I wish I were more like? I'm going to go with Cat from *Shine*, because she has courage in spades. She doesn't let the haters get to her. Sometimes I do.

How do you come up with your characters?
I follow my children around as they go through their lives and I spy on them. I wear a trench coat and carry a notepad. I am vair vair subtle.

Except, really, I do.

As an author, what's your average day like?
Oh, an average day of writing means MAKING MYSELF WRITE. And then thinking, "Oh, this is fun." And then writing some more.

What do you think books offer that other forms of entertainment don't?
Books engage readers in a more intimate way than other forms of entertainment/media, I think. They encourage critical thinking.

What is your very best life advice?
Best advice? Sheesh. Imagine life is like this: You're waiting at a red light. You're stuck there. You didn't choose to be, but there you are. How are you going to spend your time? Bitching and moaning and looking at your watch, or thinking INTERESTING thoughts? Looking at the beautiful sky? Laughing at a joke? So, use this life WISELY—we're dead a lot longer than we're alive—and leave the universe a better place than when you got here.

ACKNOWLEDGMENTS

Oh, li'l dudes, I thank you:

Liz Baltich, Kelly Dean, Todd Mitchell, Laura Pritchett, and Jack Martin, for being the best readers a girl could ask for; Derek DeCoux, poet extraordinaire and all-around cool guy; my agent, Barry Goldblatt, for assuring me that I don't suck whenever I convince myself I do; the groovy folks at Abrams, for giving me such a wonderful book-y home; Erica Finkel, goddess of cool and slave driver of scary fierceness; and the inestimable Susan Van Metre, for making me write the damn novel again and again and AGAIN. *flings self on dagger and perishes*

Thanks to Al, who wanted Maddie to say "blah, blah, blah." (And Jamie and Mirabelle, thank you, too, just for being so cute.)

And finally, huge hugs and thanks to Maria Middleton for giving this baby its sparkly new updated look!

ABOUT THE AUTHOR

LAUREN MYRACLE is the author of many books for teens and young people, including the *New York Times* bestselling Internet Girls series, *Shine, Rhymes with Witches, Bliss, The Infinite Moment of Us,* and the Flower Power series. She lives with her family in Fort Collins, Colorado. Visit her online at laurenmyracle.com.